BORN TO RUN

"Initially, I thought *Me? Read a book on running?* Then suddenly—wham!—I was drawn in, galloping along through a multi-faceted landscape that is by turns exhilarating, funny and weirdly absorbing. It's been a breathless read, but sheer endorphinous pleasure." John Gimlette, author of *At the Tomb of the Inflatable Pig*

"Driven by an intense yet subtle curiosity, Christopher McDougall gamely treads across the continent to pierce the soul and science of long-distance running. McDougall's ambitious search leads him deep into the ragged folds of Mexico's Copper Canyon, where he somehow manages the impossible: he plumbs the mystic secrets of the fleet-footed Tarahumara Indians while never losing his deep enchantment for the majesty of their culture." Hampton Sides, author of *Blood and Thunder* and *Ghost Soldiers*

"Wonderful. It's funny, insightful, captivating, and a great and beautiful discovery. There are lessons that translate to realms beyond running. The book inspires anyone who seeks to live more fully or to run faster. I just loved this book." Lynne Cox, author of *Swimming to Antarctica*

"A magnificent oddball of a book, a strange and cracked hybrid of true adventure, history, mutant road trip gone wrong, anatomy, anthropology, physiology, and personal odyssey. Christopher McDougall took a huge gamble and risked years of his life (not to mention his life itself) by journeying deep into a forbidding and dangerous canyon, where he suspected he might learn something important. He returned with ancient wisdom, powerful secrets, haunting characters and an absurdly, wonderfully, fiendishly entertaining yarn." Steve Friedman, author of *The Agony of Victory*

BORN TO RUN

THE HIDDEN TRIBE, THE ULTRA-RUNNERS,

AND THE GREATEST RACE

THE WORLD HAS NEVER SEEN

Christopher McDougall

PROFILE BOOKS

First published in Great Britain in 2009 by
PROFILE BOOKS LTD
3A Exmouth House
Pine Street
London EC1R 0JH
www.profilebooks.com

First published in the United States in 2009 by
Alfred A. Knopf, a division of Random House, Inc., New York

1 3 5 7 9 10 8 6 4 2

Printed and bound in Great Britain by
Clays, Bungay, Suffolk

A CIP catalogue record for this book is available from the
British Library.

ISBN 978 1 86197 823 3

FSC
Mixed Sources
Product group from well-managed
forests and other controlled sources
Cert no. SGS-COC-2061
www.fsc.org
© 1996 Forest Stewardship Council

The paper this book is printed on is certified by the © 1996 Forest
Stewardship Council A.C. (FSC). It is ancient-forest friendly. The
printer holds FSC chain of custody SGS-COC-2061

To John and Jean McDougall,

my parents,

who gave me everything

and keep on giving

The best runner leaves no tracks.

—*Tao Te Ching*

BORN TO RUN

CHAPTER 1

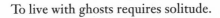

To live with ghosts requires solitude.

—ANNE MICHAELS, *Fugitive Pieces*

FOR DAYS, I'd been searching Mexico's Sierra Madre for the phantom known as *Caballo Blanco*—the White Horse. I'd finally arrived at the end of the trail, in the last place I expected to find him—not deep in the wilderness he was said to haunt, but in the dim lobby of an old hotel on the edge of a dusty desert town.

"*Sí, El Caballo está*," the desk clerk said, nodding. Yes, the Horse is here.

"For real?" After hearing that I'd *just* missed him so many times, in so many bizarre locations, I'd begun to suspect that Caballo Blanco was nothing more than a fairy tale, a local Loch Ness *monstruo* dreamed up to spook the kids and fool gullible gringos.

"He's always back by five," the clerk added. "It's like a ritual."

I didn't know whether to hug her in relief or high-five her in triumph. I checked my watch. That meant I'd actually lay eyes on the ghost in less than . . . hang on.

"But it's already after six."

The clerk shrugged. "Maybe he's gone away."

I sagged into an ancient sofa. I was filthy, famished, and defeated. I was exhausted, and so were my leads.

Some said Caballo Blanco was a fugitive; others heard he was a boxer who'd run off to punish himself after beating a man to death in the ring. No one knew his name, or age, or where he was from. He was like some Old West gunslinger whose only traces were tall tales and a whiff of cigarillo smoke. Descriptions and sightings were all over the map; villagers who lived impossible distances apart swore they'd seen him traveling on foot on the same day, and described him on a scale that swung wildly from "funny and *simpático*" to "freaky and gigantic."

But in all versions of the Caballo Blanco legend, certain basic details were always the same: He'd come to Mexico years ago and trekked deep into the wild, impenetrable Barrancas del Cobre—the Copper Canyons—to live among the Tarahumara, a near-mythical tribe of Stone Age superathletes. The Tarahumara (pronounced Spanish-style by swallowing the "h": Tara-oo-mara) may be the healthiest and most serene people on earth, and the greatest runners of all time.

When it comes to ultradistances, nothing can beat a Tarahumara runner—not a racehorse, not a cheetah, not an Olympic marathoner. Very few outsiders have ever seen the Tarahumara in action, but amazing stories of their superhuman toughness and tranquillity have drifted out of the canyons for centuries. One explorer swore he saw a Tarahumara catch a deer with his bare hands, chasing the bounding animal until it finally dropped dead from exhaustion, "its hoofs falling off." Another adventurer spent ten hours climbing up and over a Copper Canyon mountain by mule; a Tarahumara runner made the same trip in ninety minutes.

"Try this," a Tarahumara woman once told an exhausted explorer who'd collapsed at the base of a mountain. She handed him a gourd full of a murky liquid. He swallowed a few gulps, and was amazed to feel new energy pulsing in his veins. He got to his feet and scaled the peak like an overcaffeinated Sherpa. The Tarahumara, the explorer would later report, also guarded the recipe to a special energy food that leaves them trim, powerful, and unstoppable: a few mouthfuls packed enough nutritional punch to let them run all day without rest.

But whatever secrets the Tarahumara are hiding, they've hidden them well. To this day, the Tarahumara live in the side of cliffs higher than a hawk's nest in a land few have ever seen. The Barrancas are a lost world in the most remote wilderness in North America, a sort of a shorebound Bermuda Triangle known for swallowing the misfits and desperadoes who stray inside. Lots of bad things can happen down there, and probably will; survive the man-eating jaguars, deadly snakes, and blistering heat, and you've still got to deal with "canyon fever," a potentially fatal freak-out brought on by the Barrancas' desolate eeriness. The deeper you penetrate into the Barrancas, the more it feels like a crypt sliding shut around you. The walls tighten, shadows spread, phantom echoes whisper; every route out seems to end in sheer rock. Lost prospectors would be gripped by such madness and despair, they'd slash their own throats or hurl themselves off cliffs. Little surprise that few strangers have ever seen the Tarahumara's homeland—let alone the Tarahumara.

But somehow the White Horse had made his way to the depths of the Barrancas. And there, it's said, he was adopted by the Tarahumara as a friend and kindred spirit; a ghost among ghosts. He'd certainly mastered two Tarahumara skills—invisibility and extraordinary endurance—because even though he was spotted all over the canyons, no one seemed to know where he lived or when he might appear next. If anyone could translate the ancient secrets of the Tarahumara, I was told, it was this lone wanderer of the High Sierras.

I'd become so obsessed with finding Caballo Blanco that as I dozed on the hotel sofa, I could even imagine the sound of his voice. "Probably like Yogi Bear ordering burritos at Taco Bell," I mused. A guy like that, a wanderer who'd go anywhere but fit in nowhere, must live inside his own head and rarely hear his own voice. He'd make weird jokes and crack himself up. He'd have a booming laugh and atrocious Spanish. He'd be loud and chatty and . . . and . . .

Wait. I *was* hearing him. My eyes popped open to see a dusty cadaver in a tattered straw hat bantering with the desk clerk. Trail dust streaked his gaunt face like fading war paint, and the shocks of sun-bleached hair sticking out from under the hat could have been trimmed with a hunting knife. He looked like a castaway on a desert island, even to the way he seemed hungry for conversation with the bored clerk.

"Caballo?" I croaked.

The cadaver turned, smiling, and I felt like an idiot. He didn't look wary; he looked confused, as any tourist would when confronted by a deranged man on a sofa suddenly hollering "Horse!"

This wasn't Caballo. There was no Caballo. The whole thing was a hoax, and I'd fallen for it.

Then the cadaver spoke. "You know me?"

"Man!" I exploded, scrambling to my feet. "Am I glad to see you!"

The smile vanished. The cadaver's eyes darted toward the door, making it clear that in another second, he would as well.

CHAPTER 2

IT ALL BEGAN with a simple question that no one could answer.

It was a five-word puzzle that led me to a photo of a very fast man in a very short skirt, and from there it only got stranger. Soon, I was dealing with a murder, drug guerrillas, and a one-armed man with a cream-cheese cup strapped to his head. I met a beautiful blonde forest ranger who slipped out of her clothes and found salvation by running naked in the Idaho forests, and a young surfer babe in pigtails who ran straight toward her death in the desert. A talented young runner would die. Two others would barely escape with their lives.

I kept looking, and stumbled across the Barefoot Batman... Naked Guy... Kalahari Bushmen... the Toenail Amputee... a cult devoted to distance running and sex parties... the Wild Man of the Blue Ridge Mountains... and, ultimately, the ancient tribe of the Tarahumara and their shadowy disciple, Caballo Blanco.

In the end, I got my answer, but only after I found myself in the middle of the greatest race the world would never see: the Ultimate Fighting Competition of footraces, an underground showdown pitting some of the best ultradistance runners of our time against the best ultrarunners of *all* time, in a fifty-mile race on hidden trails only Tarahumara feet had ever touched. I'd be startled to discover that the ancient saying of the *Tao Te Ching*—"The best runner leaves no tracks"—wasn't some gossamer koan, but real, concrete, how-to, training advice.

And all because in January 2001 I asked my doctor this:
"How come my foot hurts?"

I'd gone to see one of the top sports-medicine specialists in the country because an invisible ice pick was driving straight up through the sole of my foot. The week before, I'd been out for an easy three-mile jog on a snowy farm road when I suddenly whinnied in pain, grabbing my right foot and screaming curses as I toppled over in the snow. When I got a grip on myself, I checked to see how badly I was bleeding. I must have impaled my foot on a sharp rock, I figured, or an old nail wedged in the ice. But there wasn't a drop of blood, or even a hole in my shoe.

"Running is your problem," Dr. Joe Torg confirmed when I limped into his Philadelphia examining room a few days later. He should know; Dr. Torg had not only helped create the entire field of sports medicine, but he also co-wrote *The Running Athlete*, the definitive radiographic analysis of every conceivable running injury. He ran me through an X-ray and watched me hobble around, then determined that I'd aggravated my cuboid, a cluster of bones parallel to the arch that I hadn't even known existed until it reengineered itself into an internal Taser.

"But I'm barely running at all," I said. "I'm doing, like, two or three miles every other day. And not even on asphalt. Mostly dirt roads."

Didn't matter. "The human body is not designed for that kind of abuse," Dr. Torg replied. "Especially not *your* body."

I knew exactly what he meant. At six feet four inches and two hundred thirty pounds, I'd been told many times that nature intended guys my size to post up under the hoop or take a bullet for the President, not pound our bulk down the pavement. And since I'd turned forty, I was starting to see why; in the five years since I'd stopped playing pickup hoops and tried turning myself into a marathoner, I'd ripped my hamstring (twice), strained my Achilles tendons (repeatedly), sprained my ankles (both, alternately), suffered aching arches (regularly), and had to walk down stairs backward on tiptoe because my heels were so sore. And now, apparently, the last docile spot on my feet had joined the rebellion.

The weird thing was, I seemed to be otherwise unbreakable. As a writer for *Men's Health* magazine and one of *Esquire* magazine's original "Restless Man" columnists, a big part of my job was experimenting with semi-extreme sports. I'd ridden Class IV rapids on a boogie board, surfed giant sand dunes on a snowboard, and mountain biked across the North Dakota Badlands. I'd also reported from three war zones for the Associated Press and spent months in some of the most lawless regions of Africa, all without a nick or a twinge. But jog a few miles down the street, and suddenly I'm rolling on the ground like I'd been gut shot in a drive-by.

Take any other sport, and an injury rate like mine would classify me as defective. In running, it makes me normal. The real mutants are the runners who *don't* get injured. Up to eight out of every ten runners are hurt *every year*. It doesn't matter if you're heavy or thin, speedy or slow, a marathon champ or a weekend huffer, you're just as likely as the other guy to savage your knees, shins, hamstrings, hips, or heels. Next time you line up for a Turkey Trot, look at the runners on your right and left: statistically, only one of you will be back for the Jingle Bell Jog.

No invention yet has slowed the carnage; you can now buy running shoes that have steel bedsprings embedded in the soles or that adjust their cushioning by microchip, but the injury rate hasn't decreased a jot in thirty years. If anything, it's actually ebbed up; Achilles tendon blowouts have seen a 10 percent increase. Running seemed to be the fitness version of drunk driving: you could get away with it for a while, you might even have some fun, but catastrophe was waiting right around the corner.

"Big surprise," the sports-medicine literature sneers. Not exactly like that, though. More like this: "Athletes whose sport involves running put enormous strain on their legs." That's what the *Sports Injury Bulletin* has declared. "Each footfall hits one of their legs with a force equal to more than twice their body weight. Just as repeated hammering on an apparently impenetrable rock will eventually reduce the stone to dust, the impact loads associated with running can ultimately break down your bones, cartilage, muscles, tendons, and ligaments." A report by the American Association of Orthopedic Surgeons concluded that distance running is "an outrageous threat to the integrity of the knee."

And instead of "impenetrable rock," that outrage is banging down on one of the most sensitive points in your body. You know what kind of nerves are in your feet? The same ones that network into your genitals. Your feet are like a minnow bucket full of sensory neurons, all of them wriggling around in search of sensation. Stimulate those nerves just a little, and the impulse will rocket through your entire nervous system; that's why tickling your feet can overload the switchboard and cause your whole body to spasm.

No wonder South American dictators had a foot fetish when it came to breaking hard cases; the bastinado, the technique of tying victims down and beating the soles of their feet, was developed by the Spanish Inquisition and eagerly adopted by the world's sickest sadists. The Khmer Rouge and Saddam Hussein's sinister son Uday were big-time bastinado fans because they knew their anatomy; only the face and hands compare with the feet for instant-messaging capability to the brain. When it comes to sensing the softest caress or tiniest grain of sand, your toes are as finely wired as your lips and fingertips.

"So isn't there anything I can do?" I asked Dr. Torg.

He shrugged. "You can keep running, but you'll be back for more of these," he said, giving a little *ting* with his fingernail to the giant needle full of cortisone he was about to push into the bottom of my foot. I'd also need custom-made orthotics ($400) to slip inside my motion-control running shoes ($150 and climbing, and since I'd need to rotate two pairs, make it $300). But that would just postpone the real big-ticket item: my inevitable next visit to his waiting room.

"Know what I'd recommend?" Dr. Torg concluded. "Buy a bike."

I thanked him, promised I'd take his advice, then immediately went behind his back to someone else. Doc Torg was getting up in years, I realized; maybe he'd gotten a little too conservative with his advice and a little too quick with his cortisone. A physician friend recommended a sports podiatrist who was also a marathoner, so I made an appointment for the following week.

The podiatrist took another X-ray, then probed my foot with his thumbs. "Looks like you've got cuboid syndrome," he concluded. "I can blast the inflammation out with some cortisone, but then you're going to need orthotics."

"Damn," I muttered. "That's just what Torg said."

He'd started to leave the room for the needle, but then he stopped short. "You already saw Joe Torg?"

"Yes."

"You already got a cortisone shot?"

"Uh, yeah."

"So what are you doing here?" he asked, suddenly looking impatient and a little suspicious, as if he thought I really enjoyed having needles shoved into the tenderest part of my foot. Maybe he suspected I was a sadomasochistic junkie who was addicted to both pain *and* painkillers.

"You realize Dr. Torg is the godfather of sports medicine, right? His diagnoses are usually well respected."

"I know. I just wanted to double-check."

"I'm not going to give you another shot, but we can schedule a fitting for the orthotics. And you should really think about finding some other activity besides running."

"Sounds good," I said. He was a better runner than I'd ever be, and he'd just confirmed the verdict of a doctor he readily admitted was the sensei of sports physicians. There was absolutely no arguing with his diagnosis. So I started looking for someone else.

It's not that I'm all that stubborn. It's not that I'm even all that crazy about running. If I totaled all the miles I'd ever run, half were aching drudgery. But it does say something that even though I haven't read *The World According to Garp* in twenty years, I've never forgotten one minor scene, and it ain't the one you're thinking of: I keep thinking back to the way Garp used to burst out his door in the middle of the workday for a five-mile run. There's something so universal about that sensation, the way running unites our two most primal impulses: fear and pleasure. We run when we're scared, we run when we're ecstatic, we run away from our problems and run around for a good time.

And when things look worst, we run the most. Three times, America has seen distance-running skyrocket, and it's always in the midst of a national crisis. The first boom came during the Great Depression, when more than two hundred runners set the trend by racing forty miles a day across the country in the Great American Footrace. Running then went dormant, only to catch fire again in the early '70s, when we were struggling to recover from Vietnam, the

Cold War, race riots, a criminal president, and the murders of three beloved leaders. And the third distance boom? One year after the September 11 attacks, trail-running suddenly became the fastest-growing outdoor sport in the country. Maybe it was a coincidence. Or maybe there's a trigger in the human psyche, a coded response that activates our first and greatest survival skill when we sense the raptors approaching. In terms of stress relief and sensual pleasure, running is what you have in your life before you have sex. The equipment and desire come factory installed; all you have to do is let 'er rip and hang on for the ride.

That's what I was looking for; not some pricey hunk of plastic to stick in my shoe, not a monthly cycle of painkillers, just a way to let 'er rip without tearing myself up. I didn't love running, but I *wanted* to. Which is what brought me to the door of M.D. No. 3: Dr. Irene Davis, an expert in biomechanics and head of the Running Injury Clinic at the University of Delaware.

Dr. Davis put me on a treadmill, first in my bare feet and then in three different types of running shoes. She had me walk, trot, and haul ass. She had me run back and forth over a force plate to measure the impact shock from my footfalls. Then I sat in horror as she played back the video.

In my mind's eye, I'm light and quick as a Navajo on the hunt. That guy on the screen, however, was Frankenstein's monster trying to tango. I was bobbing around so much, my head was disappearing from the top of the frame. My arms were slashing back and forth like an ump calling a player safe at the plate, while my size 13s clumped down so heavily it sounded like the video had a bongo backbeat.

If that wasn't bad enough, Dr. Davis then hit slow-mo so we could all settle back and really appreciate the way my right foot twisted out, my left knee dipped in, and my back bucked and spasmed so badly that it looked as if someone ought to jam a wallet between my teeth and call for help. How the hell was I even moving forward with all that up-down, side-to-side, fish-on-a-hook flopping going on?

"Okay," I said. "So what's the right way to run?"

"That's the eternal question," Dr. Davis replied.

As for the eternal answer . . . well, that was tricky. I might straighten out my stride and get a little more shock absorption if I landed on my fleshy midfoot instead of my bony heel, *buuuuūt* . . . I might just be swapping one set of problems for another. Tinkering with a new gait can suddenly load the heel and Achilles with unaccustomed stress and bring on a fresh batch of injuries.

"Running is tough on the legs," Dr. Davis said. She was so gentle and apologetic, I could tell what else she was thinking: "Especially *your* legs, big fella."

I was right back where I'd started. After months of seeing specialists and searching physiology studies online, all I'd managed was to get my question flipped around and fired back at me:

How come my foot hurts?
Because running is bad for you.
Why is running bad for me?
Because it makes your foot hurt.

But *why*? Antelope don't get shin splints. Wolves don't ice-pack their knees. I doubt that 80 percent of all wild mustangs are annually disabled with impact injuries. It reminded me of a proverb attributed to Roger Bannister, who, while simultaneously studying medicine, working as a clinical researcher, and minting pithy parables, became the first man to break the four-minute mile: "Every morning in Africa, a gazelle wakes up," Bannister said. "It knows it must outrun the fastest lion or it will be killed. Every morning in Africa, a lion wakes up. It knows it must run faster than the slowest gazelle, or it will starve. It doesn't matter whether you're a lion or a gazelle—when the sun comes up, you'd better be running."

So why should every other mammal on the planet be able to depend on its legs except us? Come to think of it, how could a guy like Bannister charge out of the lab every day, pound around a hard cinder track in thin leather slippers, and not only get faster, but never get hurt? How come some of us can be out there running all lionlike and Bannisterish every morning when the sun comes up, while the rest of us need a fistful of ibuprofen before we can put our feet on the floor?

These were very good questions. But as I was about to discover, the only ones who knew the answers—the only ones who *lived* the answers—weren't talking.

Especially not to someone like me.

———

In the winter of 2003, I was on assignment in Mexico when I began flipping through a Spanish-language travel magazine. Suddenly, a photo of Jesus running down a rock slide caught my eye.

Closer inspection revealed that while maybe not Jesus, it was definitely a man in a robe and sandals sprinting down a mountain of rubble. I started translating the caption, but couldn't figure out why it was in the present tense; it seemed to be some kind of wishful Atlantean legend about an extinct empire of enlightened superbeings. Only gradually did I figure out that I was right about everything except the "extinct" and "wishful" parts.

I was in Mexico to track down a missing pop star and her secret brainwashing cult for *The New York Times Magazine*, but the article I was writing suddenly seemed a snore compared with the one I was reading. Freakish fugitive pop stars come and go, but the Tarahumara seemed to live forever. Left alone in their mysterious canyon hideaway, this small tribe of recluses had solved nearly every problem known to man. Name your category—mind, body, or soul—and the Tarahumara were zeroing in on perfection. It was as if they'd secretly turned their caves into incubators for Nobel Prize winners, all toiling toward the end of hatred, heart disease, shin splints, and greenhouse gases.

In Tarahumara Land, there was no crime, war, or theft. There was no corruption, obesity, drug addiction, greed, wife-beating, child abuse, heart disease, high blood pressure, or carbon emissions. They didn't get diabetes, or depressed, or even old: fifty-year-olds could outrun teenagers, and eighty-year-old great-grandads could hike marathon distances up mountainsides. Their cancer rates were barely detectable. The Tarahumara geniuses had even branched into economics, creating a one-of-a-kind financial system based on booze and random acts of kindness: instead of money, they traded favors and big tubs of corn beer.

You'd expect an economic engine fueled by alcohol and freebies to spiral into a drunken grab-fest, everyone double-fisting for themselves like bankrupt gamblers at a casino buffet, but in Tarahumara Land, it works. Perhaps it's because the Tarahumara are industrious and inhumanly honest; one researcher went as far as to speculate that after so many generations of truthfulness, the Tarahumara brain was actually chemically incapable of forming lies.

And if being the kindest, happiest people on the planet wasn't enough, the Tarahumara were also the toughest: the only thing that rivaled their superhuman serenity, it seemed, was their superhuman tolerance for pain and *lechuguilla*, a horrible homemade tequila brewed from rattlesnake corpses and cactus sap. According to one of the few outsiders who'd ever witnessed a full-on Tarahumara rave, the partiers got so blitzed that wives began ripping each others' tops off in a bare-breasted wrestling match, while a cackling old man circled around trying to spear their butts with a corncob. The husbands, meanwhile, gazed on in glassy-eyed paralysis. Cancún at spring break had nothing on the Barrancas under a harvest moon.

The Tarahumara would party like this all night, then roust themselves the next morning to face off in a running race that could last not two miles, not two hours, but *two full days*. According to the Mexican historian Francisco Almada, a Tarahumara champion once ran 435 miles, the equivalent of setting out for a jog in New York City and not stopping till you were closing in on Detroit. Other Tarahumara runners reportedly went three hundred miles at a pop. That's nearly twelve full marathons, back to back to back, while the sun rose and set and rose again.

And the Tarahumara weren't cruising along smooth, paved roads, either, but scrambling up and down steep canyon trails formed only by their own feet. Lance Armstrong is one of the greatest endurance athletes of all time, and he could barely shuffle through his first marathon despite sucking down an energy gel nearly every mile. (Lance's text message to his ex-wife after the New York City Marathon: "Oh. My. God. Ouch. Terrible.") Yet these guys were knocking them out a dozen at a time?

In 1971, an American physiologist trekked into the Copper Canyons and was so blown away by Tarahumara athleticism that he had to reach back twenty-eight hundred years for a suitable scale to rank it on. "Probably not since the days of the ancient Spartans has a people achieved such a high state of physical conditioning," Dr. Dale Groom concluded when he published his findings in the *American Heart Journal*. Unlike the Spartans, however, the Tarahumara are benign as bodhisattvas; they don't use their superstrength to kick ass, but to live in peace. "As a culture, they're one of the great unsolved mysteries," says Dr. Daniel Noveck, a University of Chicago anthropologist who specializes in the Tarahumara.

The Tarahumara are so mysterious, in fact, they even go by an alias. Their real name is Rarámuri—the Running People. They were dubbed "Tarahumara" by conquistadores who didn't understand the tribal tongue. The bastardized name stuck because the Rarámuri remained true to form, running away rather than hanging around to argue the point. Answering aggression with their heels has always been the Rarámuri way. Ever since Cortés's armored invaders came jangling into their homeland and then through subsequent invasions by Pancho Villa's roughriders and Mexican drug barons, the Tarahumara have responded to attacks by running farther and faster than anyone could follow, retreating ever deeper into the Barrancas.

God, they must be unbelievably disciplined, I thought. *Total focus and dedication. The Shaolin monks of running.*

Well, not quite. When it comes to marathoning, the Tarahumara prefer more of a Mardi Gras approach. In terms of diet, lifestyle, and belly fire, they're a track coach's nightmare. They drink like New Year's Eve is a weekly event, tossing back enough corn beer in a year to spend every third day of their adult lives either buzzed or recovering. Unlike Lance, the Tarahumara don't replenish their bodies with electrolyte-rich sports drinks. They don't rebuild between workouts with protein bars; in fact, they barely eat any protein at all, living on little more than ground corn spiced up by their favorite delicacy, barbecued mouse. Come race day, the Tarahumara don't train or taper. They don't stretch or warm up. They just stroll to the starting line, laughing and bantering . . . then go like hell for the next forty-eight hours.

How come they're not crippled? I wondered. It's as if a clerical error entered the stats in the wrong columns: shouldn't *we*—the ones with state-of-the-art running shoes and custom-made orthotics—have the zero casualty rate, and the Tarahumara—who run way more, on way rockier terrain, in shoes that barely qualify as shoes—be constantly banged up?

Their legs are just tougher, since they've been running all their lives, I thought, before catching my own goof. *But that means they should be hurt* more, *not less: if running is bad for your legs, then running lots should be a lot worse.*

I shoved the article aside, feeling equal parts intrigued and annoyed. Everything about the Tarahumara seemed backward, taunting, as irritatingly ungraspable as a Zen master's riddles. The toughest guys were the gentlest; battered legs were the bounciest; the healthiest people had the crappiest diet; the illiterate race was the wisest; the guys working the hardest were having the most fun. . . .

And what did running have to do with all this? Was it a coincidence that the world's most enlightened people were also the world's most amazing runners? Seekers used to climb the Himalayas for that kind of wisdom—and all this time, I realized, it was just a hop across the Texas border.

CHAPTER 3

FIGURING OUT WHERE over the border, however, was going to be tricky.

Runner's World magazine assigned me to trek into the Barrancas in search of the Tarahumara. But before I could start looking for the ghosts, I'd need to find a ghost hunter. Salvador Holguín, I was told, was the only man for the job.

By day, Salvador is a thirty-three-year-old municipal administrator in Guachochi, a frontier town on the edge of the Copper Canyons. By night, he's a barroom mariachi singer, and he looks it; with his beer gut and black-eyed, rose-in-the-teeth good looks, he's the exact image of a guy who splits his life between desk chairs and bar stools. Salvador's brother, however, is the Indiana Jones of the Mexican school system; every year, he loads a burro with pencils and workbooks and bushwhacks into the Barrancas to resupply the canyon-bottom schools. Because Salvador is game for just about anything, he has occasionally blown off work to accompany his brother on these expeditions.

"*Hombre*, no problem," he told me once I'd tracked him down. "We can go see Arnulfo Quimare. . . ."

If he'd stopped right there, I'd have been ecstatic. While searching for a guide, I'd learned that Arnulfo Quimare was the greatest living Tarahumara runner, and he came from a clan of cousins, brothers, in-laws, and nephews who were nearly as good. The prospect of heading right to the hidden huts of the Quimare dynasty was better than I could have hoped for. The only problem was, Salvador was still talking.

". . . I'm *pretty* sure I know the way," he continued. "I've never actually been there. *"Pues, lo que sea."* Well, whatever. "We'll find it. Eventually."

Ordinarily, that would sound a little ominous, but compared with everyone else I'd talked with, Salvador was wildly optimistic. Since fleeing into no-man's-land four hundred years ago, the Tarahumara have spent their time perfecting the art of invisibility. Many Tarahumara still live in cliffside caves reachable only by long climbing poles; once inside, they pull up the poles and vanish into the rock. Others live in huts so ingeniously camouflaged, the great Norwegian explorer Carl Lumholtz was once startled to discover he'd trekked right past an entire Tarahumara village without detecting a hint of homes or humans.

Lumholtz was a true backwoods badass who'd spent years living among headhunters in Borneo before heading into Tarahumara Land in the late 1890s. But you can sense even his fortitude grinding thin after he'd dragged himself through deserts and up death-defying cliffs, only to arrive at last in the heart of Tarahumara country to find . . .

No one.

"To look at these mountains is a soul-inspiring sensation; but to travel over them is exhaustive to muscle and patience," Lumholtz wrote in *Unknown Mexico: A Record of Five Years' Exploration Among the Tribes of the Western Sierra Madre.* "Nobody except those who have travelled in the Mexican mountains can understand and appreciate the difficulties and anxieties attending such a journey."

And that's assuming you make it as far as the mountains in the first place. "On first encounter, the region of the Tarahumara appears inaccessible," the French playwright Antonin Artaud grumbled after he sweated and inched his way into the Copper Canyons in search of shamanic wisdom in the 1930s. "At best, there are a few poorly marked trails that every twenty yards seem to disappear under the ground." When Artaud and his guides finally did discover a path, they had to gulp hard before taking it: subscribing to the principle that the best trick for throwing off pursuers was to travel places where only a lunatic would follow, the Tarahumara snake their trails over suicidally steep terrain.

"A false step," an adventurer named Frederick Schwatka jotted in his notebook during a Copper Canyon expedition in 1888, "would send the climber two hundred to three hundred feet to the bottom of the canyon, perhaps a mangled corpse."

Schwatka was no prissy Parisian poet, either; he was a U.S. Army lieutenant who'd survived the frontier wars and later lived among the Sioux as an amateur anthropologist, so the man knew from mangled corpses. He'd also traveled the baddest of badlands in his time, including a hellacious two-year expedition to the Arctic Circle. But when he got to the Copper Canyons, he had to recalibrate his scoring table. Scanning the ocean of wilderness around him, Schwatka felt a quick pulse of admiration—"The heart of the Andes or the crests of the Himalayas contain no more sublime scenery than the wild, unknown fastnesses of the Sierra Madres of Mexico"—before being jerked back to morbid bewilderment: "How they can rear children on these cliffs without a loss of one hundred percent annually is to me one of the most mysterious things connected with these strange people."

Even today, when the Internet has shrunk the world into a global village and Google satellites let you spy on a stranger's backyard on the other side of the country, the traditional Tarahumara remain as ghostly as they were four hundred years ago. In the mid-1990s, an expeditionary group was pushing into the deep Barrancas when they were suddenly rattled by the feeling of invisible eyes:

"Our small party had been hiking for hours through Mexico's Barranca del Cobre—the Copper Canyon—without seeing a trace of any other human being," wrote one member of the expedition. "Now, in the heart of a canyon even deeper than the Grand Canyon, we heard the echoes of Tarahumara drums. Their simple beats were faint at first, but soon gathered strength. Echoing off stony ridges, it was impossible to tell their number or location. We looked to our guide for direction. '¿Quién sabe?' she said. 'Who knows? The Tarahumara can't be seen unless they want to be.'"

The moon was still high when we set off in Salvador's trusty four-wheel-drive pickup. By the time the sun came up, we'd left pavement far behind and were jouncing along a dirt track that was more like a creek bed than a road, grinding along in low, low gear as we pitched and rolled like a tramp steamer on stormy seas.

I tried keeping track of our location with a compass and map, but I sometimes couldn't tell if Salvador was making a deliberate turn or taking evasive action around a fallen boulder. Soon, it didn't matter—wherever we were, it wasn't part of the known world; we were still snaking along a narrow gash through the trees, but the map showed nothing but untouched forest.

"*Mucha mota por aquí*," Salvador said, swirling a finger at the hills around us. Lots of marijuana around here.

Because the Barrancas are impossible to police, they've become a base for two rival drug cartels, Los Zetas and the New Bloods. Both were manned by ex–Army Special Forces and were absolutely ruthless; the Zetas were notorious for plunging uncooperative cops into burning barrels of diesel fuel and feeding captured rivals to the gang's mascot—a Bengal tiger. After the victims stopped screaming, their scorched and tiger-gnawed heads were carefully harvested as marketing tools; the cartels liked to mark their territory by, in one case, impaling the heads of two police officers outside a government building with a sign in Spanish reading LEARN SOME RESPECT. Later that same month, five heads were rolled onto the dance floor of a crowded nightclub. Even way out here on the fringes of the Barrancas, some six bodies were turning up a week.

But Salvador seemed totally unconcerned. He drove on through the woods, throatily butchering something about a bra full of bad news named Maria. Suddenly, the song died in his mouth. He snapped off the tape player, his eyes fixed on a red Dodge pickup with smoked-black glass that had just burst through the dust ahead of us.

"*Narcotraficantes*," he muttered.

Drug runners. Salvador edged as close as he could to the cliff edge on our right and eased even further back on the gas, dropping deferentially from the ten miles per hour we'd been averaging down to a dead halt, granting the big red Dodge every bit of road he could spare.

No trouble here was the message he was trying to send. *Just minding our own, non*-mota *business. Just don't stop* . . . because what would we say if they cut us off and came piling out, demanding that we speak slowly and clearly into the barrels of their assault rifles while we explained what the hell we were doing way out here in the middle of Mexican marijuana country?

We couldn't even tell them the truth; if they believed us, we were dead. If Mexico's drug gangs hated anything as much as cops, it was singers and reporters. Not singers in any slang sense of snitches or stool pigeons; they hated real, guitar-strumming, love-song-singing crooners. Fifteen singers were executed by drug gangs in just eighteen months, including the beautiful Zayda Peña, the twenty-eight-year-old lead singer of Zayda y Los Culpables, who was gunned down after a concert; she survived, but the hit team tracked her to the hospital and blasted her to death while she was recovering from surgery. The young heartthrob Valentín Elizalde was killed by a barrage of bullets from an AK-47 just across the border from McAllen, Texas, and Sergio Gómez was killed shortly after he was nominated for a Grammy; his genitals were torched, then he was strangled to death and dumped in the street. What doomed them, as far as anyone could tell, was their fame, good looks, and talent; the singers challenged the drug lords' sense of their own importance, and so were marked for death.

The bizarre fatwa on balladeers was emotional and unpredictable, but the contract on reporters was all business. News articles about the cartels got picked up by American papers, which embarrassed American politicians, which put pressure on the Drug Enforcement Administration to crack down. Infuriated, the Zetas threw hand grenades into newsrooms, and even sent killers across the U.S. border to hunt down meddlesome journalists. After thirty reporters were killed in six years, the editor of the Villahermosa newspaper found the severed head of a low-level drug soldier outside his office with a note reading, "You're next." The death toll had gotten so bad, Mexico would eventually rank second only to Iraq in the number of killed or kidnapped reporters.

And now we'd saved the cartels a lot of trouble; a singer and a journalist had just driven smack into their backyard. I jammed my notebook down my pants and quickly scanned the front seat for more things to hide. It was hopeless; Salvador had his group's tapes scattered everywhere, a shiny red press pass was in my wallet, and right between my feet was a backpack full of tape recorders, pens, and a camera.

The red Dodge pulled alongside us. It was a glorious, sunny day with a cool, pine-scented breeze, but the truck's windows were all tightly shut, leaving the mysterious crew invisible behind their smoked-black glass. The truck slowed to a rumbling crawl.

Just keep going, I chanted inside my head. *Don't stop don'tstopdon't don'tdon't . . .*

The truck stopped. I cut my eyes hard left and saw Salvador was staring straight ahead, his hands frozen on the steering wheel. I darted my eyes forward again and didn't move a muscle.

We sat.

They sat.

We were silent.

They were silent.

Six murders a week, I was thinking. *Burned his balls off.* I could see my head rolling between panicky stilettos on a Chihuahua dance floor.

Suddenly, a roar split the air. My eyes slashed left again. The big red Dodge was spitting back to life and growling on past.

Salvador watched in the side-view mirror till the Deathmobile disappeared in a swirl of dust. Then he slapped the steering wheel and blasted his *ay-yay-yaying* tape again.

"*¡Bueno!*" he shouted. "*¡Ándale pues, a más aventuras!*" Excellent! On to more adventures!

Parts of me that had clenched tight enough to crack walnuts slowly began to relax. But not for long.

A few hours later, Salvador stomped on the brakes. He backed up, cut a hard right off the rutted path, and started winding between the trees. We wandered farther and farther into the woods, crunching over pine needles and bouncing into gullies so deep I was banging my head on the roll bar.

As the woods got darker, Salvador got quieter. For the first time since our encounter with the Deathmobile, he even turned off the music. I thought he was drinking in the solitude and stillness, so I tried to sit back and appreciate it with him. But when I finally broke the silence with a question, he grunted moodily back at me. I began to suspect what was going on: we were lost, and Salvador didn't want to admit it. I watched him more closely, and noticed he was slowing down to study the tree trunks, as if somewhere in the cuneiform bark was a decryptable road atlas.

"We're screwed," I realized. We had a one-in-four shot of this turning out well, which left three other possibilities: driving smack back into the Zetas, driving off a cliff in the dark, or driving around in the wilderness until the Clif Bars ran out and one of us ate the other.

And then, just as the sun set, we ran out of planet.

We emerged from the woods to find an ocean of empty space ahead—a crack in the earth so vast that the far side could be in a different time zone. Down below, it looked like a world-ending explosion frozen in stone, as if an angry god had been in the midst of destroying the planet, then changed his mind in mid-apocalypse. I was staring at twenty thousand square miles of wilderness, randomly slashed into twisting gorges deeper and wider than the Grand Canyon.

I walked to the edge of the cliff, and my heart started to pound. A sheer drop fell for about . . . ever. Far below, birds were swirling about. I could just make out the mighty river at the bottom of the canyon; it looked like a thin blue vein in an old man's arm. My stomach clenched. How the hell would we get down there?

"We'll manage," Salvador assured me. "The Rarámuri do it all the time."

When I didn't look any more cheerful, Salvador came up with a silver lining. "Hey, it's better this way," he said. "It's too steep for *narcotraficantes* to mess around down there."

I didn't know if he really believed it or was lying to buck me up. Either way, he should have known better.

CHAPTER 4

TWO DAYS LATER, Salvador dropped his backpack, mopped his sweating face, and said, "We're here."

I looked around. There was nothing but rocks and cactus.

"We're where?"

"*Aquí mismo*," Salvador said. "Right here. This is where the Quimare clan lives."

I didn't get what he was talking about. As far as the eye could see, it was exactly like the dark side of a lost planet we'd been hiking over for days. After ditching the truck on the rim of the canyon, we'd slid and scrambled our way down to the bottom. It had been a relief to finally walk on level ground, but not for long; after striking out upstream the next morning, we found ourselves wedged tighter and tighter between the soaring stone walls. We pushed on, holding our backpacks on our heads as we shoved against water up to our chests. The sun was slowly eclipsed by the steep walls, until we were inching our way through gurgling darkness, feeling as if we were slowly walking to the bottom of the sea.

Eventually, Salvador spotted a gap in the slick wall and we climbed through, leaving the river behind. By midday, I was longing for the gloomy dark again; with a baking sun overhead and nothing but bare rock all around, pulling ourselves up that slope was like climbing a steel sliding board. Salvador finally stopped, and I dropped against a rock to rest.

Damn, he's tough, I thought. Sweat was pouring down Salvador's sunburned face, but he stayed on his feet. He had a strange, expectant look on his face.

"*¿Qué pasa?*" I asked. "What's up?"

"They're right here," Salvador said, pointing to a little hill.

I hauled myself back up. I followed him through a crack between the rocks, and found myself facing a dark opening. The hill was actually a small hut, fashioned from mud bricks and contoured into the hillside so that it was invisible until you were literally on top of it.

I took another look around to see if I'd missed any other camouflaged homes, but there wasn't a hint of another human in any direction. The Tarahumara prefer to live in such isolation, even from each other, that members of the same village don't like to be close enough to see each other's cook smoke.

I opened my mouth to call out, then shut it. Someone was already there, standing in the dark, watching us. Then Arnulfo Quimare, the most feared of Tarahumara runners, stepped outside.

"*Kuira-bá,*" Salvador said in the only words he knew in the Tarahumara language. "We're all one."

Arnulfo was looking at me.

"*Kuira-bá,*" I repeated.

"*Kuira,*" Arnulfo breathed, his voice as soft as a sigh. He put out his hand for the Tarahumara handshake, a soft sliding of fingertips. Then he vanished back inside. We waited and . . . waited some more. Was that it? There wasn't a whisper from inside the hut, not a sign that he intended to come back out. I edged around the corner to see if he'd slipped out the back. Another Tarahumara man was napping in the shade of the back wall, but there was no sign of Arnulfo.

I shuffled over to Salvador. "Is he coming back?"

"*No sé,*" Salvador said, shrugging. "I don't know. We might have really pissed him off."

"Already? How?"

"We shouldn't have just come up like that." Salvador was kicking himself. He'd gotten overexcited, and violated a key rule of Tarahumara etiquette. Before approaching a Tarahumara cave, you have to take a seat on the ground a few dozen yards away and wait. You then look off in the opposite direction for a while, as if you'd just happened to be wandering by with nothing better to do. If someone appears and invites you into the cave, great. If not, you get up and go. You do not go walking right up to the entrance, the way Salvador and I had. The Tarahumara like to be visible only if they decide to be; laying eyes on them without invitation was like barging in on someone naked in the bathroom.

Luckily, Arnulfo turned out to be the forgiving type. He returned a few moments later, carrying a basket of sweet limes. We'd turned up at a bad time, he explained; his whole family was down with the flu. That body behind the hut was his big brother, Pedro, who was too conked out with fever to even get up. Still, Arnulfo invited us to rest.

"*Assag*," he said. Have a seat.

We sprawled in whatever shade we could find and began peeling limes, gazing at the tumbling river. As we chomped and spat seeds in the dirt, Arnulfo stared off silently at the water. Every once in a while, he turned and gave me an appraising look. He never asked who we were or why we were there; it seemed like he wanted to figure it out for himself.

I tried not to stare, but it's hard to keep your eyes off a guy as good-looking as Arnulfo. He was brown as polished leather, with whimsical dark eyes that glinted with bemused self-confidence from under the bangs of his black bowl-cut. He reminded me of the early Beatles; *all* the early Beatles, rolled into one shrewd, amused, quietly handsome composite of raw strength. He was dressed in typical Tarahumara garb, a thigh-length skirt and a fiery red tunic as billowy as a pirate's blouse. Every time he moved, the muscles in his legs shifted and re-formed like molten metal.

"You know, we've met," Salvador told him in Spanish.

Arnulfo nodded.

Three years in a row, Arnulfo had hiked for days to show up in Guachochi for a sixty-mile race through the canyons. It's an annual all-comers race pitting Tarahumara from throughout the Sierras, plus the rare handful of Mexican runners willing to test their legs and luck against the tribesmen. Three years in a row, Arnulfo won. He took the title from his brother, Pedro, and was followed in second and third by a cousin, Avelado, and his brother-in-law, Silvino.

Silvino was an odd case, a Tarahumara who straddled the line between old and new worlds. Years ago, a Christian Brother who ran a small Tarahumara school had trekked with Silvino to a marathon somewhere in California. Silvino won, and came home with enough money for an old pickup truck, a pair of jeans, and a new wing for the schoolhouse. Silvino kept his truck at the top of the canyon, occasionally hiking up to drive into Guachochi. But even though he'd found a surefire way to make cash, he'd never returned to race again.

When it comes to the rest of the planet, the Tarahumara are living contradictions: they shun outsiders, but are fascinated by the outside world. In one way, it makes sense: when you love running extraordinary distances, it must be tempting to cut loose and see where, and how far, your legs can take you. A Tarahumara man once turned up in Siberia; he'd somehow strayed onto a tramp steamer and vagabonded his way across the Russian steppes before being picked up and shipped back to Mexico. In 1983, a Tarahumara woman in her swirling native skirts was discovered wandering the streets of a town in Kansas; she spent the next twelve years in an insane asylum before a social worker finally realized she was speaking a lost language, not gibberish.

"Would you ever race in the United States?" I asked Arnulfo.

He continued to chomp limes and spit seeds. After a while, he shrugged.

"Are you going to run again in Guachochi?"

Chomp. Chomp. Shrug.

Now I knew what Carl Lumholtz meant about Tarahumara men being so bashful that if it weren't for beer, the tribe would be extinct. "Incredible as it may sound," Lumholtz had marveled, "I do not hesitate to state that in the ordinary course of his existence the uncivilised Tarahumare is too bashful and modest to enforce his matrimonial rights and privileges; and that by means of tesvino chiefly the race is kept alive and increasing." Translation: Tarahumara men couldn't even muster the nerve to get romantic with their own wives if they didn't drown their bashfulness in home brew.

Only later did I find out that I'd thrown my own wrench into the social wheels with big blunder Number 2: Quizzing Him Like a Cop. Arnulfo wasn't being rude with his silence; I was being creepy with my questions. To the Tarahumara, asking direct questions is a show of force, a demand for a possession inside their head. They certainly wouldn't abruptly open up and spill their secrets to a stranger;

strangers were the reason the Tarahumara were hidden down here in the first place. The last time the Tarahumara had been open to the outside world, the outside world had put them in chains and mounted their severed heads on nine-foot poles. Spanish silver hunters had staked their claim to Tarahumara land—and Tarahumara labor—by decapitating their tribal leaders.

"Raramuri men were rounded up like wild broncos and impressed into slave labor in the mines," one chronicler wrote; anyone who resisted was turned into a human horror show. Before dying, the captured Tarahumara were tortured for information. That was all the surviving Tarahumara needed to know about what happens when curious strangers come calling.

The Tarahumara's relationship with the rest of the planet only got worse after that. Wild West bounty hunters were paid one hundred dollars apiece for Apache scalps, but it didn't take long for them to come up with a vicious way to maximize the reward while eliminating the risk; rather than tangling with warriors who'd fight back, they simply massacred the peaceful Tarahumara and cashed in on their look-alike hair.

Good guys were even deadlier than the villains. Jesuit missionaries showed up with Bibles in their hands and influenza in their lungs, promising eternal life but spreading instant death. The Tarahumara had no antibodies to combat the disease, so Spanish flu spread like wildfire, wiping out entire villages in days. A Tarahumara hunter would leave his family for a week in search of game, and come home to find nothing but corpses and flies.

No wonder the Tarahumara's mistrust of strangers had lasted four hundred years and led them here, to a last refuge at the bottom of the earth. It also led to a meat cleaver of a vocabulary when it comes to describing people. In the Tarahumara tongue, humans come in only two forms: there are *Rarámuri*, who run from trouble, and *chabochis*, who cause it. It's a harsh view of the world, but with six bodies a week tumbling into their canyons, it's hard to say they're wrong.

As far as Arnulfo was concerned, he'd met his social obligation with the limes. He'd made sure the travelers were rested and refreshed, then he withdrew into himself the way his people withdrew into the canyons. I could sit there all day and pursue him with all the questions I could think of. But I wasn't going to find him.

CHAPTER 5

"YES, YOU'D HAVE to be down here a *looonnng* time before they'd feel comfortable with you," I was told later that night by Ángel Nava López, who ran the Tarahumara schoolhouse in Muñerachi a few miles downriver from the Quimares' hut. "*Años y años*— years and years. Like Caballo Blanco."

"Wait," I interrupted. "Who?"

The White Horse, Ángel explained, was a tall, thin, chalky white man who jabbered his own strange language and would emerge from the hills with no warning, just materializing on the trail and loping on into the settlement. He first appeared ten years before, shortly after lunch on a hot Sunday afternoon. The Tarahumara don't have a written language, let alone written records of weird hominid sightings, but Ángel was dead certain about the day, year, and strangeness of the encounter, because he's the one who did the encountering.

Ángel had been outside at the time, scanning the canyon walls to keep an eye on kids returning to school. His students slept over during the week, then scattered on Friday, climbing high into the mountains to their families' homes. On Sunday, they came traipsing back to school again. Ángel liked to do a head count as they trekked in, which is why he happened to be out in the hot noon sun when two boys came tearing down the mountainside.

The boys hit the river at full speed, churning through as though they were being chased by demons. Which, they gasped to Ángel when they made it to the schoolhouse, they probably were.

They'd been out herding goats on the mountain, they said, when a weird creature darted through the trees above them. The Creature had the shape of a man, but was taller than any human they'd ever seen. It was deathly pale and bony as a corpse, and had shocks of flame-colored hair jutting out of its skull. It was also naked. For a giant, nude cadaver, the Creature was pretty quick on its feet; it vanished into the brush before the boys could get more than a glimpse.

Not that they hung around for more glimpsing. The two boys hightailed it back to the village, wondering who—or *what*—they'd just seen. After they reached Ángel, though, they began to calm down and catch their breath, and they realized who it was.

"That's the first *chuhuí* I ever saw," one of the boys said.

"A ghost?" Ángel said. "What makes you think it was a ghost?"

By this point, several Rarámuri elders had ambled up to see what was going on. The boys repeated their story, describing the Creature's skeletal appearance, its wild shocks of hair, the way it ran along the trail above them. The elders heard the boys out, then set them straight. The canyon shadows could play tricks on anyone's mind, so it was no surprise the boys' imaginations had run a little wild. Still, they shouldn't be allowed to panic the younger kids with wild stories.

"How many legs did it have?" the elders asked.

"Two."

"Did it spit on you?"

"No."

Well, there you had it. "That was no ghost," the elders said. "That was just an *ariwará*."

A soul of the dead; yes, that did make a lot more sense. Ghosts were evil phantoms who traveled by night and galloped around on all fours, killing sheep and spitting in people's faces. Souls of the dead, on the other hand, meant no harm and were just tidying up loose ends. Even in death, the Tarahumara are fanatics about elusiveness. After they die, their souls hustle around to retrieve any footprints or stray hair the body left behind. The Tarahumara technique for getting a trim was to pull their hair taut in the crotch of a tree and saw it off with a knife, so all those leftover hanks had to be picked up. Once the dead soul has erased all signs of its earthbound existence, it can venture on to the afterlife.

"The journey takes three days," the elders reminded the boys. "Four, if it's a woman." So naturally the *ariwará* is going to look a little bushy, what with all that chopped hair jammed back on its head; and of course it'll be moving top speed, with only a long weekend to knock out a ton of chores. Come to think of it, it was pretty impressive the boys managed to spot the *ariwará* at all; Tarahumara souls usually run so fast, all you see is swirl of dust sweeping across the countryside. Even in death, the elders reminded the boys, they're still the Running People.

"You're alive because your father can run down a deer. *He's* alive because his grandfather could outrun an Apache war pony. That's how fast we are when we're weighed down by our *sapá*, our fleshiness. Imagine how you'll fly once you shuck it."

Ángel listened, wondering if he should bother pointing out another possibility. Ángel was an oddity in Muñerachi, a half-Mexican Tarahumara who had actually left the canyon for a while and gone to school in a Mexican village. He still wore traditional Tarahumara sandals and the *koyera* hairband, but unlike the other elders around him, Ángel had on faded work pants instead of a breechcloth. He'd changed on the inside, as well; though he still worshipped the Tarahumara gods, he had to wonder if this Wild Thing in the Wilderness wasn't just a *chabochi* who'd wandered in from the outside world.

Granted, it was probably even more of a long shot than sharing the trail with a traveling spirit. No one ever penetrated this far unless they had a very good reason. Maybe he was a fugitive hiding from the law? A mystic seeking visions? A gold digger driven mad by the heat?

Ángel shrugged. A lone *chabochi* could be any of the above, and still not be the first of his kind to surface in Tarahumara territory. It's a natural law (or supernatural, if you're so inclined) that weird things appear where people tend to disappear. African jungles, Pacific islands, Himalayan wastelands—wherever expeditionary parties go missing, that's where lost species, Stonehengey stone idols, the flitting shadows of yetis, and ancient, unsurrendering Japanese soldiers are sure to pop up.

The Copper Canyons are no different, and in some regards, considerably worse. The Sierra Madres are the middle link of a mountain chain that stretches practically uninterrupted from Alaska to Patagonia. A desperado with a knack for backcountry navigation could hold up a bank in Colorado and slink to safety in the Copper Canyons, darting across desolate passes and desert ranges without coming within ten miles of the next human being.

As the best open-air safe house on the continent, consequently, the Copper Canyons not only spawn bizarre beings but also attract them. Over the past hundred years, the canyons have played host to just about every stripe of North American misfit: bandits, mystics, murderers, man-eating jaguars, Comanche warriors, Apache marauders, paranoid prospectors, and Pancho Villa's rebels have all shaken pursuit by slipping into the Barrancas.

Geronimo used to skeedaddle into the Copper Canyons when he was on the run from the U.S. Cavalry. So did his protégé, the Apache Kid, who "moved like a ghost in the desert," as one chronicler put it. "He followed no pattern. No one knew where he would show up next. It was unnerving to work cattle or mine a claim when every shadow, every slight noise, could be the Apache Kid closing in for the kill. One worried settler said it best: 'Usually, by the time you saw the Apache Kid it was entirely too late.' "

Pursuing them into the maze meant running the risk of never finding a way back out again. "To look at this country is grand; to travel in it, is Hell," a U.S. Cavalry captain named John Bourke wrote after barely surviving another unsuccessful pursuit of Geronimo into the Copper Canyons. The click of a tumbling pebble would echo around crazily, getting louder and louder rather than fainter, the sound bouncing from right, to left, to overhead. The rasp of two juniper branches would have an entire company of cavalrymen yanking out their pistols, their own shadows contorting monstrously against the stone walls as they searched wildly in all directions.

More than just echoes and jumpy imaginations made the Copper Canyons seem haunted; one torment could transform into another so quickly, it was hard not to believe the Barrancas were guarded by some wrathful spirit with a sadistic sense of humor. After days of baking under a merciless sun, soldiers would welcome the relief of a few dark clouds. Within minutes, they'd be trapped in a surge of floodwater as powerful as a fire hose, scrambling desperately to escape up the slippery rock walls. That's exactly how another Apache rebel named Massai once wiped out an entire cavalry squad: "By bringing them into a shallow gorge just in time to be swept away by a mountain cloudburst."

The Barrancas were so treacherous, even a quick sip of fresh water could kill you. The Apache chief Victorio used to lead U.S. Cavalry troops on a cat-and-mouse chase deep into the canyons, then lie in wait by the only water hole. The cavalrymen must have known he'd be there, but couldn't help themselves. Lost and crazed by the heat, they would rather risk a quick bullet in the head than a slow choking from a thirst-thickened tongue.

Not even the two toughest hombres in U.S. military history were any match for the Barrancas. When Pancho Villa's forces attacked a town in New Mexico in 1916, President Woodrow Wilson personally directed both Black Jack Pershing *and* George Patton to haul him out of his Copper Canyon lair. Ten years later, the Jaguar was still on the loose. Even with the full might of the U.S. armed forces at their disposal, Patton and Pershing had to be bewildered by ten thousand miles of raw wilderness, with their only possible information source, the Tarahumara, disappearing at the sound of a sneeze. The result: Black Jack and Old Blood and Guts could whip the Germans in two world wars, but surrendered to the Copper Canyons.

Over time, the Mexican *federales* learned to take a more be-careful-what-you-wish-for strategy. What was hell for pursuers, they realized, couldn't be a whole lot nicer for the pursued. Whatever happened to the fugitives in there—starvation, jaguar attack, dementia, a life sentence of voluntary solitary confinement—was probably more ghastly than anything the Mexican court system would have meted out. So, often as not, the *federales* would rein in their horses and allow any bandit who reached the canyons to try his luck in the prison of his own making.

Many adventurers who slunk in never slunk back out again, giving the canyons their reputation as the Bermuda Triangle of the borderlands. The Apache Kid and Massai galloped over Skeleton Pass into the Copper Canyons one last time and were never seen again. Ambrose Bierce, the celebrity newspaper columnist and author of the satiric hit *The Devil's Dictionary*, was reportedly en route to a ren-

dezvous with Pancho Villa in 1914 when he strayed into the Copper
Canyons' gravitational pull and was never seen again. Imagine
Anderson Cooper vanishing on assignment for CNN, and you get
the sense of the search that was launched for Bierce. But no trace was
ever found.

Did the lost souls of the canyons suffer a terrible fate, or wreak
terrible fates on each other? No one knows. In the old days, they'd be
killed off by mountain lions, scorpions, coral snakes, thirst, cold,
hunger, or canyon fever, and you could now add a sniper's bullet to
that list. Ever since the drug cartels had moved into the Copper
Canyons, they'd guarded their crops through telescopic scopes powerful enough to see a leaf quiver from miles away.

Which made Ángel wonder if he'd ever see the Creature at all. A
lot of things could kill him out there, and probably would. If the
Creature didn't know enough to keep his distance from the marijuana fields, he wouldn't even hear the shot that took off his head.

"*¡Hoooooolaaaaaa! ¡Amigoooooooooos!*"

The mystery of the lone wanderer was solved even sooner than
Ángel had expected. He was still squinting into the sun, watching out
for returning schoolkids, when he heard an echoing yodel and spotted a naked guy waving and running down the trail toward the river.

On closer inspection, the Creature wasn't entirely naked. He
wasn't exactly dressed either, certainly not by Tarahumara standards.
For a people who prefer not to be seen, the Tarahumara always look
fantastic. The men wear bright blouses over a long white cloth
bound around the groin and left hanging, skirtlike, in the front and
rear. They cinch it all together with a rainbow-colored sash, and
accessorize with a matching headband. Tarahumara women are even
more magnificent, wearing brilliantly colored skirts and matching
blouses, their lovely umber skin highlighted by coral-colored stone
necklaces and bracelets. No matter what kind of fancy hiking duds
you've got on, you're guaranteed to feel underdressed among the
Tarahumara.

Even by sun-crazed-prospector standards, the Creature was seriously shabby. He only had on some dirt-colored *chabochi* shorts, a
pair of sandals, and an old baseball cap. That was it. No backpack, no

shirt, and apparently no food, because as soon as he reached Ángel, he asked in awkward Spanish for *agua* and made shoveling gestures toward his mouth—maybe he could have something to eat?

"*Assag*," Ángel told him in Tarahumara, gesturing for him to sit. Someone produced a cup of *pinole*, the Tarahumara corn gruel. The stranger slurped it down hungrily. Between gulps, he tried to communicate. He pumped his arms and let his tongue loll like a panting dog.

"*¿Corriendo?*" the teacher asked. You've been running?

The Creature nodded. "*Todo día*," he said in pidgin Spanish. "All day."

"*¿Por qué?*" Ángel asked. "*¿Y a dónde?*" Why? And where to?

The Creature launched into a long tale, which Ángel found highly entertaining as performance art but barely intelligible as narrative. From what Ángel could make out, the lone wanderer was either totally nuts or not so lone after all; he claimed to have an even more mysterious sidekick, some kind of Apache warrior he called Ramón Chingón—"Ray, the Mean Motherfucker."

"*¿Y tú?*" Ángel asked. "What's your name?"

"Caballo Blanco," he said. The White Horse.

"*Pues, bueno*," the teacher said, shrugging. Good enough.

The White Horse didn't linger; once he'd gulped some water and a second cup of *pinole*, he waved good-bye and went trotting back up the trail. He stomped and shrieked like a wild stallion as he went, amusing the kids, who laughed and chased at his heels until he disappeared, once again, back into the wild.

"*Caballo Blanco es muy amable*," Ángel said, concluding his story, "*pero un poco raro.*" The White Horse is a good guy, in other words, if you like 'em a little loony.

"So you think he's still out there?" I asked.

"Hombre, *claro*," Ángel said. "He was here yesterday. I gave him a drink with that cup."

I looked around. There was no cup.

"The cup was there, too," Ángel insisted.

From what Ángel had picked up over the years, Caballo lived in a hut he'd built himself somewhere across the Batopilas mountain. Whenever he turned up at Ángel's school, he arrived with just the sandals on his feet, the shirt on his back (if that), and a bag of dry pinole hanging from his waist, like the Tarahumara. He seemed to live off the land when he ran, depending on *korima*, the cornerstone of Tarahumara culture.

Korima sounds like karma and functions the same way, except in the here and now. It's your obligation to share whatever you can spare, instantly and with no expectations: once the gift leaves your hand, it was never yours to begin with. The Tarahumara have no monetary system, so *korima* is how they do business: their economy is based on trading favors and the occasional cauldron of corn beer.

The White Horse looked and dressed and sounded nothing like the Tarahumara, but in a deeper way, he was one of them. Ángel had heard of Tarahumara runners who used the Horse's hut as a way station during long journeys through the canyons. The Horse, in return, was always welcome to a meal and a place to rest when he came roaming through Ángel's village on his rambling runs.

Ángel waved his arm, a brusque sweep of his arm out thataway—beyond the river and the canyon top, toward non-Tarahumara country whence no good can come.

"There's a village called Mesa de la Yerbabuena," he said. "Do you know it, Salvador?"

"Mm-hm," Salvador murmured.

"Do you know what happened to it?"

"Mm-*HM*," Salvador replied, his inflection conveying *Hell, yeah*.

"Many of the best runners were from Yerbabuena," Ángel said. "They had a very good trail which would let them cover a lot of distance in a day, much farther than you could get to from here."

Unfortunately, the trail was so good that the Mexican government eventually decided to slick it with asphalt and turn it into a road. Trucks began showing up in Yerbabuena, and in them, foods the Tarahumara had rarely eaten—soda, chocolate, rice, sugar, butter, flour. The people of Yerbabuena developed a taste for starch and treats, but they needed money to buy them, so instead of working their own fields, they began hitching rides to Guachochi, where they worked as dishwashers and day laborers, or selling junk crafts at the train station in Divisadero.

"That was twenty years ago," Ángel said. "Now, there are no runners in Yerbabuena."

The Yerbabuena story really scares Ángel, because now there's talk that the government has found a way to run a road along the canyon floor and right into this settlement. Why they would put a road in here, Ángel doesn't have a clue; the Tarahumara don't want it, and they're the only ones who live here. Only drug lords and illegal loggers benefit from Copper Canyon roads, which makes the Mexican government's obsession with backcountry road-building rather bewildering—or, considering how many soldiers and politicians are linked to the drug trade, rather not.

"That's exactly what Lumholtz was afraid would happen," I thought to myself. A century ago, the farseeing explorer was already warning that the Tarahumara were in danger of disappearing.

"Future generations will not find any other record of the Tarahumares than what scientists of the present age can elicit from the lips of the people and from the study of their implements and customs," he predicted. "They stand out to-day as an interesting relic of a time long gone by; as a representative of one of the most important stages in the development of the human race; as one of those wonderful primitive tribes that were the founders and makers of the history of mankind."

"There are Rarámuri who don't respect our traditions as much as Caballo Blanco," Ángel lamented. "*El Caballo sabe*—the Horse gets it."

I slumped against the wall of Ángel's schoolhouse, my legs twitching and head pounding from exhaustion. It had been grueling enough to get this far, and now it looked like the hunt had just begun.

CHAPTER 6

"WHAT A CON JOB."

Salvador and I set off the next morning, racing the sun to the rim of the canyon. Salvador set a brutal pace, often ignoring switchbacks and using his hands to scrabble straight up the cliff face like a convict scaling a prison wall. I did my best to keep up, despite my growing certainty that we'd just been tricked.

The farther we left Ángel's village behind, the more the idea nagged that the weird White Horse story was a last line of defense against outsiders who came nosing around in search of Tarahumara secrets. Like all great cons, the story of a Lone Wanderer of the High Sierras teetered between perfect and implausible; the news that there was a modern-world disciple of the ancient Tarahumara arts was better than I could have hoped for, which made it too good to believe. The White Horse seemed more myth than man, making me think that Ángel had gotten tired of my questions, dreamed up a decoy, and pointed us toward the horizon knowing we'd be hundreds of hard miles away before we wised up.

I wasn't being paranoid; it wouldn't be the first time a tall tale had been used to blow a smokescreen around the Running People. Carlos Castaneda, author of the wildly popular Don Juan books of the '60s, was almost unquestionably referring to the Tarahumara when he described magical Mexican shamans with astonishing wisdom and endurance. But in an apparent twinge of compassion, Castaneda deliberately misidentified the tribe as the Yaquis. Castaneda apparently felt that, in the event that his books launched an invasion of peyote-hungry hippies, the badass Yaquis could hold their own a lot better than the gentle Tarahumara.

But despite my suspicion that I'd just been Castanedaed, one odd incident helped spur me to stay on the hunt. Ángel had let us spend the night in the only room he had free, a tiny mud-brick hut used as the school's infirmary. The next morning, he kindly invited us to join him for a breakfast of beans and hand-patted corn tortillas before we set off. It was a frosty morning, and as we sat outside, warming our hands around the steaming bowls, a torrent of kids came swarming past us out of the schoolhouse. Rather than having the cold kids suffer in their seats, the teacher cut them loose to warm up Tarahumara-style—meaning I'd lucked into a chance to witness a *rarájipari*, the Tarahumara running game.

Ángel pulled himself to his feet and divided the kids into two teams, girls and boys together. He then produced two wooden balls, each about the size of a baseball, and flipped one to a player on each team. He held up six fingers; they'd be running six laps from the schoolhouse to the river, a total distance of about four miles. The two boys dropped the balls into the dust and arched one of their feet, so the ball was balanced on top of their toes. Slowly, they coiled themselves down into a crouch and . . .

¡Vayan! Go!

The balls whistled past us, flip-kicked off the boys' feet like they'd been fired out of a bazooka, and the kids went stampeding after them down the trail. The teams looked pretty evenly matched, but my pesos were on the gang led by Marcelino, a twelve-year-old who looked like the Human Torch; his bright red shirt flowed behind him like flames and his white skirt whipped his legs like a trail of smoke. The Torch caught up with his team's ball while it was still rolling. He wedged it expertly against the front of his toes and zinged it down the trail with barely a hitch in his stride.

Marcelino's running was so amazing, it was hard to take it all in at once. His feet were jitterbugging like crazy between the rocks, but everything above his legs was tranquil, almost immobile. Seeing him from the waist up, you'd think he was gliding along on skates. With his chin high and his black hair streaming off his forehead, he looked as if he'd burst straight out of the Steve Prefontaine poster on the bedroom wall of every high school track star in America. I felt as if I'd discovered the Future of American Running, living five hundred years in the past. A kid that talented and handsome was born to have his face on a cereal box.

"*Sí, de acuerdo*," Ángel said. Yes, I hear you. "It's in his blood. His father is a great champion."

Marcelino's father, Manuel Luna, could beat just about anyone at an all-night *rarájipari*, the grown-ups' version of the game I was watching. The real *rarájipari* was the heart and soul of Tarahumara culture, Ángel explained; everything that made the Tarahumara unique was on display during the heat of a *rarájipari*.

First, two villages would get together and spend the night making bets and pounding *tesgüino*, a homemade corn beer that could blister paint. Come sunup, the villages' two teams would face off, with somewhere between three and eight runners on each side. The runners would race back and forth over a long strip of trail, advancing their ball like soccer players on a fast break. The race could go on for twenty-four hours, even forty-eight, whatever had been agreed to the night before, but the runners could never zone out or relax into an easy rhythm; with the ball ricocheting around and up to thirty-two fast-moving legs on all sides, the runners had to be constantly on their toes as they surged, veered, and zigzagged.

"We say the *rarájipari* is the game of life," Ángel said. "You never know how hard it will be. You never know when it will end. You can't control it. You can only adjust."

And, he added, no one gets through it on their own. Even a superstar like Manuel Luna couldn't win without a village behind him. Friends and family fueled the racers with cups of *pinole*. Come nightfall, the villagers spark up sticks of *acate*, sap-rich pine branches, and the runners race through the dark by torchlight. To endure a challenge like that, you had to possess all the Tarahumara virtues—strength, patience, cooperation, dedication, and persistence. Most of all, you had to love to run.

"That one's going to be as good as his father," Ángel said, nodding toward Marcelino. "If I let him, he'd go like that all day."

Once Marcelino reached the river, he wheeled around and drilled the ball to a little six-year-old who'd lost one sandal and was struggling with his belt. For a few glorious moments, Little One-Shoe was leading his team and loving it, hopping on one bare foot while grappling to keep his skirt from falling off. That's when I began to glimpse the real genius of the *rarájipari*. Because of gnarly trails and back-and-forth laps, the game is endlessly and instantly self-handicapping; the ball ricocheted around as if it were coming off a pinball paddle, allowing the slower kids to catch up whenever Marcelino had to root it out of a crevice. The playing field levels the playing field, so everyone is challenged and no one is left out.

The boys and girls were all hurtling up and down the hilly trail, but no one really seemed to care who won; there was no arguing, no showboating, and, most noticeably, no coaching. Ángel and the schoolteacher were watching happily and with intense interest, but not yelling advice. They weren't even cheering. The kids accelerated when they felt frisky, downshifted when they didn't, and caught an occasional breather under a shady tree when they overdid it and started sucking wind.

But unlike most of the other players, Marcelino never seemed to slow. He was tireless, flowing uphill as lightly as he coasted down, his legs scissoring in a surprisingly short, mincing stride that somehow still looked smooth, not choppy. He was on the tall side for a Tarahumara boy, and had the same thrill-of-the-game grin that always used to creep across Michael Jordan's face as the clock was ticking down. On his team's final lap, Marcelino fired a bank shot off a big rock to the left, calculated the ricochet, and was in position to receive his own pass, picking the ball up on the fly and covering fifty yards in a matter of seconds over a trail as rocky as a riverbed.

Ángel banged on an iron bar with the back of a hatchet. Game over. The kids begin filing back inside the schoolhouse, the older ones carrying wood for the school's open fireplace. Few returned our greeting; many had only heard their first words of Spanish the day they started school. Marcelino, however, stepped out of line and came over. Ángel had told him what we were up to.

"*Que vayan bien,*" Marcelino said. Good luck with your trip. "*Caballo Blanco es muy norawa de mi papá.*"

Norawa? I'd never heard the word before. "What's he mean?" I asked Salvador. "Caballo is a legend his dad knows? Some kind of story he tells?"

"No," Salvador said. "*Norawa* means *amigo.*"

"Caballo Blanco is good *friends* with your dad?" I asked.

"*Sí.*" Marcelino nodded, before disappearing inside the school-house. "He's a really good guy."

Okay, I thought later that afternoon. *Maybe Ángel would buffalo us, but I gotta trust the Torch.* Ángel told us Caballo might be heading to the town of Creel, but we had to hurry: if we didn't catch him, there was no telling where he'd turn up next. The Horse would often vanish for months at a time; no one knew where he went or when he'd be back. Miss him, and we might not get another chance.

And Ángel sure hadn't lied about one thing, as I was discovering by the surprising strength in my legs: just before we began our long climb out of the canyon, he'd handed me a dented tin cup full of something he promised would help.

"You'll like this," he assured me.

I peered inside. The cup was full of gooey slime that looked like rice pudding without the rice, lots of black-flecked bubbles I was pretty sure were frog eggs in midhatch. If I were anywhere else, I'd think it was a gag; it looked exactly like a kid had scooped the scum out of his aquarium to see if he could trick me into tasting it. Best guess, it was some kind of fermented root mixed with river water— meaning if the taste didn't make me hurl, the bacteria would.

"Great," I said, looking around for a cactus I could dump it behind. "What is it?"

"*Iskiate.*"

That sounded familiar . . . and then I remembered. The indomitable Lumholtz had once staggered into a Tarahumara home looking for food while he was in the middle of a grueling expedition. Looming ahead was a mountain he had to summit by nightfall. Lumholtz was exhausted and despairing; there was no way he had the strength left for the climb.

"I arrived late one afternoon at a cave where a woman was just making this drink," Lumholtz later wrote. "I was very tired and at a loss how to climb the mountain-side to my camp, some two thousand feet above. But after having satisfied my hunger and thirst with some *iskiate,*" he went on, "I at once felt new strength, and, to my own astonishment, climbed the great height without much effort. After this I always found *iskiate* a friend in need, so strengthening and refreshing that I may almost claim it as a discovery."

Home-brewed Red Bull! Now this I had to try. "I'll save it for later," I told Ángel. I poured the *iskiate* into a hip bottle that was half full of water I'd purified with iodine pills, then tossed in a couple of extra pills for good measure. I was dog tired, but unlike Lumholtz, I wasn't desperate enough to risk a yearlong bout of chronic diarrhea from waterborne bacteria.

Months later, I'd learn that *iskiate* is otherwise known as *chia fresca*—"chilly *chia*." It's brewed up by dissolving *chia* seeds in water with a little sugar and a squirt of lime. In terms of nutritional content, a tablespoon of *chia* is like a smoothie made from salmon, spinach, and human growth hormone. As tiny as those seeds are, they're superpacked with omega-3s, omega-6s, protein, calcium, iron, zinc, fiber, and antioxidants. If you had to pick just one desert-island food, you couldn't do much better than *chia*, at least if you were interested in building muscle, lowering cholesterol, and reducing your risk of heart disease; after a few months on the *chia* diet, you could probably swim home. *Chia* was once so treasured, the Aztecs used to deliver it to their king in homage. Aztec runners used to chomp *chia* seeds as they went into battle, and the Hopis fueled themselves on *chia* during their epic runs from Arizona to the Pacific Ocean. The Mexican state of Chiapas is actually named after the seed; it used to rank right up there with corn and beans as a cash crop. Despite its liquid-gold status, *chia* is ridiculously easy to grow; if you own a Chia Pet, in fact, you're only a few steps away from your own batch of devil drink.

And a damn tasty devil drink at that, as I discovered once the iodine had melted enough to risk a few swigs. Even with the medicinal after-bite from the pills, the *iskiate* went down like fruit punch with a nice limey tang. Maybe the excitement of the hunt had something to do with it, but within minutes, I felt fantastic. Even the low-throbbing headache I'd had all morning from sleeping on a frosty dirt floor the night before had vanished.

Salvador kept pushing us hard, racing daylight to the canyon rim. We almost made it, too. But when we had a good two hours' worth of climbing still ahead, the sun vanished, plunging the canyon into darkness so deep that all I could make out were varying shades of black. We debated rolling out our sleeping bags and camping right there for the night, but we'd run out of food and water over an hour earlier and the temperature was dropping below freezing. If we could just feel our way up another mile, we might catch enough light above the rim to make it out. We decided to go for it; I hated the idea of shivering all night on a sliver of trail on the edge of a cliff.

It was so dark, I could only follow Salvador by the crunch of his boots. How he was finding the turns on those steep switchbacks without straying over the edge, I didn't really want to know. But he'd proven me wrong with his psychic navigation when he was driving us through the woods, so I owed it to him to shut up, pay careful attention to his every move, and . . . and . . .

Wait. What happened to the crunching?

"Salvador?"

Nothing. Shit.

"Salvador!"

"*¡No pases por aquí!*" he called from somewhere ahead of me. Don't go this way!

"What's the prob—"

"*Calla.*" Shut up.

I *calla*ed and stood in the dark, wondering what the hell was wrong. Minutes passed. Not a sound from Salvador. "He'll be back," I told myself. "He would have screamed if he had fallen. You'd have heard something. A crash. Something. But damn, he's taking a long—"

"*Bueno.*" A shout came from somewhere above me and off to the right. "Good here. But go slow!" I twisted toward the sound of his voice and slowly inched along. To my left, I felt the ground drop abruptly away. How close Salvador had come to stepping into empty air, I didn't want to know.

By ten that night, we'd made it to the rim of the cliff and crawled into our bags, chilled to the bone and just as weary. The next morning, we were up before the sun and fast-hiking back to the truck. By the time dawn broke, we were already well on the bouncing, meandering, word-of-mouth trail of the White Horse.

Every time we came to a farm or tiny village, we hit the brakes and asked if anyone knew Caballo Blanco. Everywhere—in the village of Samachique, at the schoolhouse in Huisichi—we heard the same thing: *Sí*, of course! He passed through last week . . . a few days ago . . . yesterday. . . . You *just* missed him. . . .

We came to a little cluster of ramshackle cabins and stopped for food. "*Ahhh, ten cuidado con ese,*" the old woman behind the counter of a roadside stand said as she passed me a dust-covered bag of chips and a warm Coke with her thin, trembly hands. "Be careful with that one. I heard about that Caballo. He was a fighter who went loco. A man died, and he went loco. He can kill you with his hands. And," she added, in case I'd forgotten, "he's loco."

The last place he'd been spotted was the old mining town of Creel, where a woman in a taco stand told us she'd seen him that very morning, walking the train tracks toward the edge of town. We followed the tracks to the end of the line, asking all the way, until we reached the final building: the Casa Pérez hotel. Where, I was both thrilled and nervous to hear, he was supposed to be at that moment.

Maybe it was a good thing I fell asleep on the corner sofa. That way, at least, I was hidden in the shadows and managed to get a good look at the lone wanderer—before he saw me, and bolted right back into the wild.

CHAPTER 7

LUCKILY, I WAS closer to the door.

"Hey! Uh, do you know Ángel?" I stammered as I stepped between Caballo and his only way out. "The teacher at the Tarahumara school? And Esidro in Huisichi? And, um, Luna, Miguel Luna . . ." I kept shotgunning names, hoping he'd hear one he recognized before body-slamming me against the wall and escaping into the hills behind the hotel. ". . . No, *Manuel.* Not Miguel Luna. Manuel. His son said you guys were friends. Marcelino? You know Marcelino?"

But the more I talked, the more his scowl deepened, until it looked downright menacing. I snapped my mouth shut. I'd learned my lesson after the Debacle at the Quimare Compound; maybe he'd cool out if I kept quiet and gave him a chance to size me up on his own. I stood silently while he squinted, suspicious and scornful, from under the brim of his straw campesino's hat.

"Yeah," he grunted. "Manuel is an amigo. Who the hell are you?"

Since I didn't really know what was making him skittish, I started with who I wasn't. I wasn't a cop or a DEA agent, I told him. I was just a writer and busted-up runner who wanted to learn the secrets of the Tarahumara. If he was a fugitive, that was his own business. If anything, it boosted his credibility: anyone who could dodge the law for all these years with no getaway vehicle except his own two legs had sure made his bones as a wannabe Rarámuri. I could set aside my obligations to justice long enough to hear what had to be the escape tale of a lifetime.

Caballo's scowl didn't fade—but he didn't try to get around me, either. Only later would I discover that I'd gotten extraordinarily lucky and stumbled across him at a strange time in his very strange life: in his own way, Caballo Blanco was looking for me, too.

"Okay, man," he said. "But I've got to get some beans."

He led me out of the hotel and down a dusty alley to a small, unmarked door. We stepped over a little boy playing with a kitten on the doorstep and right into a tiny living room. An old woman looked up from an ancient gas stove in an adjoining alcove, where she was stirring a fragrant pot of frijoles.

"*Hola, Caballo,*" she called.

"*¿Cómo está, Mamá?*" Caballo Blanco called back. We took seats at a rickety wooden table in the living room. He's got "*mamás*" all over the canyons, he said, little old ladies who'd fill him up on beans and tortillas for only a few centavos during his rambling vagabond runs.

Despite Mamá's nonchalance, I could see why the Tarahumara were spooked when Caballo first came whisking through their woods. Fantastic feats of endurance under an unforgiving sun have left Caballo a little on the savage side. He's well over six feet tall, with naturally fair skin that has weathered into shades ranging from pink on his nose to walnut on his neck. He's so long-limbed and lean-muscled, he looks like the endoskeleton of a bulkier beast; melt the Terminator in a cauldron of acid, and Caballo Blanco is what comes out.

The desert glare had scrunched his eyes into a permanent squint, leaving his face capable of only two expressions: skepticism or amusement. No matter what I said for the rest of the night, I could never tell if he thought I was hilarious or full of shit. When Caballo turns his attention on you, he locks in hard; he listens as attentively as a hunter tracking game, seeming to get as much from the warbles of your voice as from the meaning of your words. Oddly, though, he still has an abominable ear for accents—after more than a decade in Mexico, his Spanish clanged so badly it sounded as if he were sounding it out from phonics cards.

"What freaked me out about you—," Caballo began, but suddenly stopped, bug-eyed with hunger, as Mamá plopped big bowls in front of us and futzed over them with chopped cilantro and jalapeños and squirts of lime. The snarling look he'd given me back at the hotel wasn't because I was standing between him and freedom; it was because I was standing between him and food. Caballo had set out that morning for a short hike to a natural thermal pool in the woods, but once he spotted a faint trail through the trees he'd never seen before, hike and hot tub were history. He took off running, and was still going hours later. He hit a mountain, but instead of turning back, he bent himself into a three-thousand-foot ascent, the equivalent of climbing to the top of the Empire State Building twice. Eventually, he linked onto a path back into Creel, turning what should have been a relaxing soak into a grueling trail marathon. By the time I shanghaied him in the hotel, he hadn't eaten since sunup and was nearly delirious with hunger.

"I'm always getting lost and having to vertical-climb, water bottle between my teeth, buzzards circling over head," he said. "It's a beautiful thing." One of the first and most important lessons he learned from the Tarahumara was the ability to break into a run anytime, the way a wolf would if it suddenly sniffed a hare. To Caballo, running has become as much of a first option in transportation as driving is to suburbanites; everywhere he goes, he goes at a lope, setting off as lightly equipped as a Neolithic hunter and with just as little concern about where—or how far away—he'll end up.

"Look," he said, pointing to his ancient hiking shorts and Dumpster-ready pair of Teva sandals. "That's all I wear, and I'm always wearing them."

He paused to shovel steaming mounds of spicy beans into his mouth, washing them down with long, thirsty pulls on a bottle of Tecate. Caballo polished off one bowl and was refilled by Mamá so quickly that he barely slowed his spoon, moving his hand from bowl to mouth to beer bottle with such ergonomic efficiency that dinner seemed less like the end of his long workout and more like its next phase. Listening to him from across the table was like listening to gas pumping into the tank of a car: *scoop, chomp, chomp, gurgle, gurgle, scoop, chomp, chomp, gurgle . . .*

Every once in a while, he'd lift his head and deliver a brief torrent of storytelling, then dip back down to his bowl. "Yeah, I used to be a fighter, man, ranked fifth in the world." Back to the spoonwork.

"What freaked me out was, you just came blaring at me out of nowhere. We've had kidnappings and murders down here. Drug nastiness. Guy I know was kidnapped, wife paid a big ransom, then they killed him anyway. Nasty stuff. Good thing I got nothing. I'm just a gringo Indio, man, running humbly with the Rarámuri."

"Sorry—," I began, but his face was already back in the beans.

I didn't want to bug Caballo with questions just yet, even though listening to him was like watching an art-house film in fast forward; traumas, jokes, fantasies, flashbacks, grudges, guilt over grudges, tantalizing fragments of ancient wisdom—they all came calliope-ing past in a blur too quick and disjointed to catch. He'd tell a story, move on to the next, skip ahead to the third, go back and correct a detail in the first, gripe about the guy in the second, then apologize for griping because, man, he'd spent his life trying to control his anger, and *that* was another story altogether. . . .

His name was Micah True, he said, and he came from Colorado. Well, California, actually. And if I really wanted to understand the Rarámuri, I should have been there when this ninety-five-year-old man came hiking twenty-five miles over the mountain. Know why he could do it? Because no one ever told him he couldn't. No one ever told him he oughta be off dying somewhere in an old age home. You live up to your own expectations, man. Like when he named himself after his dog. That's where the name "True" really came from, his old dog. He didn't always measure up to good old True Dog, but *that* was another story, too. . . .

I waited, scraping at the label of my beer bottle with a fingernail, wondering if he'd ever simmer down enough for me to figure out what the hell he was talking about. Gradually, Caballo's spoonwork slowed and came to a stop. He drained his second bottle of Tecate and sat back, satisfied.

"*Guadajuko!*" he said with a toothy grin. "Good word to learn. That's Rarámuri for 'cool.'"

I pushed a third Tecate across the table. He eyed it with that skeptical, sun-scorched squint. "I don't know, man," he said. "Not eating all day, I can't hold it like the Rarámuri."

But he picked it up and took a sip. Thirsty work, rambling up skyscraping mesas. He took a long, chugging pull, then relaxed way back in his chair, tipping the front legs up and lacing his fingers across his lean belly. Something had just clicked inside him; I could tell before he even said another word. Maybe he needed those last twelve ounces of beer to loosen up, or maybe he'd just had to blow out some pent-up steam before relaxing into his story.

Because when Caballo started to talk this time, he kept me spell-bound. He talked deep into the night, telling an amazing story that spanned the ten years since his disappearance from the outside world and was full of bizarre characters, amazing adventures, and furious fights. And, in the end, a plan. An audacious plan.

A plan, I gradually realized, that involved me.

CHAPTER 8

TO APPRECIATE Caballo's vision, you have to go back to the early '90s, when a wilderness photographer from Arizona named Rick Fisher was asking himself the obvious question: if the Tarahumara were the world's toughest runners, why weren't they ripping up the world's toughest races? Maybe it was time they met the Fisherman.

Total score all around, the way Fisher saw it. Some spit-chaw towns bag a ton of TV for their oddball races, the Fisherman turns into the Crocodile Hunter of Lost Tribes, and the Tarahumara get primo PR and become media sweethearts. Okay, so the Tarahumara are the most publicity-shy people on the planet and have spent centuries *fleeing* any kind of relations with the public, but . . .

Well, Fisher would have to deal with that speed bump later; he already had far stickier problems to handle. Like, he didn't know jack about running and barely spoke a lick of Spanish, let alone Rarámuri. He had no idea where to find Tarahumara runners, and no clue how he'd persuade them to follow him out of the safety of their caves and up into the lair of the Bearded Devils. And those were only the minor details: assuming he did assemble an all-Tarahumara track team, how the hell was he going to get them out of the canyons without cars and into America without passports?

Luckily, Fisher had some special talents going for him. Top of the list was his amazing internal GPS; Fisher was like one of those house cats who reappear at home in Wichita after getting lost on a family vacation in Alaska. His ability to sniff his way through the most bewildering canyons may be unrivaled on the planet, and it appears to be mostly raw instinct. Fisher had never seen anything deeper than a ditch before leaving the midwest for the University of Arizona, but once there, he immediately began plunging into places better left unplunged. He was still a student when he began exploring Arizona's mazelike Mogollon canyon range, venturing in just after the head of Phoenix's Sierra Club was killed there in a not-uncommon flash flood. Fisher, with zero experience and Boy Scout–grade gear, not only survived, but came back with breathtaking photos of an underground wonderland.

Even Jon Krakauer, the adventure überexpert and author of *Into Thin Air*, was impressed. "Rick Fisher can fairly lay claim to being the world's leading authority on the Mogollon canyons and the myriad secrets they contain," Krakauer concluded early in Fisher's career, after Fisher had led him to "an utterly spellbinding slice of earth, like no place I'd even seen"—a Willy Wonka world of lime-green pools and pink crystal towers and subterranean waterfalls.

Which brings up Rick Fisher's other skill set: when it comes to grabbing a spotlight and persuading people to do things they'd rather not, Fisher could put a televangelist to shame (well, as much as that's possible). Take this classic Fish tale that Krakauer tells about a rafting trip Fisher made into the Copper Canyons in the mid-1980s. Fisher really didn't know where he was going, even though he was attempting, by Krakauer's estimation, "the canyoneering equivalent of a major mountaineering expedition in the Himalaya." Yet he still managed to convince two pals—a guy and his girlfriend—to come along. Everything was going grand . . . until Fisher accidentally beached the raft next to a marijuana field. Suddenly, a drug sentinel popped up with a cocked assault rifle.

No problem. Fisher just whipped out a packet of news articles about himself he carries everywhere he goes (yup, even on very wet rafts through non-English-speaking Mexican badlands). *See! You don't want to mess with me. I'm, uh, whatchacallit—importante! ¡Muy importante!*

The bewildered sentinel let them paddle on, only to have Fisher come to shore at *another* drug encampment. This time, it got really ugly. Fisher's little band was surrounded by a band of thugs who—being womanless in the wilderness—were drunk and dangerously lusty. One of the thugs grabbed the American woman. When her boyfriend tried to pull her back, a rifle barrel was slammed into his chest.

That did it for Fisher. No fanning out his scrapbook this time; instead, he went berserk. "You're *muy malos hombres!*" he screamed in an absolute spitting fury, calling the thugs "naughty, naughty men" in his junior-high Spanish. "*¡Muy, muy malos!*" He kept screeching and raving until, as Krakauer tells it, the thugs finally silenced the shrill lunatic by shoving him aside and walking away. Fisher had just brazened his way out of a death sentence—and, naturally, he made sure that the journalist Krakauer heard about it.

Fisher loved the sound of his own horn, no doubt about it, and that spurred him to keep finding reasons to toot it. While most wild-men in the '80s were pushing skyward, racing Reinhold Messner to scale the fourteen highest peaks in the Himalayas, Rick Fisher was burrowing down to more exotic kingdoms right beneath their feet. Using notes from Captain Frederick Bailey, a British secret agent who'd stumbled across a hidden valley in Tibet in the 1930s while reconnoitering with rebel groups in Asia, Fisher helped locate the fabled Kintup Falls, a thundering cascade that conceals the entrance to the deepest canyon on the planet. From there, Fisher moled his way into lost worlds on five continents, sliding through war zones and murderous militias to pioneer descents in Bosnia, Ethiopia, China, Namibia, Bolivia, and China.

Secret agents, whizzing bullets, prehistoric kingdoms... even Ernest Hemingway would have shut up and surrendered the floor if Fisher walked into the bar. But no matter where he roamed, Fisher kept circling back home to his greatest passion: the bewitching girl next door, the Copper Canyons.

During one expedition into the Barrancas, Fisher and his fiancée, Kitty Williams, became friends with Patrocinio López, a young Tarahumara man who'd wandered into the modern world when a new logging road pushed into his homeland. Patrocinio was Hollywood handsome and musically gifted on the two-string Tarahumara *chabareke*, and so agreeable to working with the Bearded Devils that the Chihuahua Tourism Department adopted him as the face for the Copper Canyon Express, a luxury vintage train that makes whistle-stops along the rim of the Barrancas and allows tourists in air-conditioned railcars to be served by bow-tied waiters while peering at the savage country below. Patrocinio's job was to pose for posters with a violin he'd carved by hand (a handicraft legacy from the Span-ish slave days), as if to suggest that the life of the Tarahumara down yonder was all hunky guys and fiddle music.

Rick and Kitty asked Patrocinio if he could take them to a *raráji-pari*, the ancient Tarahumara ball race. *Maybe*, Patrocinio replied, before demonstrating that he'd adopted the modern world as much as it had adopted him: *If you're willing to pay*. He made Rick and Kitty an offer—he'd roust some runners, if they'd pony up food for his entire village.

Deal?

Deal.

Rick and Kitty delivered the chow, and Patrocinio delivered one hell of a race. When Rick and Kitty arrived at the village, they didn't find some rinky-dink fun run awaiting them; instead, thirty-four Tarahumara men were stripping down to breechcloths and sandals, getting prerace rubdowns from medicine men, and slamming back last-minute cups of *iskiate*. At the bark of the village elder, they were off, charging down the dirt trail in a sixty-mile, no mercy, dawn-to-dusk, semi-controlled stampede, flowing past Rick and Kitty with the speed and near-telepathic precision of migrating sparrows.

Yow! Now THAT's *running!* Kitty, a seasoned ultrarunner herself, was enthralled. She'd grown up watching her father, Ed Williams, turn himself into an unstoppable mountain racer despite living along the lowland banks of the Mississippi. Testament to Ed's toughness was the fact that of all races in the world, his favorite was one of the scariest: the notorious Leadville Trail 100, a hundred-mile ultra-marathon held in Colorado, which he'd finished twelve times and was still running *at age seventy*.

A beautiful marriage was forming in Rick's mind: Patrocinio could get him runners, and future dad-in-law Ed could get him inside juice with a prestigious race. All he had left to do was hit up some charities for corn donations to tempt the Tarahumara, and maybe get a shoe company to put them in something sturdier than those sandals, and . . .

Fisher schemed on, clueless that he was fine-tuning a fiasco.

CHAPTER 9

Make friends with pain, and you will never be alone.

—KEN CHLOUBER,
Colorado miner and creator of the Leadville Trail 100

THE BIG, fat flaw in Rick Fisher's plan was the fact that the
Leadville race happens to be held in Leadville.

Hunkered in a valley two miles up in the Colorado Rockies,
Leadville is the highest city in North America and, many days, the
coldest (the fire company couldn't ring its bell come winter, afraid it
would shatter). One look at those peaks had the first settlers shaking
in their coonskins. "For there, before their unbelieving eyes, loomed
the most powerful and forbidding geological phenomenom they had
ever seen," recounts Leadville historian Christian Buys. "They might
as well have been on another planet. It was that remote and threatening to all but the most adventuresome."

Of course, things have improved since then: the fire company
now uses a horn. Otherwise, well . . . "Leadville is a home for miners,
muckers, and mean motherfuckers," says Ken Chlouber, who was an
out-of-work, bronco-busting, Harley-riding, hard-rock miner when
he created the Leadville Trail 100, in 1982. "Folks who live at ten
thousand feet are cut from a different kind of leather."

Dog-toy-tough or not, when Leadville's top physician heard what
Ken had in mind, he was outraged. "You can*not* let people run a hundred miles at this altitude," railed Dr. Robert Woodward. He was so
pissed off he had a finger in Ken's face, which didn't bode well for his
finger. If you've seen Ken, with those steel-toed boots on his size 13
stompers and that mug as craggy as the rock he blasted for a living,

you figure out pretty quick you don't put a hand near his face unless you're dead drunk or dead serious.

Doc Woodward wasn't drunk. "You're going to kill anyone foolish enough to follow you!"

"Tough shit!" Ken shot back. "Maybe killing a few folks will get us back on the map."

Shortly before Ken's showdown with Doc Woodward on that cold autumn day in 1982, the Climax Molybdenum mine had suddenly shut down, taking with it nearly every paycheck in Leadville. "Moly" is a mineral used to strengthen steel for battleships and tanks, so once the Cold War fizzled, so did the moly market. Almost overnight, Leadville stopped being a bustling little burg with an old-timey ice-cream parlor on its old-timey main street and was transformed into the most desperate, jobless city in North America. Eight out of every ten workers in Leadville punched the clock at Climax, and the few who didn't depended on the ones who did. Once boasting the highest per capita income in Colorado, it soon found itself the county seat of one of the poorest counties in the state.

It couldn't get worse. And then it did.

Ken's neighbors were drinking hard, punching their wives, sinking into depression, or fleeing town. A sort of mass psychosis was overwhelming the city, an early stage of civic death: first, people lose the means to stick it out; then, after the knife fights, arrests, and foreclosure warnings, they lose the desire.

"People were packing up and leaving by the hundreds," recalls Dr. John Perna, who ran Leadville's emergency room. His ER was as busy as a MASH unit and confronting an ugly new trend of injuries; instead of job-site ankle sprains and smashed fingers, Dr. Perna was amputating toes from drunk miners who'd passed out in the snow, and calling the police for wives who arrived in the middle of the night with broken cheekbones and scared children.

"We were slipping into lethal doldrums," Dr. Perna told me. "Ultimately, we faced the disappearance of the city." So many miners had already left, the last citizens of Leadville couldn't fill the bleachers at a minor-league ballpark.

Leadville's only hope was tourism, which was no hope at all. What kind of idiot would vacation in a place with nine months of freezing weather, no slopes worth skiing, and air so thin that breathing counted as a cardio workout? Leadville's backcountry was so brutal that the army's elite 10th Mountain Division used to train there for Alpine combat.

Making things worse, Leadville's reputation was as scary as its geography. For decades, it was the wildest city in the Wild West, "an absolute death trap," as one chronicler put it, "that seemed to take pride in its own depravity." Doc Holliday, the dentist turned gun-slinging gambler, used to hang out in the Leadville saloons with his quick-drawin' O.K. Corral buddy Wyatt Earp. Jesse James used to slink through as well, attracted by the stages loaded with gold and excellent hideouts just a lick away in the mountains. Even as late as the 1940s, the 10th Mountain Division commandos were forbidden to set foot in downtown Leadville; they might be fierce enough for the Nazis, but not for the cutthroat gamblers and prostitutes who ruled State Street.

Yeah, Leadville was a tough place, Ken knew. Full of tough men, and even tougher women, and—

And *damn*! God*damn*! That was it.

If all Leadville had left to sell was grit, then step right up for your hot grits. Ken had heard about this guy in California, a long-haired mountain man named Gordy Ainsleigh, whose mare went lame right before the world's premier horse endurance event, the Western States Trail Ride. Gordy decided to race anyway. He showed up at the starting line in sneakers and set out to run all one hundred miles through the Sierra Nevada on foot. He slurped water from creeks, got his vitals checked by veterinarians at the medical stops, and beat the twenty-four-hour cutoff for all horses with seventeen minutes to spare. Naturally, Gordy wasn't the only lunatic in California, so the next year, another runner crashed the horse race . . . and another the year after that . . . until, by 1977, the horses were crowded out and Western States became the world's first one-hundred-mile footrace.

Ken had never even run a marathon himself, but if some Califor-nia hippie could go one hundred miles, how hard could it be? Besides, a normal race wouldn't cut it; if Leadville was going to sur-vive, it needed an event with serious holy-shit power, something to set it apart from all the identical, ho-hum, done-one-done-'em-all 26.2-milers out there.

So instead of a marathon, Ken created a monster.

To get a sense of what he came up with, try running the Boston Marathon two times in a row with a sock stuffed in your mouth and then hike to the top of Pikes Peak.

Done?

Great. Now do it all again, this time with your eyes closed. That's pretty much what the Leadville Trail 100 boils down to: nearly four full marathons, half of them in the dark, with twin twenty-six-hundred-foot climbs smack in the middle. Leadville's starting line is twice as high as the altitude where planes pressurize their cabins, and from there you only go up.

"The hospital does make a lot of money off us," Ken Chlouber happily agrees today, twenty-five years after the inaugural race and his showdown with Doc Woodward. "It's the only weekend when all the beds in the hotels *and* the emergency room are full at the same time."

Ken should know; he's run every Leadville race, despite having been hospitalized with hypothermia during his first attempt. Leadville racers routinely fall off bluffs, break ankles, suffer over-exposure, get weird heart arrhythmias and altitude sickness.

Fingers crossed, Leadville has yet to polish anyone off, probably because it beats most runners into submission before they collapse. Dean Karnazes, the self-styled Ultramarathon Man, couldn't finish it the first two times he tried; after watching him drop out twice, the Leadville folks gave him their own nickname: "Ofer" ("O fer one, O fer two . . ."). Less than half the field makes it to the finish every year.

Not surprisingly, an event with more flameouts than finishers tends to attract a rare breed of athlete. For five years, Leadville's reigning champion was Steve Peterson, a member of a Colorado higher-consciousness cult called Divine Madness, which seeks nirvana through sex parties, extreme trail running, and affordable housecleaning. One Leadville legend is Marshall Ulrich, an affable dog-food tycoon who perked up his times by having his toenails surgically removed. "They kept falling off anyway," Marshall said.

When Ken met Aron Ralston, the rock climber who sawed off his own hand with the chipped blade of a multitool after getting pinned by a boulder, Ken made an astonishing offer: if Aron ever wanted to run Leadville, he wouldn't have to pay. Ken's invitation stunned everyone who heard about it. The defending champ has to pay his way back into the race. Heroic grand master Ed Williams still has to pay. *Ken* has to pay. But Aron got a free ride—and why?

"He's the essence of Leadville," Ken said. "We've got a motto here—you're tougher than you think you are, and you can do more than you think you can. Guy like Aron, he shows the rest of us what we can do if we dig deep."

You might think poor Aron had already suffered enough, but little more than a year after his accident, he took Ken up on the offer. New prosthetic swinging by his side, Aron made it to the finish under the thirty-hour cutoff and went home with a silver belt buckle, thereby stating better than Ken ever could what it takes to toe the line at Leadville:

You don't have to be fast. But you'd better be fearless.

CHAPTER 10

PERFECT! Leadville was exactly the kind of wild, Rock'em-Sock'em thrill show Rick Fisher was looking for. As usual, he was out to make a big splash, and a carnival like Leadville was just the ticket. You telling him that ESPN wouldn't jump at the chance for footage of good-looking guys in skirts smashing records on a mythical man-eater? Hell yeah!

So in August 1992, Fisher came roaring back to Patrocinio's village in his big old Chevy Suburban. He'd gotten travel papers from the Mexican Tourism Board, and a promised payoff in corn for the racers. Meanwhile, Patrocinio had cajoled five of his fellow villagers to trust this strange, intense *chabochi* whose name got stuck in their mouths. Spanish has no "sh" sound, so Fisher soon got a taste of sly Tarahumara humor when he heard his new team calling him Pescador—the Fisherman. Sure, it was easier to pronounce; but it also nailed his Ahabness, the constant hunger to hook a big one that radiated off him like heat waves off a car hood.

Whatever. As far as Fisher was concerned, they could call him Dr. Dumbass, as long as they got serious once the race started. The Pescador squeezed his team into the Chevy and hit the gas for Colorado.

Just before 4 a.m. on race day, the crowd at the Leadville starting line tried not to stare as five men in skirts struggled with the unfamiliar laces of the black canvas basketball sneakers the Pescador had gotten for them. The Tarahumara shared a last few drags on a black tobacco cigarette, then moved shyly to the very back of the pack as the other two hundred ninety ultrarunners chanted *Three . . . two . . .*

Boooom! Leadville's mayor blasted his big old blunderbuss of a shotgun, and the Tarahumara raced off to show their stuff.

For a while. Before they even made it halfway, every one of the Tarahumara runners had dropped out. Damn, Fisher moaned into every ear he could grab. I never should have stuffed them into those sneaks, and no one told them they were allowed to eat at the aid stations. Totally my bad. They'd never seen flashlights before, so they were pointing them straight up like torches. . . .

Yeah, yeah, check's in the mail. Same old Tarahumara letdown; same old Tarahumara excuses. Few but the most obsessive track historians know it, but Mexico tried using a pair of Tarahumara runners in the Olympic marathon in both the 1928 Amsterdam games and the 1968 Mexico City games. Both times, the Tarahumara finished out of the medals. The excuse those times was that 26.2 miles was too short; the dinky little marathon was over before the Tarahumara got a chance to shift into high gear.

Maybe. But if these guys were really such superhuman speedsters, how come they never beat anybody? Nobody cares if you're a great three-point shooter in your backyard; what matters is whether you stick them on game day. And for a century, the Tarahumara had never competed in the outside world without stinking up the joint.

Fisher puzzled over it during the long drive back to Mexico, and then the lightbulb flashed. Of *course!* Same reason you can't grab five kids off a Chicago schoolyard and expect to beat the Bulls: just because you're a Tarahumara runner doesn't mean you're a *great* Tarahumara runner. Patrocinio had tried to make life easier for Fisher by enlisting runners who lived near the new paved road, figuring they'd be more comfortable around outsiders and easier to gather for the trip. But as the Mexican Olympic Committee should have realized years ago, the easiest Tarahumara to recruit may not be the ones worth recruiting.

"Let's try again," Patrocinio urged. Fisher's sponsors had donated a pile of corn to Patrocinio's village, and he hated to lose the windfall.

This time, he'd open the team to runners from outside his own village. He'd head back into the canyons—and back in time. Team Tarahumara was going old-school.

Yep, "old" pretty much nailed it.

Ken was none too impressed with the new band of Tarahumara who showed up at the next Leadville. The team captain looked like a Keebler elf who'd taken early retirement in Miami Beach: he was a short fifty-five-year-old grandfather in a blue robe with flashy pink flowers, topped off by a happy-go-lucky grin, a pink scarf, and a wool cap yanked down over his ears. Another guy had to be in his forties, and the two scared kids behind him looked young enough to be his sons. The whole operation was even worse equipped than last year's; no sooner had Team Tarahumara arrived than they disappeared into the town dump, emerging with strips of tire rubber that they began fashioning into sandals. No chafing black Chuckies this time around.

Seconds before the race was about to begin, the Tarahumara vanished. *Same eye of the tiger as last year,* Ken thought dismissively; just as before, the timid Tarahumara had hidden themselves at the very rear of the pack. At the blast of the shotgun, they trotted off in last place. And in last place they remained, ignored and inconsequential . . .

. . . until mile 40, when Victoriano Churro (the Keebler look-alike with a taste for pastels) and Cerrildo Chacarito (the forty-something goat farmer) began quietly, almost nonchalantly, pitter-pattering their way along the edges of the trail, picking off a few runners at a time as they began the three-mile mountain climb to Hope Pass. Manuel Luna caught up and locked in beside them, the three elders leading the younger Tarahumara like a wolf pack on the hunt.

Heeya! Ken whooped and hollered like a bullrider when he saw the Tarahumara heading back toward him after the fifty-mile turn-around. Something strange was going on; Ken could tell by the weird look on their faces. He'd seen every single Leadville runner for the past decade, and not one of them had ever looked so freak-ishly . . . *normal.* Ten straight hours of mountain running will either knock you on your ass or plant its flag on your face, no exceptions. Even the best ultrarunners by this point are heads down and digging deep, focusing hard on the near-impossible task of getting each foot to follow the other. But that old guy? Victoriano? Totally cool. Like he just woke up from a nap, scratched his belly, and decided to show the kids how the big boys play this game.

By mile 60, the Tarahumara were *flying*. Leadville has aid stations every fifteen miles or so where helpers can resupply their runners with food, dry socks, and flashlight batteries, but the Tarahumara were moving so fast, Rick and Kitty couldn't drive around the mountain fast enough to keep up with them.

"They seemed to move with the ground," said one awestruck spectator. "Kind of like a cloud, or a fog moving across the mountains."

This time, the Tarahumara weren't two lonely tribesmen adrift in a sea of Olympians. They weren't five confused villagers in awful canvas sneakers who hadn't run since the road was bulldozed into their village. This time, they were locked into a formation they'd practiced since childhood, with wily old vets up front and eager young bucks pushing from behind. They were sure-footed and sure of themselves. They were the Running People.

Meanwhile, a rather different endurance contest was taking place a few blocks from the finish line. Every year, Leadville's Sixth Street partyers cowboy up and spend the weekend trying to outlast the runners. They start pounding at the blast of the starting gun, and keep downing 'em until the race officially ends, thirty hours later. Between Jäger and Jell-O shots, they also perform a critical advisory function: their job is to alert the timers at the finish line by going apeshit the second they spot a runner emerging from the dark. This time, the boozers nearly blew it; at two in the morning, old Victoriano and Cerrildo came whisking by so quickly and quietly—"a fog moving across the mountains"—they almost went unnoticed.

Victoriano hit the tape first, with Cerrildo right behind in second. Manuel Luna, whose new sandals had fallen apart at mile 83 and left his unprotected feet raw and bleeding, still surged back over the rocky trail around Turquoise Lake to finish fifth. The first non-Tarahumara finisher was nearly a full hour behind Victoriano—a distance of roughly six miles.

The Tarahumara hadn't just gone from last to first; they'd done serious damage to the record book in the process. Victoriano was the oldest winner in race history, eighteen-year-old Felipe Torres was the youngest finisher, and Team Tarahumara was the only squad to ever grab three of the top five spots—even though its two top finishers had a combined age of nearly one hundred.

"It was amazing," a hard-to-amaze participant named Harry Dupree would tell *The New York Times*. After running Leadville twelve times himself, Dupree thought his days of being surprised by anything in the race were over. Then he watched Victoriano and Cerrildo whiz past.

"Here were these little guys wearing sandals who never actually trained for the race. And they blew away some of the best long-distance runners in the world."

CHAPTER 11

"I TOLD YOU!" Rick Fisher crowed.

He was right about something else, too: suddenly, everybody wanted a piece of the Running People. Fisher promised that Team Tarahumara would be back next year, and that was the magic wand that transformed Leadville from a little-known gruelathon into a major media event. ESPN grabbed broadcast rights; *Wide World of Sports* aired a Who-Are-These-Super-Jocks special; Molson beer signed on as a Leadville sponsor. Rockport Shoes even became official backers of the only running team in the world that hated running shoes.

Reporters from *The New York Times*, *Sports Illustrated*, *Le Monde*, *Runner's World*, you name it, kept calling Ken with the same question:

"Can anyone beat these guys?"

"Yep," Ken replied. "Annie can."

Ann Trason. The thirty-three-year-old community-college science teacher from California. If you said you could spot her in a crowd, you were either her husband or a liar. Ann was sort of short, sort of slender, sort of schlumpy, sort of invisible behind her mousy-brown bangs—sort of what you'd expect, basically, in a community-college science teacher. Until someone fired a gun.

Watching Ann bolt at the start of a race was like watching a mild-mannered reporter yank off his glasses and sling on a crimson cape.

Her chin came up, her hands curled into fists, her hair flowed around her face like a jet stream, the bangs blowing back to reveal glinting brown cougar eyes. In street clothes, Ann is a pinch over five feet; in running shorts, she reconfigures to Brazilian model proportions, all lean legs and ballerina-straight back and sun-browned belly hard enough to break a bat.

Ann had run track in high school, but got sick to death of "hamstering" around and around an artificial oval, as she put it, so she gave it up in college to become a biochemist (which pretty much makes the case for how tedious track was, if periodic tables were more spellbinding). For years, she ran only to keep from going nuts: when her brain got fried from studying, or after she'd graduated and started a demanding research job in San Francisco, Ann would blow out the stress with a quick patter around Golden Gate Park.

"I love to run just to feel the wind in my hair," she'd say. She could care less about races; she was just hooked on the joy of bustin' out of prison. It wasn't long before she began defusing job stress in advance by jogging the nine miles to the lab each morning. And once she realized that her legs were fresh again by punch-out time, she began running back home again as well. Oh, and what the heck; as long as she was racking up eighteen miles a day during the workweek, it was no big deal to unwind on a lazy Saturday with twenty at a pop . . .

. . . or twenty-five . . .

. . . or thirty . . .

One Saturday, Ann got up early and ran twenty miles. She relaxed over breakfast, then headed back out for twenty more. She had some plumbing chores around the house, so after finishing run No. 2, she hauled out her toolbox and got to work. By the end of the day, she was pretty pleased with herself; she'd run forty miles and taken care of a messy job on her own. So as a reward, she treated herself to another fifteen miles.

Fifty-five miles in one day. Her friends had to wonder, and worry. Did Ann have an eating disorder? An exercise obsession? Was she fleeing some subconscious Freudian demon by literally running away? "My friends would tell me I'm not addicted to crack, I'm addicted to endorphins," Trason would say, and her comeback didn't much put their minds at ease: she liked to tell them that running huge miles in the mountains was "very romantic."

Gotcha. Grueling, grimy, muddy, bloody, lonely trail-running equals moonlight and champagne.

But yeah, Ann insisted, running *was* romantic; and no, of course her friends didn't get it because they'd never broken through. For them, running was a miserable two miles motivated solely by size 6 jeans: get on the scale, get depressed, get your headphones on, and get it over with. But you can't muscle through a five-hour run that way; you have to relax into it, like easing your body into a hot bath, until it no longer resists the shock and begins to enjoy it.

Relax enough, and your body becomes so familiar with the cradle-rocking rhythm that you almost forget you're moving. And once you break through to that soft, half-levitating flow, that's when the moonlight and champagne show up: "You have to be in tune with your body, and know when you can push it and when to back off," Ann would explain. You have to listen closely to the sound of your own breathing; be aware of how much sweat is beading on your back; make sure to treat yourself to cool water and a salty snack and ask yourself, honestly and often, exactly how you feel. What could be more sensual than paying exquisite attention to your own body? Sensual counted as romantic, right?

Just goofing around, Ann was logging more miles than many serious marathoners, so by 1985, she figured it was time to see how she stacked up against some real runners. Maybe the L.A. Marathon? Yawn; she might as well be back hamstering around behind the high school if she was going to spend three hours circling city blocks. She wanted a race so wild and fun she'd get lost in it, just the way she did with her mountain jaunts.

Now this looks interesting, she thought as she eyed an ad in a local sports magazine. Like Western States, the American River 50-Mile Endurance Run was a horseless horse race, a cross-country ramble over a course previously used for backcountry roughriders. It's hot, hilly, and hazardous. ("Poison oak flourishes along the trail," racers are warned. "You may also encounter horses and rattlesnakes. It is recommended that you yield to both.") Sidestep the fangs and hooves, and you've still got a final punch in the face waiting before you finish: after forty-seven miles of trail-running, you hit a one-thousand-foot climb for the last three miles.

So, to recap: Ann's first race would be a double marathon featuring snakebites and skin eruptions under a sizzling sun. Nope, no risk of boredom there.

And, no big surprise, Ann's ultramarathon debut started miserably. The thermometer was hitting sauna levels, and she was too raw a rookie to realize that maybe carrying a water bottle on a 108-degree day might be a smart idea. She knew zip about pacing (was this thing going to take her seven hours? Ten? Thirteen?) and even less about trail-race tactics (those guys who walked uphill and flew past her on the descents were really starting to piss her off. Run like a man, goddammit!).

But once the jitters wore off, she relaxed into her cradle-rocking stride. Her head came up, those bangs blew back, and she started feeling that jungle-cat confidence. By the thirty-mile mark, dozens of runners were wobbling in the damp heat, feeling as if they were trapped in the middle of a freshly baked muffin. But despite being badly dehydrated, Ann only seemed to get stronger; so strong, in fact, that she beat every other woman in the race and broke the female course record, finishing two back-to-back trail marathons in seven hours and nine minutes.

That shock victory was the beginning of a scorching streak. Ann went on to become the female champion of the Western States 100 — the Super Bowl of trail-running—*fourteen times*, a record that spans three decades and makes Lance Armstrong, with his piddlin' little seven Tour de France wins, look like a flash in the pan. And a pampered flash in the pan, at that: Lance never pedaled a stroke without a team of experts at his elbow to monitor his caloric intake and transmit microsecond split analyses into his earbud, while Ann only had her husband, Carl, waiting in the woods with a Timex and half a turkey sandwich.

And unlike Lance, who trained and peaked for a single event every year, Ann was a girl gone wild for competition. During one stretch, she averaged an ultramarathon every other month *for four years*. Such a relentless battering should have wasted her, but Ann had the recovery powers of a mutant superhero; she seemed to recharge on the move, getting stronger when she should have been wilting. She got faster with every month, and came within a flu shot of a perfect record: she won twenty races over those four years, only dropping to second place the time she ran a sixty-miler when she should have been on the sofa with Kleenex and Cup-a-Soup.

Of course, there was a weak spot in her armor. There had to be. Except . . . no one could ever find it. Ann was like a circus strongman who fights the toughest guy in any town: she won on roads and trails . . . on smooth tracks and scrabbly mountains . . . in America, Europe, and Africa. She smashed world records at 50 miles, 100 kilometers, and 100 miles, and set ten more world bests on both track and road. She qualified for the Olympic Marathon Trials, ran 6:44 a mile for 62 miles to win the World Ultra Title, and then won Western States and Leadville in the same month.

But one prize kept slipping out of her fingers: for years, Ann could never win a major ultra outright. She'd beaten every man and woman in the field in plenty of smaller races, but when it came to the top showdowns, at least one man had always beaten her by a few minutes.

No more. By 1994, she knew her time had come.

CHAPTER 12

THE WEIRDNESS STARTED as soon as Rick Fisher's dusty Chevy rolled to a stop outside Leadville race headquarters and two guys in white wizard capes stepped out.

"Hey!" Ken Chlouber called as he came outside to greet them. "The speed demons are here!" Ken stuck out his hand and tried to remember the phonetics for "welcome" that the Spanish teacher over at the high school had taught him.

"Uh . . . Bee en benny—," he began.

One of the guys in the capes smiled and put out his hand. Suddenly, Fisher shoved his body between them.

"No!" Fisher said. "You must not touch them in a controlling way, or you'll pay. In their culture that's considered criminal assault."

What the—Ken could feel the blood swelling in his head. *You want to see some criminal assault, buddy? Try grabbing my arm again.* Fisher sure as hell never had a handshake problem when he was begging Ken to find his guys free housing. So what, now he's got a winner and a pocketful of Rockport sponsorship money and everyone's supposed to treat them like royalty? Ken was ready to drive a steel toe up Fisher's tail, but then he thought of something that made him exhale, relax, and chalk it up to nerves.

Annie must really be making him edgy, Ken thought. *Especially the way the media is playing this thing.*

The news stories had shifted dramatically since Ann confirmed that she'd be at Leadville. Instead of asking whether the Tarahumara would win, they were now wondering whether Rick Fisher's team would be humiliated—again. "The Tarahumara consider it shameful to lose to a woman," article after article repeated. It was an irresistible story: the shy science teacher heading bravely into the Rockies to battle the macho Mexican tribesmen and anyone else, male or female, who got between her and the tape in one of the sport's premier events.

Of course, there was one way Fisher could ease the media pressure on Team Tarahumara: he could shut up. No one had ever mentioned Tarahumara machismo until Fisher began telling reporters about it. "They don't lose to women," he said. "And they don't plan to start now." It was a fascinating revelation—especially to the Tarahumara, who wouldn't have known what he was talking about.

The Tarahumara are actually an extraordinarily egalitarian society; men are gentle and respectful to women, and are commonly seen toting infants around on the small of their backs, just like their wives. Men and women race separately, that's true, but mostly for logistical reasons: moms with a passel of younguns to look after aren't free to spend two days traipsing across the canyons. They've got to stay close to home, so their races tend to be short (by Tarahumara standards, "short" clocks in at forty to sixty miles). Women are still respected as crackerjack runners, and often serve as the *cho' kéame*—a combination team captain and chief bookie—when the men race. Compared with NFL-revering American guys, Tarahumara men are Lilith Fair fans.

Fisher had already been embarrassed once when his entire team had crapped out. Now, thanks to his own mistake, he found himself in the spotlight of a nationally televised Battle of the Sexes that, quite likely, he was going to lose. Ann's best time at Leadville two years before was only thirty minutes behind Victoriano's 20:03, and she'd improved phenomenally since then. Look at Western States; she'd gotten ninety minutes faster in the space of just one year. There was no telling what she'd do when she came roaring into Leadville with a score to settle.

Plus, Ann was holding all the aces: Victoriano and Cerrildo weren't coming back this year (they had corn to plant and had no time for another fun run), so Fisher had lost his two best racers.

Ann had won Leadville twice before, so unlike whatever newcomers Fisher had drafted, she had the huge advantage of knowing every bewildering twist in the trail. Miss one marker at Leadville, and you could wander in the dark for miles before getting back on course.

Ann also acclimated effortlessly to high altitude, and knew better than anyone alive how to analyze and attack the logistical problems of a one-hundred-mile footrace. At its essence, an ultra is a binary equation made up of hundreds of yes/no questions: Eat now or wait? Bomb down this hill, or throttle back and save the quads for the flats? Find out what is itching in your sock, or push on? Extreme distance magnifies every problem (a blister becomes a blood-soaked sock, a declined PowerBar becomes a woozy inability to follow trail markers), so all it takes is one wrong answer to ruin a race. But not for honor-student Ann; when it came to ultras, she always aced her quizzes.

In short: thumbs up to the Tarahumara for being amazing amateurs, but this time, they were meeting the top pro in the business (literally; Ann was now a hired gun backed by Nike money). The Tarahumara had their brief, shining moment as Leadville champions; now they were coming back as underdogs.

Which explained the guys in the wizard capes.

Desperate to replace his two missing veterans, Fisher had followed Patrocinio up a nine-thousand-foot climb to the mountaintop village of Choguita. There, he found Martimano Cervantes, a forty-two-year-old master of the ball game, and his protégé, twenty-five-year-old Juan Herrera. Choguita is bitterly cold at night and sun-scorched by day, so even when running, the Choguita Tarahumara protect themselves with fine woolen ponchos that hang nearly to their feet. As they fly down the trail, capes flowing around them, they look like magicians appearing from a puff of smoke.

Juan and Martimano were doubtful. They'd never left their village before, and this sounded like a long time alone among the Bearded Devils. Fisher cut right through their objections; he had cash and was ready to talk turkey. It had been a dry winter and worse spring in the Choguita highlands, and he knew food supplies were dangerously low. "Come race with us," Fisher promised them, "and I'll give your village one ton of corn and a half ton of beans."

Hmm. Fifty bags of corn wasn't a lot for a village . . . but at least it was guaranteed. Maybe if they had some companionship, it would be okay.

We have other runners here who are also very fast, they told Fisher. Can some of them come?

No dice, Fisher replied. Just you two.

Secretly, the Pescador was working on a little social-engineering scheme: by taking runners from as many different villages as possible, he hoped to pit the Tarahumara against each other. *Let them tear after each other*, he figured, *and win Leadville in the bargain*. It was a shrewd plan—and totally misguided. If Fisher had known more about Tarahumara culture, he'd have understood that racing doesn't divide villages; it *unites* them. It's a way for distant tribesmen to tighten the bonds of kinship and buddyhood, and make sure everyone in the canyon is in fine enough fettle to come through in an emergency. Sure it's competitive, but so is family touch football on Thanksgiving morning. The Tarahumara saw racing as a festival of friendship; Fisher saw a battlefield.

Men versus women, village versus village, race director versus race team manager—within minutes of arriving in Leadville, Fisher had storms brewing on three fronts. And then he really got down to business.

"Hey, okay if we take a picture together?" a Leadville runner asked when he spotted the Tarahumara in town before the race.

"Sure," Fisher replied. "You got twenty bucks?"

"For what?" the startled runner asked.

For crimes against humanity. For the fact that "white guys" had taken advantage of the Tarahumara and other indigenous people for centuries, Fisher would explain. And if you don't like it, too bad: "I couldn't care less about the ultra community," Fisher would say. "I don't care about white people. I like for the Tarahumara to kick white butt."

White butt? Must have been a while since Fisher swiveled around for a look at his own behind. And what was he here for, anyway: a race, or a race war?

No one could chat with the Tarahumara, or even pat them on the back and say "Good luck," without the Pescador forcing his way between them. Even Ann Trason found a wall of hostility facing her. "Rick kept the Tarahumara unnecessarily secluded," she would later complain. "He wouldn't even let us talk to them."

The Rockport executives were bewildered. They'd just launched a trail-running shoe, and the whole marketing campaign was based around the Leadville race. The shoe was even *named* the Leadville Racer. When Rick Fisher called them for sponsorship ("Keep in mind, he came to *us*," then Rockport vice president Tony Post told me), Rockport made it clear that the Tarahumara would be a big part of the promos. Rockport would kick in cash, and in return, the Tarahumara would wear the banana-yellow shoes, work the crowd, appear in some ads. Was that cool?

Totally, Fisher promised.

"Then I get to Leadville and meet this strange guy," Tony Post went on. "He seemed like an inconsolable hothead. That was the contradiction. Here you had these really gentle people, being managed by the worst of American culture. It was like . . ." Post paused to reflect, and in the silence you could almost hear the realization dawning and forming in his mind. "It's like he was jealous they were the ones getting all the attention."

And so, with battles brewing all around them, the Tarahumara snuffed out their cigarettes and edged in awkwardly beside the other runners in front of Leadville's courthouse, same place they used to hang the horse thieves. Among the hugs and handshakes, the we-who-are-about-to-die camaraderie shared by the other runners during the final countdown, the Tarahumara looked lonely and alone.

Manuel Luna's genial smile disappeared and his face hardened into oak. Juan Herrera adjusted his Rockport cap and shifted his feet in his new $110 screaming-yellow Rockports with the thick hiking-boot sole. Martimano Cervantes huddled inside his cape in the freezing Rocky Mountain night. Ann Trason stepped in front of all of them, shook herself loose, and stared into the darkness ahead.

CHAPTER 13

He who loves his body more than
dominion over the empire
can be given custody of the empire.

—LAO TZU, *Tao Te Ching*

DR. JOE VIGIL, a sixty-five-year-old army of one, warmed his
hands around his coffee as he waited for the first flashlight beams to
come stabbing toward him through the woods.

No other elite coach in the world was anywhere near Leadville,
because no other elite coach could give a hoot what was going on at
that giant outdoor insane asylum in the Rockies. Self-mutilators,
mean mothermuckers or whatever they called themselves—what did
they have to do with real running? With *Olympic* running? As a sport,
most track coaches ranked ultras somewhere between competitive
eating and recreational S&M.

Super, Vigil thought, as he stomped his feet against the chill. *Go
ahead and sleep, and leave the freaks to me*—because he knew the freaks
were onto something.

The secret to Vigil's success was spelled out right in his name: no
other coach was more vigilant about detecting the crucial little
details that everyone else missed. He'd been that way his entire competitive life, ever since he was a puny Latino kid trying to play high-
school football in a conference that didn't have many Latinos, let
alone puny ones. Joey Vigil couldn't outmuscle the meat slabs on the
other side of the line, so he out-scienced them; he studied the tricks

of leverage, propulsion, and timing, figuring out ways to position his feet so he popped up from a crouch like a spring-loaded anvil. By the time he graduated from college, the puny Latino kid was a first-team All-Conference guard. He then turned to track, and used that tireless bloodhound nose to become the greatest distance-running mind America has ever seen.

Besides his Ph.D. and two master's degrees, Vigil's pursuit of the lost art of distance running had taken him deep into the Russian outback, high into the mountains of Peru, and far across Kenya's Rift Valley highlands. He'd wanted to learn why Russian sprinters are forbidden to run a single step in training until they can jump off a twenty-foot ladder in their bare feet, and how sixty-year-old goatherds at Machu Picchu can possibly scale the Andes on a starvation diet of yogurt and herbs, and how Japanese runners trained by Suzuki-san and Koide-san could mysteriously alchemize slow walking into fast marathons. He'd tracked down the old masters and picked their brains, vacuuming up their secrets before they disappeared into the grave. His head was a Library of Congress of running lore, much of it vanished from every place on the planet except his memory.

His research paid off sensationally. At his alma mater, Adams State College in Alamosa, Colorado, Vigil took over the dying cross-country program and engineered it into an absolute terror. Adams State harriers won twenty-six national titles in thirty-three years, including the most awe-inspiring show of strength ever displayed in a national championship race: in 1992, Vigil's runners took the first five places in the NCAA Division II Championship meet, scoring the only shutout ever achieved at a national championship. Vigil also guided Pat Porter to *eight* U.S.A. Cross Country titles (twice as many as Olympic marathon gold medalist Frank Shorter, four times as many as silver medalist Meb Keflezighi), and was named College National Coach of the Year a record fourteen times. In 1988, Vigil was appointed the distance coach for American runners heading to the Seoul Olympics.

And that explained why, at that moment, old Joe Vigil was the only coach in America shivering in a freezing forest at four in the morning, waiting for a glimpse of a community-college science teacher and seven men in dresses. See, nothing about ultrarunning added up; and when Vigil couldn't do the math, he knew he was missing something big.

Take this equation: how come nearly all the women finish Leadville and fewer than half the men do? Every year, more than 90 percent of the female runners come home with a buckle, while 50 percent of the men come up with an excuse. Not even Ken Chlouber can explain the sky-high female finishing rate, but he can damn well exploit it: "All my pacers are women," Chlouber says. "They get the job done."

Or try this word problem: subtract the Tarahumara from last year's race, and what do you get?

Answer: a woman lunging for the tape.

In all the hubbub over the Tarahumara, few besides Vigil paid much attention to the remarkable fact that Christine Gibbons was just nosed out for third place. If Rick Fisher's van had blown a fan belt in Arizona, a woman would have been thirty-one seconds from winning the whole show.

How was that possible? No woman ranked among the top fifty in the world in the mile (the female world record for the mile, 4:12, was achieved a century ago by men and rather routinely now by high school boys). A woman *might* sneak into the top twenty in a marathon (in 2003, Paula Radcliffe's world-best 2:15:25 was just ten minutes off Paul Tergat's 2:04:55 men's record). But in ultras, women were taking home the hardware. Why, Vigil wondered, did the gap between male and female champions get smaller as the race got *longer*—shouldn't it be the other way around?

Ultrarunning seemed to be an alternative universe where none of planet Earth's rules applied: women were stronger than men; old men were stronger than youngsters; Stone Age guys in sandals were stronger than everybody. And the *mileage*! The sheer stress on their legs was off the charts. Running one hundred miles a week was supposed to be a straight shot to a stress injury, yet the ultrafreaks were doing one hundred miles in a *day*. Some of them were doing double that every week in training and still not getting hurt. Was ultrarunning self-selective, Vigil wondered—did it attract only runners with unbreakable bodies? Or had ultrarunners discovered the secret to megamileage?

So Joe Vigil had hauled himself stiffly out of bed, tossed a thermos of coffee in his car, and driven through the night to watch the body geniuses do their thing. The best ultrarunners in the world, he suspected, were on the verge of rediscovering secrets that the Tarahumara had never forgotten. Vigil's theory had brought him to the brink of a very important decision, one that would change his life and, he hoped, millions of others. He just needed to see the Tarahumara in person to verify one thing. It wasn't their speed; he probably knew more about their legs than they did. What Vigil was dying for was a look inside their heads.

Suddenly, he caught his breath. Something had just come floating out of the trees. Something that looked like ghosts . . . or magicians, appearing from a puff of smoke.

Right from the gun, Team Tarahumara caught everyone by surprise. Instead of hanging back as they had the last two years, they surged in a pack, hopping up on the Sixth Street sidewalk to patter around the crowd and take command of the front-running positions.

They were moving out fast—*Much too fast, it seemed*, thought Don Kardong, the 1976 Olympic marathoner and veteran *Runner's World* writer watching from the sidelines. Last year, Victoriano had shown shrewd restraint by steadily climbing along from last to first, gradually getting faster as he got closer to the finish line. *That's* how you run one hundred miles.

But Manuel Luna had spent a year reflecting on gringo-style racing, and he'd done a nice job of briefing his new teammates. The course is wide open under the streetlights, he told them, then suddenly funnels onto a dark single-track trail as it enters the woods. If you're not up front, you hit a solid wall of bodies as runners pause to fumble with flashlights and then caterpillar along in single file. Better to move out early and avoid the jam-up, Luna advised them, then ease back later.

Despite the dangerous pace, Johnny Sandoval of nearby Gypsum, Colorado, stuck tight with Martimano Cervantes and Juan Herrera. *Let everyone go nuts over Ann and the Tarahumara*, he thought, *while I stealth myself to a trophy*. After finishing ninth the previous year in 21:45, Sandoval had the best training year of his life. Quietly, he'd been coming to Leadville throughout the summer, running each segment of the course over and over until he'd memorized every twist, quirk, and creek crossing. A nineteen-hour run should win it, Sandoval figured, and he was ready to run one.

Ann Trason had expected to be in front, but an eight-minute mile right out of the box was just nuts. So she contented herself with staying within sight of Team Tarahumara's bobbing flashlights as they entered the woods around Turquoise Lake, confident she'd reel them in soon enough. The trail ahead was dark and knotted with rocks and roots, and that played to one of Ann's peculiar strengths: she absolutely loved night runs. Even back in college, midnight was her favorite time to grab a flashlight and a friend and trot through the silent campus, the world reduced to glitters and sparkles in a tiny orb of light. If anyone could make up time running blindly on a treacherous trail, it was Ann.

But by the first aid station, Sandoval and the Tarahumara had opened a good half-mile lead. Sandoval checked in, got his split—about 1:55 for 13.5 miles—and shot right back on the trail. The Tarahumara, however, veered into the parking lot and ran over to Rick Fisher's van. They began kicking off their yellow Rockports like they were crawling with fire ants. Rick and Kitty, as planned, were already standing by with their huaraches. So much for product endorsement.

The Tarahumara knelt, looping the leather thong around and around their ankles and high up on their calves, adjusting the tautness as carefully as you'd tune a guitar string. It's a fine art, custom-fitting a strip of rubber to the bottom of your foot with a single lash of leather so it doesn't shift or flop for eighty-seven miles of gritty, rocky trail. Then they were up and gone, hard on Johnny Sandoval's heels. By the time Ann Trason arrived at the aid station, Martimano Cervantes and Juan Herrera were out of sight.

Sick pace, Sandoval thought, as he shot a glance over his shoulder. Anyone tell these guys it had been raining here for the past two weeks? Sandoval knew they were heading straight into a world of slop around the Twin Lakes marshes and down the muddy back end of Hope Pass. The Arkansas River would be a roaring mess; they'd have to haul themselves hand over hand along a safety rope to cross, and then claw their way two thousand feet to the top of Hope Pass. Then spin around and do the same again coming home.

Okay, this is suicide, Sandoval decided after he came through mile

23.5 in three hours and twenty minutes. *I'll save my strength and cream those guys when their tires go flat.* He let Martimano Cervantes and Juan Herrera go—and almost immediately, he was passed by Ann Trason. *Where the hell did she come from?* Ann should know better; this was crash-and-burn speed.

At the thirty-mile mark in Half Moon campground, Martimano and Juan were ready for breakfast. Kitty Williams slapped thin bean burritos into their hands. They ran on, chomping contentedly, and were soon swallowed up by the thick woods around Mount Elbert.

Ann raced in a few minutes later, pissed off and shouting. "Where's Carl? *Where the hell is he?*" It was now 8:20 in the morning and she was ready to shuck weight by dumping her headlamp and jacket. But she was so far under record pace, her husband hadn't yet made it to the aid station.

To hell with him; Ann kept her night gear, and disappeared on the trail of the invisible Tarahumara.

At mile 40, the crowd milled around the ancient wood firehouse in the tiny cabin village of Twin Lakes, checking their watches. The first runners probably wouldn't show up for another, oh, about—

"There she is!"

Ann had just crested the hill. Last year, it took Victoriano seven hours and twelve minutes to get this far; Ann had done it in less than six. "No woman has ever led at this point in the race before," said an incredulous Scott Tinley, the two-time world champion Ironman triathlete who was doing TV commentary for *ABC's Wide World of Sports.* "We're witnessing the most incredible demonstration of raw courage in sports today."

Less than a minute later, Martimano and Juan popped out of the woods and came scrambling down the hill behind her. Tony Post of Rockport was so swept up in the drama, he didn't care for the moment that his boys were not only losing but had also shit-canned the shoes he was paying them to wear. "It was the most amazing thing," said Post, once a nationally ranked marathoner himself, with times in the low 2:20s. "We were just flipping out, watching this woman take control."

Luckily, Ann's husband was in position this time. He got a banana into Ann's hands, then ushered her into the little firehouse for her medical exam. All Leadville runners need to have their pulse and weight checked at the forty-mile mark, because shedding pounds too quickly is an early warning sign of dangerous dehydration. Only with Doc Perna's okay are they cleared to plunge into the meat grinder ahead: there, looming across the marsh, was the twenty-six-hundred-foot climb to the top of Hope Pass.

Ann munched the banana while a nurse named Cindy Corbin adjusted the scale. A moment later, Martimano stepped up on the scale beside Ann.

"¿Cómo estás?" Kitty Williams asked Martimano, laying an encouraging hand on his back. How are you feeling after nearly six straight hours of high-altitude hill running at impossibly fast speed?

"Ask him how it feels to get beat by a woman," Ann called out. Nervous laughter rippled through the room, but Ann wasn't smiling; she glared at Martimano as if she were a black belt and he was a stack of bricks. Kitty shot her an appalled look, but Ann ignored it and kept her eyes locked on Martimano. Martimano turned questioningly toward Kitty, but Kitty chose not to translate. In all her years of running ultras and pacing them for her dad, it was the first time Kitty had ever heard one runner taunt another.

Despite what most people in the room heard, a video of the incident would later suggest that what Ann actually said was, "Ask him how it feels to compete with a woman." But while her exact words were debatable, her attitude was unmistakable: Ann didn't just win by running hard; she won by *racing* hard. This thing was going to be a death match.

As Martimano got off the scale, Ann pushed past him and hurried out the door. She slung on her fanny pack—freshly loaded with carbohydrate gel, gloves, and a slicker in case she hit sleet or freezing winds above the timberline—and began trotting down the road toward the snow-capped mountain. She was outa there so fast, Martimano and Juan were still biting into slices of orange while Ann was heading around the corner and out of sight.

What was wrong with her? The trash talk, the hasty exit—Ann didn't even take time to slip on a dry shirt and socks, or get a few more calories down her neck. And why was she even in the lead at all? Mile 40 was only round one of a very long fight. Once you jump ahead, you're vulnerable; you surrender all element of surprise, and become a prisoner of your own pace. Even middle-school milers know that the smart tactic is to sit on the leader's shoulder, go only as fast as you have to, then jam 'er into gear and blow past on the bell lap.

Classic example: Steve Prefontaine. Pre came out too quickly *twice* in the same race in the '72 Olympics; both times, he was chased down. By the home stretch, Pre had nothing left and faded out of the medals to fourth. That historic defeat pounded home the lesson: nobody gives up the pursuit position if they don't have to. Not unless you're foolish, or reckless—or Garry Kasparov.

In the 1990 World Chess Championship, Kasparov made a horrible mistake and lost his queen right at the start of a decisive game. Chess grand masters around the world let out a pained groan; the bad boy of the chessboard was now road kill (a less-gracious observer for *The New York Times* visibly sneered). Except it wasn't a mistake; Kasparov had deliberately sacrificed his most powerful piece in exchange for an even more powerful psychological advantage. He was deadliest when swashbuckling, when he was chased into a corner and had to slash, scramble, and improvise his way out. Anatoly Karpov, his by-the-book opponent, was too conservative to pressure Kasparov early in the game, so Kasparov put the pressure on himself with a Queen's Gambit—and won.

That's what Ann was doing. Instead of hunting the Tarahumara, she'd hit on the risky, inspired strategy of letting the Tarahumara hunt her. Who's more committed to winning, after all: predator or prey? The lion can lose and come back to hunt another day, but the antelope gets only one mistake. To defeat the Tarahumara, Ann knew she needed more than willpower: she needed fear. Once she was out front, every cracking twig would spur her toward the finish.

"To move into the lead means making an act requiring fierceness and confidence," Roger Bannister once noted. "But fear must play some part . . . no relaxation is possible, and all discretion is thrown to the wind."

Ann had fierceness and confidence to burn. Now she was deep-sixing discretion and letting fear play its part. Ultrarunning was about to see its first Queen's Gambit.

CHAPTER 14

SHE'S INSANE! *She's . . . awesome.*

Coach Vigil was a hard-data freak, but as he watched Ann plunge into the Rockies with her ballsy do-or-die game plan, he loved the fact that ultrarunning had no science, no playbook, no training manual, no conventional wisdom. That kind of freewheeling self-invention is where big breakthroughs come from, as Vigil knew (and Columbus, the Beatles, and Bill Gates would happily agree). Ann Trason and her compadres were like mad scientists messing with beakers in the basement lab, ignored by the rest of the sport and free to defy every known principle of footwear, food, biomechanics, training intensity . . . *everything.*

And whatever breakthroughs they came up with, they'd be legit. With ultrarunners, Vigil had the refreshing peace of mind of dealing with pure lab specimens. He wasn't being hoodwinked by a phony superperformance, like the "miraculous" endurance of Tour de France cyclists, or the gargantuan power of suddenly melon-headed home-run hitters, or the blazing speed of female sprinters who win five medals in one Olympics before going to jail for lying to the feds about steroids. "Even the brightest smile," one observer would say of disgraced wondergirl Marion Jones, "can hide a lie."

So whose could you trust? Easy; the smiles on the oddballs in the woods.

Ultrarunners had no reason to cheat, because they had nothing to gain: no fame, no wealth, no medals. No one knew who they were, or cared who won their strange rambles through the woods. They didn't even get prize money; all you get for winning an ultra is the same belt buckle as the guy who comes in last. So, as a scientist, Vigil could rely on the data from an ultramarathon; as a fan, he could enjoy the show without scorn or skepticism. There's no EPO in Ann Trason's blood, no smuggled blood in her fridge, no ampules of Eastern European anabolics on her FedEx account.

Vigil knew that if he could understand Ann Trason, he'd grasp what one amazing person could do. But if he could understand the Tarahumara, he'd know what *everyone* could do.

Ann sucked air with deep, shuddering gasps. The final push up Hope Pass was agony, but she kept reminding herself that ever since the time Carl cursed her out, no one had beaten her on a big climb. About two years earlier, she and Carl were running on a rainy day when Ann began grousing about the endless, slippery hill ahead. Carl got tired of hearing her kvetch, so he blistered her with the most obscene name he could think of.

"A wimp!" Ann would later say. "The big W! Right then, I decided I was going to work to be a better hill climber than he was." Not only better than Carl, but better than everybody; Ann developed into such a relentless mountain goat that hills became her favorite place to drop the hammer and leave the competition behind.

But now, as she approached the Hope Pass peak, she could glance back and see Martimano and Juan steadily closing the gap, looking as light and breezy as the capes that swirled around them.

"God," Ann panted. She was so hunched over, she could almost pull herself up the slope with her hands. "I don't know how they do it."

A little farther down the mountain, Manuel Luna and the rest of Team Tarahumara were also catching up. They'd gotten scattered in the early miles by the startlingly fast pace, but now—like an alien protoplasm that re-forms and gets stronger every time you blast it to bits—they were tightening back into a pack behind Manuel Luna.

"God!" Ann exclaimed again.

She finally reached the peak. The view was spectacular; if Ann turned around, she could see all forty-five miles of tumbling green wilderness between her and Leadville. But she didn't even pause for a slurp of water. She had an ace in her hand, and she had to play it now. She was woozy from the thin air and her hamstrings were screaming, but Ann pushed straight over the top and started chop-stepping downhill.

This was a Trason specialty: using terrain to recharge on the move. After a steep first drop, the backside descent quickly softens into long, gently sloped switchbacks, so Ann could lean back, make her legs go limp, and let gravity do the work. After a bit, she could feel the knots easing in her calves and the strength creeping back into her thighs. By the time she reached bottom, her head was up and the glint was back in her cougar eyes.

Time to fire the jets. Ann veered off the muddy trail and onto hard-packed road, her legs spinning fast and loose from the hip as she accelerated into the last three miles to the turnaround.

Juan and Martimano, meanwhile, had gotten a little sidetracked. As soon as they'd broken past the tree line above, they were startled to see a giant herd of strange, woolly beasts—and among them, some animals. "SOUP'S ON, FELLAS," a hoarse voice bellowed to the uncomprehending Tarahumara from somewhere inside the herd. The Tarahumara had just made first contact with another wilderness tribe: the Hopeless Crew.

Twelve years earlier, Ken Chlouber had mustered enough of his neighbors to staff a good half-dozen aid stations, but he refused to put anyone at the top of Hope Pass; even the tough-guy miner who delighted in his race's high hospitalization rate considered that inhumane. A volunteer on Hope Pass would have to haul enough supplies up the mountain to feed, water, and bandage an endless parade of battered runners, and then camp out for two nights on a snowy peak with gale-force gusts. Nothin' doin'; if Ken sent anyone up there, he'd have hell to pay when they didn't come back down.

Luckily, a group of Leadville llama farmers shrugged and said, Eh, what the hell. Sounded like a party. They loaded their llamas with enough food and booze to make it through the weekend, and hammered in tent stakes at 12,600 feet. Since then, the Hopeless Crew has grown into an army eighty-some strong of llama owners and friends. For two days, they endure fierce winds and frostbitten fingers while dispensing first aid and hot soup, packing injured runners out by llama and partying in between like a tribe of amiable yetis. "Hope Pass is a bad son of a bitch on a *good* day," Ken says. "If it weren't for those llamas, we'd have lost a good many lives."

Juan and Martimano shyly returned high fives as they jogged through the raucous Hopeless gauntlet. They stopped to drink in the sight of the weird gypsy camp (as well as cups of some really tasty noodle soup someone shoved into their hands), then began quick-stepping down the back side of the mountain. Ann was nowhere to be seen.

Ann hit the fifty-mile mark at 12:05 p.m., nearly two hours ahead of Victoriano's time from the previous year. Carl loaded her up with sports drink and Cytomax carbohydrate gel, then snapped on his own fanny pack and gave his shoelaces a tug. According to Leadville rules, a "mule" can run alongside a racer for the last fifty miles, which meant Ann would now have a personal pit crew by her side all the way to the finish.

A good pacer is a huge help during an ultra, and Ann had one of the best: not only was Carl fast enough to push her, but experienced enough to take over if Ann's brain fritzed out. After twenty or so hours of nonstop running, an ultrarunner can get too mind numb to replace flashlight batteries, or comprehend trail markers, or even, in the unfortunate true case of a Badwater runner in 2005, distinguish between an imminent bowel movement and an occurring one.

And those are the runners who are really keeping it together. Hallucinations are no strangers to the rest; one ultrarunner kept screaming and leaping into the woods whenever he saw a flashlight, convinced it was an oncoming train. One runner enjoyed the company of a smokin' young hottie in a silver bikini who Rollerbladed by his side for miles across Death Valley until, to his regret, she dissolved into heat shimmers. Six out of twenty Badwater runners reported hallucinations that year, including one who saw rotting corpses along the road and "mutant mice monsters" crawling over the asphalt. One pacer got a little freaked out after she saw her runner stare into space for a while and then tell the empty air, "I know you're not real."

A tough pacer, consequently, can save your race; a sharp one can save your life. Too bad for Martimano, then, that the best he could hope for was that the shaggy goofball he'd met in town would actually show up—and could actually run.

The night before, Rick Fisher had brought the Tarahumara to a prerace spaghetti dinner at the Leadville VFW hall to see if he could recruit a few pacers. It wouldn't be easy; pacing is so grueling and thankless, usually only family, fools, and damn good friends let themselves get talked into it. The job means shivering in the middle of nowhere for hours until your runner shows up, then setting off at sunset for an all-night run through wind-whistling mountains. You'll get blood on your shins, vomit on your shoes, and not even a T-shirt for completing two marathons in a single night. Other job requirements can include staying awake while your runner catches a nap in the mud; popping a blood blister between her butt cheeks with your fingernails; and surrendering your jacket, even though your teeth are chattering, because her lips have gone blue.

At the spaghetti dinner, Martimano locked eyes with some long-haired local who, for some bizarre reason, immediately began cracking up. Martimano started laughing, too; he found the shaggy guy totally cool and hilarious. "It's you and me, brother," Shaggy said. "You follow? *Tú* and *yo*. If you want a mule, I'm your man."

"Whoa, whoa, hang on," Fisher interjected. "You sure you're fast enough for these guys?"

"You're not doing me any favor," Shaggy shrugged. "Who else you got lined up?"

"Yeah," Fisher said. "Okay, then."

And just as he'd promised, Shaggy was hollering and waving by the aid station the next afternoon when Juan and Martimano came running into the fifty-mile turnaround. They took a long, cool drink of water and grabbed some *pinole* and thin bean burritos from Kitty Williams. Rick Fisher had also roped in another pacer, an elite ultrarunner from San Diego who'd been a longtime student of Tarahumara lore. The four runners traded Tarahumara handshakes—that soft caressing of fingertips—and turned toward Hope Pass. Ann was already out of sight.

"Saddle up, guys," Shaggy said. "Let's go get the *bruja*."

Juan and Martimano barely understood anything the guy said, but they caught that all right: Shaggy was calling Ann a witch. They looked closely to see if he was serious, decided he wasn't, and started laughing. This guy was going to be a kick.

"Yeah, she's a *bruja*, but that's cool," Shaggy went on. "We've got stronger mojo. You understand that, mojo? No? Doesn't matter. We're gonna run the *bruja* down like a deer. Like a *venado*. Yeah, a *venado*. Got it? We're gonna run the *bruja* down like a *venado*. *Poco a poco*—little bit at a time."

But the bruja wasn't backing off. By the time she summited Hope Pass for the second time, Ann had widened her lead from four minutes to seven. "I was heading up Hope Pass, and she just blew by me going the other direction—*vroo-o-o-om!*" a Leadville runner named Glen Vaassen later told *Runner's World*. "She was *cruisin'*."

She threaded her way to the bottom of the switchbacks and plunged back through the Arkansas River, fighting to keep from being swept downstream in the waist-deep water. It was 2:31 p.m. when she and Carl arrived back at the Twin Lakes fire station at mile 60. Ann checked in, got her medical clearance, and trudged up the twenty-foot dirt ramp to the trailhead. By the time Shaggy and the Tarahumara arrived, Ann had been gone for twelve minutes.

Coincidentally, Ken Chlouber was just arriving at the Twin Lakes aid station heading outbound when Juan and Martimano came through on their return trip. Everyone in the firehouse was buzzing about Ann's record pace and ever-growing lead, but as Ken watched Juan and Martimano exit the firehouse, he was struck by something else: when they hit the dirt ramp, they hit it laughing.

"Everybody else walks that hill," Chlouber thought, as Juan and Martimano churned up the slope like kids playing in a leaf pile. "*Everybody*. And they sure as hell ain't laughin' about it."

CHAPTER 15

The flesh about my body felt soft and relaxed, like an
experiment in functional background music.

—RICHARD BRAUTIGAN, *Trout Fishing in America*

"SUCH A SENSE of joy!" marveled Coach Vigil, who'd never
seen anything like it, either. "It was quite remarkable." Glee and
determination are usually antagonistic emotions, yet the Tarahumara
were brimming with both at once, as if running to the death made
them feel more alive.

Vigil had been furiously taking mental notes (*Look how they point
their toes down, not up, like gymnasts doing the floor exercise. And their
backs! They could carry water buckets on their heads without spilling a drop!
How many years have I been telling my kids to straighten up and run from
the gut like that?*). But it was the smiles that really jolted him.

That's it! Vigil thought, ecstatic. *I found it!*

Except he wasn't sure what "it" was. The revelation he'd been
hoping for was right in front of his eyes, but he couldn't quite grasp
it; he could only catch the glim around the edges, like spotting the
cover of a rare book in a candlelit library. But whatever "it" was, he
knew it was exactly what he was looking for.

Over the previous few years, Vigil had become convinced that the
next leap forward in human endurance would come from a dimen-
sion he dreaded getting into: character. Not the "character" other
coaches were always rah-rah-rah-ing about; Vigil wasn't talking
about "grit" or "hunger" or "the size of the fight in the dog." In fact,

he meant the exact opposite. Vigil's notion of character wasn't toughness. It was compassion. Kindness. Love.

That's right: love.

Vigil knew it sounded like hippie-dippy drivel, and make no mistake, he'd have been much happier sticking to good, hard, quantifi-
able stuff like VO$_2$ max and periodized-training tables. But after
spending nearly fifty years researching performance physiology,
Vigil had reached the uncomfortable conclusion that all the easy
questions had been answered; he was now learning more and more
about less and less. He could tell you exactly how much of a head
start Kenyan teenagers had over Americans (eighteen thousand miles
run in training). He'd discovered why those Russian sprinters were
leaping off ladders (besides strengthening lateral muscles, the trauma
teaches nerves to fire more rapidly, which decreases the odds of training injuries). He'd parsed the secret of the Peruvian peasant diet
(high altitude has a curious effect on metabolism), and he could talk
for hours about the impact of a single percentage point in oxygen-
consumption efficiency.

He'd figured out the body, so now it was on to the brain. Specifi-
cally: How do you make anyone actually want to do any of this stuff?
How do you flip the internal switch that changes us all back into the
Natural Born Runners we once were? Not just in history, but in our
own lifetimes. Remember? Back when you were a kid and you had to
be yelled at to slow down? Every game you played, you played at top
speed, sprinting like crazy as you kicked cans, freed all, and attacked
jungle outposts in your neighbors' backyards. Half the fun of doing
anything was doing it at record pace, making it probably the last time
in your life you'd ever be hassled for going too fast.

That was the real secret of the Tarahumara: they'd never forgotten what it felt like to love running. They remembered that running
was mankind's first fine art, our original act of inspired creation. Way
before we were scratching pictures on caves or beating rhythms on
hollow trees, we were perfecting the art of combining our breath and
mind and muscles into fluid self-propulsion over wild terrain. And
when our ancestors finally did make their first cave paintings, what
were the first designs? A downward slash, lightning bolts through the
bottom and middle—behold, the Running Man.

Distance running was revered because it was indispensable; it was the way we survived and thrived and spread across the planet. You ran to eat and to avoid being eaten; you ran to find a mate and impress her, and with her you ran off to start a new life together. You had to love running, or you wouldn't live to love anything else. And like everything else we love—everything we sentimentally call our "passions" and "desires"—it's really an encoded ancestral necessity. We were born to run; we were born *because* we run. We're all Running People, as the Tarahumara have always known.

But the American approach—*ugh*. Rotten at its core. It was too artificial and grabby, Vigil believed, too much about getting stuff and getting it now: medals, Nike deals, a cute butt. It wasn't art; it was business, a hard-nosed quid pro quo. No wonder so many people hated running; if you thought it was only a means to an end—an investment in becoming faster, skinnier, richer—then why stick with it if you weren't getting enough quo for your quid?

It wasn't always like that—and when it wasn't, we were awesome. Back in the '70s, American marathoners were a lot like the Tarahumara; they were a tribe of isolated outcasts, running for love and relying on raw instinct and crude equipment. Slice the top off a '70s running shoe, and you had a sandal: the old Adidas and Onitsuka Tigers were just a flat sole and laces, with no motion control, no arch support, no heel pad. The guys in the '70s didn't know enough to worry about "pronation" and "supination"; that fancy running-store jargon hadn't even been invented yet.

Their training was as primitive as their shoes. They ran way too much: "We ran twice a day, sometimes three times," Frank Shorter would recall. "All we did was run—run, eat, and sleep." They ran way too hard: "The modus operandi was to let a bunch of competitive guys have at each other every day in a form of road rage," one observer put it. And they were *waaay* too buddy-buddy for so-called competitors: "We liked running together," recalled Bill Rodgers, a chieftain of the '70s tribe and four-time Boston Marathon champ. "We had fun with it. It wasn't a grind."

They were so ignorant, they didn't even realize they were supposed to be burned out, overtrained, and injured. Instead, they were fast; *really* fast. Frank Shorter won the '72 Olympic marathon gold and the '76 silver, Bill Rodgers was the No. 1 ranked marathoner in the world for three years, and Alberto Salazar won Boston, New

York, *and* the Comrades ultramarathon. By the early '80s, the Greater Boston Track Club had half a dozen guys who could run a 2:12 marathon. That's six guys, in one amateur club, in one city. Twenty years later, you couldn't find a single 2:12 marathoner anywhere in the country. The United States couldn't even get one runner to meet the 2:14 qualifying standard for the 2000 Olympics; only Rod DeHaven squeaked into the games under the 2:15 "B" standard. He finished sixty-ninth.

So what happened? How did we go from leader of the pack to lost and left behind? It's hard to determine a single cause for any event in this complex world, of course, but forced to choose, the answer is best summed up as follows:

$

Sure, plenty of people will throw up excuses about Kenyans having some kind of mutant muscle fiber, but this isn't about why other people got faster; it's about why we got *slower.* And the fact is, American distance running went into a death spiral precisely when cash entered the equation. The Olympics were opened to professionals after the 1984 Games, which meant running-shoe companies could bring the distance-running savages out of the wilderness and onto the payroll reservation.

Vigil could smell the apocalypse coming, and he'd tried hard to warn his runners. "There are two goddesses in your heart," he told them. "The Goddess of Wisdom and the Goddess of Wealth. Everyone thinks they need to get wealth first, and wisdom will come. So they concern themselves with chasing money. But they have it backwards. You have to give your heart to the Goddess of Wisdom, give her all your love and attention, and the Goddess of Wealth will become jealous, and follow you." Ask nothing from your running, in other words, and you'll get more than you ever imagined.

Vigil wasn't beating his chest about the purity of poverty, or fantasizing about a monastic order of moneyless marathoners. Shoot, he wasn't even sure he had a handle on the problem, let alone the solution. All he wanted was to find one Natural Born Runner—someone who ran for sheer joy, like an artist in the grip of inspiration—and study how he or she trained, lived, and thought. Whatever that thinking was, maybe Vigil could transplant it back into American culture like an heirloom seedling and watch it grow wild again.

Vigil already had the perfect prototype. There was this Czech soldier, a gawky dweeb who ran with such horrendous form that he looked "as if he'd just been stabbed through the heart," as one sportswriter put it. But Emil Zatopek loved running so much that even when he was still a grunt in army boot camp, he used to grab a flashlight and go off on twenty-mile runs through the woods at night.

In his combat boots.

In winter.

After a full day of infantry drills.

When the snow was too deep, Zatopek would jog in the tub on top of his dirty laundry, getting a resistance workout along with clean tighty whities. As soon as it thawed enough for him to get outside, he'd go nuts; he'd run four hundred meters as fast as he could, over and over, for ninety repetitions, resting in between by jogging two hundred meters. By the time he was finished, he'd done more than thirty-three miles of speedwork. Ask him his pace, and he'd shrug; he never timed himself. To build explosiveness, he and his wife, Dana, used to play catch with a javelin, hurling it back and forth to each other across a soccer field like a long, lethal Frisbee. One of Zatopek's favorite workouts combined all his loves at once: he'd jog through the woods in his army boots with his ever-loving wife riding on his back.

It was all a waste of time, of course. The Czechs were like the Zimbabwean bobsled team; they had no tradition, no coaching, no native talent, no chance of winning. But being counted out was liberating; having nothing to lose left Zatopek free to try any way to win. Take his first marathon: everyone knows the best way to build up to 26.2 miles is by running long, slow distances. Everyone, that is, except Emil Zatopek; he did hundred-yard dashes instead.

"I already know how to go slow," he reasoned. "I thought the point was to go fast." His atrocious, death-spasming style was punchline heaven for track scribes ("The most frightful horror spectacle since Frankenstein." . . . "He runs as if his next step would be his last." . . . "He looks like a man wrestling with an octopus on a conveyor belt"), but Zatopek just laughed along. "I'm not talented enough to run and smile at the same time," he'd say. "Good thing it's not figure skating. You only get points for speed, not style."

And dear God, was he a Chatty Cathy! Zatopek treated competition like it was speed dating. Even in the middle of a race, he liked to natter with other runners and try out his smattering of French and English and German, causing one grouchy Brit to complain about Zatopek's "incessant talking." At away meets, he'd sometimes have so many new friends in his hotel room that he'd have to give up his bed and sleep outside under a tree. Once, right before an international race, he became pals with an Australian runner who was hoping to break the Australian 5,000-meter record. Zatopek was only entered in the 10,000-meter race, but he came up with a plan; he told the Aussie to drop out of his race and line up next to Zatopek instead. Zatopek spent the first half of the 10,000-meter race pacing his new buddy to the record, then sped off to attend to his own business and win.

That was pure Zatopek, though; races for him were like a pub crawl. He loved competing so much that instead of tapering and peaking, he jumped into as many meets as he could find. During a manic stretch in the late '40s, Zatopek raced nearly every other week for three years *and never lost*, going 69–0. Even on a schedule like that, he still averaged up to 165 miles a week in training.

Zatopek was a bald, self-coached thirty-year-old apartment-dweller from a decrepit Eastern European backwater when he arrived for the 1952 Olympics in Helsinki. Since the Czech team was so thin, Zatopek had his choice of distance events, so he chose them all. He lined up for the 5,000 meters, and won with a new Olympic record. He then lined up for the 10,000 meters, and won his second gold with another new record. He'd never run a marathon before, but what the hell; with two golds already around his neck, he had nothing to lose, so why not finish the job and give it a bash?

Zatopek's inexperience quickly became obvious. It was a hot day, so England's Jim Peters, then the world-record holder, decided to use the heat to make Zatopek suffer. By the ten-mile mark, Peters was already ten minutes under his own world-record pace and pulling away from the field. Zatopek wasn't sure if anyone could really sustain such a blistering pace. "Excuse me," he said, pulling alongside Peters. "This is my first marathon. Are we going too fast?"

"No," Peters replied. "Too slow." If Zatopek was dumb enough to ask, he was dumb enough to deserve any answer he got.

Zatopek was surprised. "You say too slow," he asked again. "Are you sure the pace is too slow?"

"Yes," Peters said. Then he got a surprise of his own.

"Okay. Thanks." Zatopek took Peters at his word, and took off.

When he burst out of the tunnel and into the stadium, he was met with a roar: not only from the fans, but from athletes of every nation who thronged the track to cheer him in. Zatopek snapped the tape with his third Olympic record, but when his teammates charged over to congratulate him, they were too late: the Jamaican sprinters had already hoisted him on their shoulders and were parading him around the infield. "Let us live so that when we come to die, even the undertaker will be sorry," Mark Twain used to say. Zatopek found a way to run so that when he won, even other teams were delighted.

You can't pay someone to run with such infectious joy. You can't bully them into it, either, which Zatopek would unfortunately have to prove. When the Red Army marched into Prague in 1968 to crush the pro-democracy movement, Zatopek was given a choice: he could get on board with the Soviets and serve as a sports ambassador, or he could spend the rest of his life cleaning toilets in a uranium mine. Zatopek chose the toilets. And just like that, one of the most beloved athletes in the world disappeared.

At the same time, coincidentally, his rival for the title of world's greatest distance runner was also taking a beating. Ron Clarke, a phenomenally talented Australian with Johnny Depp's dark, dreamy beauty, was exactly the kind of guy that Zatopek, by all rights, should hate. While Zatopek had to teach himself to run in the snow at night after sentry duty, the Australian pretty boy was enjoying sunny morning jogs along the beaches of Mornington Peninsula and expert coaching. Everything Zatopek could wish for, Clarke had to spare: Freedom. Money. Elegance. Hair.

Ron Clarke was a star—but still a loser in the eyes of his nation. Despite breaking nineteen records in every distance from the half-mile to six miles, "the bloke who choked" never managed to win the big ones. In the summer of '68, he blew his final chance: in the 10,000-meter finals at the Mexico City Games, Clarke was knocked out by altitude sickness. Anticipating a barrage of abuse back home, Clarke delayed his return by stopping off in Prague to pay a courtesy call to the bloke who never lost. Toward the end of their visit, Clarke glimpsed Zatopek sneaking something into his suitcase.

"I thought I was smuggling some message to the outside world for him, so I did not dare to open the parcel until the plane was well away," Clarke would say. Zatopek sent him off with a strong embrace. "Because you deserved it," he said, which Clarke found cute and very touching; the old master had far worse problems of his own to deal with, but was still playful enough to grant a victory-stand hug to the young punk who'd missed his chance to mount one.

Only later would he discover that Zatopek wasn't talking about the hug at all: in his suitcase, Clarke found Zatopek's 1952 Olympic 10,000-meters gold medal. For Zatopek to give it to the man who'd replaced his name in the record books was extraordinarily noble; to give it away at precisely the moment in his life when he was losing everything else was an act of almost unimaginable compassion.

"His enthusiasm, his friendliness, his love of life, shone through every movement," an overcome Ron Clarke said later. "There is not, and never was, a greater man than Emil Zatopek."

So here's what Coach Vigil was trying to figure out: was Zatopek a great man who happened to run, or a great man *because* he ran? Vigil couldn't quite put his finger on it, but his gut kept telling him that there was some kind of connection between the capacity to love and the capacity to love *running*. The engineering was certainly the same: both depended on loosening your grip on your own desires, putting aside what you wanted and appreciating what you got, being patient and forgiving and undemanding. Sex and speed—haven't they been symbiotic for most of our existence, as intertwined as the strands of our DNA? We wouldn't be alive without love; we wouldn't have survived without running; maybe we shouldn't be surprised that getting better at one could make you better at the other.

Look, Vigil was a scientist, not a swami. He hated straying into this Buddha-under-the-lotus-tree stuff, but he wasn't going to ignore it, either. He'd made his bones by finding connections where everyone else saw coincidence, and the more he examined the compassion link, the more intriguing it became. Was it just by chance that the pantheon of dedicated runners also included Abraham Lincoln ("He could beat all the other boys in a footrace") and Nelson Mandela (a college cross-country standout who, even in prison, continued to run seven miles a day in place in his cell)? Maybe Ron Clarke wasn't being poetic in his description of Zatopek—maybe his expert eye was clinically precise: *His love of life shone through every movement.*

Yes! Love of life! Exactly! That's what got Vigil's heart thumping when he saw Juan and Martimano scramble happy-go-luckily up that dirt hill. He'd found his Natural Born Runner. He'd found an entire *tribe* of Natural Born Runners, and from what he'd seen so far, they were just as joyful and magnificent as he'd hoped.

Vigil, an old man alone in the woods, suddenly felt a burst of immortality. He was onto something. Something huge. It wasn't just how to run; it was how to *live*, the essence of who we are as a species and what we're meant to be. Vigil had read his Lumholtz, and at that moment the great explorer's words revealed their hidden treasure; so that's what Lumholtz meant when he called the Tarahumara "the founders and makers of the history of mankind." Perhaps all our troubles—all the violence, obesity, illness, depression, and greed we can't overcome—began when we stopped living as Running People. Deny your nature, and it will erupt in some other, uglier way.

Vigil's mission was clear. He had to trace the route back from what we've become to what the Tarahumara have always been, and figure out where we got lost. Every action flick depicts the destruction of civilization as some kind of crash-boom-bang, a nuclear war or hurtling comet or a self-aware-cyborg uprising, but the true cataclysm may already be creeping up right under our eyes: because of rampant obesity, one in three children born in the United States is at risk of diabetes—meaning, we could be the first generation of Americans to outlive our own children. Maybe the ancient Hindus were better crystal-ball-gazers than Hollywood when they predicted the world would end not with a bang but with a big old yawn. Shiva the Destroyer would snuff us out by doing . . . nothing. Lazing out. Withdrawing his hot-blooded force from our bodies. Letting us become slugs.

Coach Vigil wasn't a maniac, though. He wasn't proposing we all run off to the canyons with the Tarahumara to live in caves and gnaw mice. But there had to be transferable skills, right? Basic Tarahumara principles that could survive and take root in American soil?

Because my God, imagine the payoff. What if you could run for decades and never get injured . . . and log hundreds of weekly miles and enjoy every one of them . . . and see your heart rate drop and your stress and anger fade while your energy soared? Imagine crime, cholesterol, and greed melting away as a nation of Running People finally rediscovered its stride. More than his Olympic runners, more than his triumphs and records, this could be Joe Vigil's legacy.

He didn't have all the answers yet—but watching the Tarahumara whisk past in their wizard capes, he knew where he would find them.

CHAPTER 16

FUNNY, because Shaggy was looking at the same thing and all he saw was a middle-aged guy with a demonic knee.

Shaggy's ear caught the problem first. For hours, he'd been listening to the faint *whish . . . whish . . . whish* of Juan's and Martimano's sandals, a sound like a drummer beating rhythm with the brushes. Their soles didn't hit the ground so much as caress it, scratching back lightly as each foot kicked toward their butts and circled around for the next stride. Hour after hour: *whish . . . whish . . . whish . . .*

But as they came down Mount Elbert on the single-track trail toward mile 70, Shaggy detected a little hitch in the beat. Martimano seemed to be babying one foot, placing it carefully rather than whipping it right around. Juan noticed, too; he kept glancing back at Martimano uncertainly.

"*¿Qué pasa?*" Shaggy asked. "What's up?"

Martimano didn't answer right away, most likely because he was mentally scanning the previous twelve hours to see if he could pinpoint the cause of his pain: was it running those thirteen miles wearing trail shoes for the first time in his life? Or pivoting around those jagged switchbacks in the dark? Or slip-sliding over slick stones in a raging river? Or was it . . .

"*La bruja*," Martimano said; must've been the witch. The whole episode back at the firehouse suddenly made sense. Ann's glare, the mumbo jumbo she spat at him, the shocked look on people's faces,

Kitty's refusal to repeat it in English, Shaggy's comment—it was obvious. Ann had cursed him. "I passed her," Martimano said later, "but then she cast a spell on my knee."

Martimano had been afraid something like this would happen ever since the Pescador had refused to bring along their shaman. Back home in the Barrancas, the shamans protect the *iskiate* and *pinole* from witchcraft, and combat any spells in the runner's hips and knees and butts by massaging them with smooth stones and mashed medicinal herbs. But the Tarahumara had no shaman by their side in Leadville, and look what happened: for the first time in forty-two years, Martimano's knee was giving out.

When Shaggy realized what was going on, he felt a sudden pang of affection. *They're not gods*, he realized. *They're just guys.* And like every guy, the thing they loved most could bring them the most misery and confusion. Running a hundred miles wasn't painless for the Tarahumara, either; they had to face their doubts, and silence the little devil on their shoulder who kept whispering excellent reasons in their ear for quitting.

Shaggy looked over at Juan, who was torn between taking off or sticking with his mentor. "Go ahead," Shaggy told Juan and his pacer. "I've got your boy. Go run that *bruja* down like a deer!"

Juan nodded, and soon disappeared around a bend in the trail.

Shaggy gave Martimano a wink. "It's *tú y yo, amigo*."

"*Guadajuko*," Martimano said. Cool by me.

The scent of the finish line was tickling Ann's nose. By the time Juan made it to the Halfmoon aid station at mile 72, Ann had nearly doubled her lead; she was twenty-two minutes ahead with just twenty-eight miles to go.

Just to pull even, Juan would have to steal back close to one minute every mile, and he was about to enter the worst possible place to start trying: a seven-mile stretch of asphalt. Ann, with her road-racing expertise and air-injected Nikes, could uncoil her long legs and let fly. Juan, who'd never touched blacktop until that day, would have to handle the strange surface in homemade sandals.

"His feet are really going to suffer," Juan's pacer called out to a TV crew by the roadside. As soon as Juan came off the dirt and hit the hardtop, he bent his knees and shortened his stride, getting all the shock absorption he needed from the up-and-down compression of his legs. He adjusted so well, in fact, that his amazed pacer began falling back, unable to keep up.

Juan chased Ann on his own. He covered the seven miles to the Fish Hatchery in almost exactly the time it had taken him that morning, then cut left and onto the muddy trail leading to the dreaded Powerline Climb. Many Leadville runners fear Powerline nearly as much as Hope Pass. "I've seen people sitting by the side of the trail, crying," one Leadville vet recalled. But Juan leaned into it like he'd been waiting for it all day, running up near-vertical pitches that force most runners to push their knees down with their hands.

Ahead, Ann was approaching the peak, but her eyes were nearly closed with exhaustion, as if she couldn't bear to even look at the last bit of slope. Switchback by switchback, Juan steadily reeled her in— until abruptly, he pulled up short and started hopping on one foot. Disaster had struck; the thong on one of his sandals had snapped, and he had nothing to replace it with. As Ann was cresting the mountain, Juan was taking a seat on a rock and examining what was left of the strap. He rethreaded the sandal, and found there was just enough thong left to hold the sole on his foot. He knotted the shortened strap carefully and gave it a couple of test steps. Good to go.

Ann, meanwhile, had made it to the homestretch. All she had left was the ten miles of rolling dirt trail around Turquoise Lake before the screams of the Sixth Street party animals hauled her uphill to the finish line. It was just past eight in the evening and the woods around her were sinking into darkness—and that's when something burst out of the trees behind her. It came on her so fast, Ann couldn't even react; she froze in place in the middle of the trail, too startled to move, as Juan darted to her left with one stride and back onto the trail with the next, his white cape swirling around him as he whisked past Ann and disappeared down the trail.

He didn't even look tired! It's like he was just . . . having fun! Ann was so crushed, she decided to quit. She was less than an hour from the finish line, but the Tarahumara joyfulness that so excited Joe Vigil had totally disheartened her. Here she was, absolutely *killing* herself to hold the lead, and this guy looked like he could have snatched it any time he pleased. It was humiliating; she now realized that as soon as she'd sprung her Queen's Gambit, Juan had marked her for the kill. Her husband eventually got her moving again, and just in time; Martimano and the rest of the Tarahumara pack were coming up fast.

Juan crossed the finish line in 17:30, setting a new Leadville course record by twenty-five minutes. (He also established another first by shyly ducking under the tape instead of breasting it, never having seen one before.) Ann finished nearly a half hour later, in 18:06. Right behind her, Martimano and his bewitched knee finished third, with Manuel Luna and the rest of the Tarahumara charging home in fourth, fifth, seventh, tenth, and eleventh.

"Wow, what a race!" Scott Tinley raved for the TV audience as he pushed a microphone into Ann Trason's face. She blinked into the camera lights, looking like she was about to faint, but managed to rally one last burst of fight.

"Sometimes," she said, "it takes a woman to bring out the best in a man."

Hey, and right back atcha, the Tarahumara could have replied; thanks to Ann's heroic attempt to single-handedly defeat an entire team of distance-running savants, she had smashed her own Leadville best by more than two hours, setting a new women's record that has never been broken.

But the Tarahumara weren't free to say anything at the moment, even if they'd been so inclined. They'd stepped off the racecourse and into a shit storm.

This should have been their moment. Finally, after centuries of horror and fear, after being hunted for their scalps, enslaved for their strength, and bullied for their land, the Tarahumara were respected. They had proven themselves, indisputably, the greatest ultrarunners on earth. The world would see they had fantastic skills worth studying, a way of life worth preserving, a homeland worth protecting.

Joe Vigil was already selling his house and quitting his job; that's how excited *he* was. Now that Leadville had built a bridge between American and Tarahumara culture, he was ready to carry out a plan he'd been contemplating for a long time. At sixty-five years old, he was ready to retire from Adams State anyway. He and his wife, Caroline, would move to Arizona's Mexican border, where he'd set up a base camp for Tarahumara studies. It might take another few years, but in the meantime, he'd come back to Leadville every summer and tighten his relationship with the Tarahumara racers. He'd start learning their language . . . get them on a treadmill with heart-rate and maximal-oxygen-consumption monitors . . . maybe even arrange workshops with his Olympians! Because that was the cool part—Ann had been right there with them, which meant whatever the Tarahumara were doing, the rest of us could learn!

It was beautiful. For about a minute.

If you think you're using one goddamn picture of my Tarahumara, Rick Fisher declared when Tony Post and the other Rockport executives hurried over with their congratulations, you'd better come up with some money.

Tony Post was appalled. "He really went off. He came across like he was totally enraged, like the kind of guy who'd hunt you down and kill you. Not literally," Post hastened to add. "He just seemed like this hothead who would argue forever and never admit he was wrong."

"He was a pain in the ass," Ken Chlouber added. According to Ken, Fisher demanded that Rockport come up with an extra $5,000 bonus for the Tarahumara—instantly. "He wasn't a pain in the ass until we had big-time sponsors and TV crews, and then he held Rockport hostage to use film of the Indians. He tried to make life miserable for me as the race president, he was totally self-serving, and he didn't take care of them at all."

That's how steamed Chlouber was, and the worst was yet to come. Fisher still had one last bomb to drop. "They had a blonde, blue-eyed female they wanted to win, and she didn't win," Fisher would say. Pushed into a corner, Fisher fought back by going sort of nuts, just the way he had that time when he was surrounded by drug thugs in the Copper Canyons and only survived by going berserk. Accusing Ken and Rockport of favoring Ann Trason made no sense at all, but it accomplished one goal: it got people yelling about something besides the five grand he was demanding.

The Tarahumara watched the *chabochis* scream at each other. They heard the angry words, and saw the angry arms chopping in their direction. The Tarahumara didn't know what was being said, but they got the message. Confronted by hostility, the world's greatest underground athletes reacted as they always had; they headed back home to their canyons, fading like a dream and taking their secrets with them. After their triumph in 1994, the Tarahumara would never return to Leadville.

One man followed them. He was never seen in Leadville again either. It was the Tarahumara's strange new friend, Shaggy—soon to be known as Caballo Blanco, lone wanderer of the High Sierras.

CHAPTER 17

And now what shall become of us without any barbarians?
Those people were some kind of solution.

—Constantine Cavafy, "Waiting for the Barbarians"

"THAT WAS TEN years ago," Caballo told me, wrapping up his tale. "And I've been here ever since."

Mamá had kicked us out of her living-room restaurant hours before and gone to bed. Caballo, still talking, had led me down the deserted streets of Creel and into a back-alley bodega. We closed that place, too. By the time Caballo had brought me from 1994 to the present, it was two in the morning and my head was spinning. He'd told me more than I'd even hoped for about the Tarahumara's flash across the American ultra landscape (and tipped me to how I could learn the rest by tracking down Rick Fisher, Joe Vigil, and company), but in all those tales, he'd never answered the only question I'd asked:

Dude, who *are* you?

It was as if he'd done nothing in his life before running through the woods with Martimano—or else he'd done plenty he wouldn't talk about. Every time I probed, he sidestepped with either a joke or a non-answer that slammed the topic shut like a dungeon door ("How do I make money? I do stuff for rich people who won't do it for themselves"). Then he'd power off on another yarn. The choice was clear; I could be a pest and piss him off, or I could back off and hear some great stories.

I did learn that after the '94 Leadville race, Rick Fisher went on the rampage. There were other races out there and other Tarahumara runners, and it wasn't long before Fisher had regrouped and was careening from mayhem to mayhem like a frat boy on a road trip. First, Team Tarahumara was thrown out of the Angeles Crest 100-Mile Endurance Run in California because Fisher kept barging into a runners-only section of the course in the middle of the race. "The last thing I want to do is disqualify a runner," the race director said, "but Rick left us no choice."

Then, three Tarahumara runners were disqualified after finishing first, second, and fourth in Utah's Wasatch Front 100 because Fisher had refused to pay the entry fee. Then it was on to Western States, where Fisher threw another finish-line tantrum, accusing race volunteers of secretly switching trail markers to trick the Tarahumara and—true story—*stealing their blood*. (All the Western States racers were asked for a blood sample as part of a scientific study on endurance, but Fisher alone somehow smelled a ruse and blew up. "The Tarahumara blood is very, very rare," he's reported to have said. "The medical world wants to get its hands on it for genetic testing.")

By that point, even the Tarahumara seemed to be sick of dealing with the Pescador. They also noticed that he kept trading up for newer and nicer SUVs, while all they got for the long, lonely weeks away from home and their hundreds of miles of mountain running were a few bags of corn. Once again, dealing with the *chabochis* had left the Tarahumara feeling like slaves. That was the end of Team Tarahumara. They disbanded—forever.

Micah True (or whatever his name really was) felt such kinship with the Tarahumara and such disgust with the behavior of his fellow Americans that he felt compelled to make amends. Immediately after he'd paced Martimano in the '94 Leadville race, he talked his way onto a radio station in Boulder, Colorado, and asked anyone with an old coat to come drop it off. Once he had a pile, he bundled them up and set off for the Copper Canyons.

He had no clue where he was going, putting his odds of actually finding his buddy Martimano on a par with Shackleton making it back from Antarctica. He wandered across the desert and through the canyons, repeating Martimano's name to anyone he met, until he stunned both himself and Martimano by actually arriving at the top of a nine-thousand-foot mountain and the center of Martimano's village. The Tarahumara made him welcome in their own wordless way: they barely spoke to him, but when Caballo awoke every morning, he found a little pile of handmade tortillas and fresh *pinole* by his campsite.

"The Rarámuri have no money, but nobody is poor," Caballo said. "In the States, you ask for a glass of water and they take you to a homeless shelter. Here, they take you in and feed you. You ask to camp out, and they say, 'Sure, but wouldn't you rather sleep inside with us?'"

But Choguita gets cold at night, too cold for a skinny guy from California (or wherever he was really from), so after giving away all his coats, Micah waved *adiós* to Juan and Martimano and struck off on his own, pushing into the warm depths of the canyons. He meandered blindly past drug dens and desperadoes, avoided diseases and canyon fever, and eventually discovered a spot he liked by a bend in the river. He hauled up rocks to build a hut, and made himself at home.

"I decided I was going to find the best place in the world to run, and that was it," he told me as we walked back to the hotel that night. "The first view made my jaw drop. I got all excited because I couldn't wait to get out on the trail. I was so overwhelmed, I didn't know where to begin. But it's wild out there. I had to give it some time."

He had no choice, anyway. The reason he was pacing at Leadville instead of racing was because his legs had begun betraying him after he turned forty. "I used to have trouble with injuries, especially with my ankle tendons," Micah said. Over the years, he'd tried every remedy—wraps, massage, more expensive and supportive shoes— but nothing really helped. When he arrived in the Barrancas, he decided to chuck logic and trust that the Tarahumara knew what they were doing. He wasn't going to take the time to try figuring out their secrets; he'd just tackle it swimming-hole style, by leaping in and hoping for the best.

He got rid of his running shoes and began wearing nothing but sandals. He started eating *pinole* for breakfast (after learning how to cook it like oatmeal with water and honey), and carrying it dry with him in a hip bag during his rambles through the canyons. He took some vicious falls and sometimes barely made it back to his hut on his own two feet, but he just gritted his teeth, soaked his wounds in the icy river, and chalked it up as an investment. "Suffering is humbling. It pays to know how to get your butt kicked," Caballo said. "I learned pretty fast you'd better have respect for the Sierra Madre, 'cause she'll chew you up and crap you out."

By his third year, Caballo was tackling trails that were invisible to the non-Tarahumara eye. With butterflies in his stomach, he'd push himself over the lip of jagged descents that were longer, steeper, and more serpentine than any black-diamond ski run. He'd slip-scramble-sprint downhill for miles, barely in control, relying on his canyon-honed reflexes but still awaiting the *pop* of a knee cartilage, the rip of a hamstring, the fiery burn of a torn Achilles tendon he knew was coming any second.

But it never came. He never got hurt. After a few years in the canyons, Caballo was stronger, healthier, and faster than he'd ever been in his life. "My whole approach to running has changed since I've been here," he told me. As a test, he tried running a trail through the mountains that takes three days on horseback; he did it in seven hours. He's not sure how it all came together, what proportions of sandals and *pinole* and *korima*, but—

"Hey," I interrupted him. "Could you show me?"

"Show you what?"

"How to run like that."

Something about his smile made me instantly regret asking. "Yeah, I'll take you for a run," he said. "Meet me here at sunup."

"Huh! Huh!"

I was trying to shout, but it kept turning into a pant. "*Horse*," I finally got out, catching Caballo Blanco's ear just before he vanished around an uphill bend. We had set out in the hills behind Creel, on a rocky, pine-needled trail climbing through the woods. We'd been running for less than ten minutes and already I was dying for air. It's not that Caballo is so fast; it's just that he seems so *light*, as though he wills himself uphill by mind power instead of muscle.

He turned and trotted back down. "Okay, man, lesson one. Get right behind me." He started to jog, more slowly this time, and I tried to copy everything he did. My arms floated until my hands were rib-high; my stride chopped down to pitty-pat steps; my back straightened so much I could almost hear the vertebrae creaking.

"Don't fight the trail," Caballo called back over his shoulder. "Take what it gives you. If you have a choice between one step or two between rocks, take three." Caballo has spent so many years navigating the trails, he's even nicknamed the stones beneath his feet: some are *ayudantes*, the helpers which let you spring forward with power; others are "tricksters," which look like *ayudantes* but roll treacherously at takeoff; and some are *chingoncitos*, little bastards just dying to lay you out.

"Lesson two," Caballo called. "Think *Easy, Light, Smooth,* and *Fast.* You start with easy, because if that's all you get, that's not so bad. Then work on light. Make it effortless, like you don't give a shit how high the hill is or how far you've got to go. When you've practiced that so long that you forget you're practicing, you work on making it *smooooooth.* You won't have to worry about the last one—you get those three, and you'll be fast."

I kept my eyes on Caballo's sandaled feet, trying to duplicate his odd, sort of tippy-toeing steps. I had my head down so long, I didn't notice at first that we'd left the forest.

"Wow!" I exclaimed.

The sun was just rising over the Sierras. Pine smoke scented the air, rising from dented stovepipes in the lodge-pole shacks on the edge of town. In the distance, giant standing stones like Easter Island statues reared from the mesa floor, with snow-dusted mountains in the background. Even if I hadn't been sucking wind, I'd have been breathless.

"I told ya," Micah gloated.

We'd hit our turnaround point, but even though I knew it would be foolish for me to try going more than eight miles, it was such a kick loping these trails that I hated heading back. Caballo knew exactly what I meant.

"I've felt that way for ten years," he said. "And I'm still just learning my way around." But he had to hustle; he was heading home to his hut that day, and he'd barely have enough time to make it before dark. And that's when he began to explain what he was doing in Creel in the first place.

"You know," Caballo began, "a lot has happened since that Leadville race." Ultrarunning used to be just a handful of freaks in the woods with flashlights, but over the past few years, it had been transformed by an invasion of Young Guns. Like Karl Meltzer, who rocked "Strangelove" through his iPod while winning the Hardrock 100 three times in a row; and the "Dirt Diva," Catra Corbett, a beautiful and kaleidoscopically-tattooed Goth chick who once, just for fun, ran all 211 miles of the John Muir trail across Yosemite National Park and then turned around and ran all the way back; and Tony "Naked Guy" Krupicka, who rarely wore more than skimpy shorts and spent a year sleeping in a friend's closet while training to win the Leadville 100; and the Fabulous Flying Skaggs Brothers, Eric and Kyle, who hitchhiked to the Grand Canyon before setting a new record for the fastest round-trip run from rim to rim.

These Young Guns wanted something fresh, tough, and exotic, and they were flocking to trail-running in such numbers that, by 2002, it had become the fastest-growing outdoor sport in the country. It wasn't just the racing they loved; it was the thrill of exploring the brave new world of their own bodies. Ultra god Scott Jurek summed up the Young Guns' unofficial creed with a quote from William James he stuck on the end of every e-mail he sent: "Beyond the very extreme of fatigue and distress, we may find amounts of ease and power we never dreamed ourselves to own; sources of strength never taxed at all because we never push through the obstruction."

As the Young Guns took to the woods, they brought everything that had been learned about sports science over the past decade. Matt Carpenter, a mountain runner in Colorado Springs, began spending hundreds of hours on a treadmill to measure the variations in body oscillations when, for instance, he took a sip of water (the most biomechanically efficient way to hold a water bottle was tucked into his armpit, not held in his hand). Carpenter used a belt sander and a straight razor to shave micro-ounces off his running shoes and plunged them in and out of the bathtub to gauge water retention and drying speed. In 2005, he used his obsessive knowledge to blast the record at Leadville—he finished in a stunning 15:42, nearly two hours faster than the fastest Tarahumara ever had.

But! What could the Tarahumara do if pushed? See, that's what Caballo wanted to know. Victoriano and Juan had run like hunters, the way they'd been taught: just fast enough to capture their quarry and no faster. Who knew how much faster they might have gone against a guy like Carpenter? And *no one* knew what they could do on their home terrain. As defending champs, didn't they deserve the right to the home-field advantage at least once?

If the Tarahumara couldn't go back to America, Caballo reasoned, then the Americans would have to come to the Tarahumara. But he knew the fiercely shy canyon-dwellers would vanish back into the hills if surrounded by a pack of question-firing, camera-clicking American runners.

However—and this was Caballo's brainstorm—what if he set up a race the Tarahumara way? It would be like an old-time guitar picker's battle—a week of sparring, trading secrets, studying each other's style and techniques. On the last day, all the runners would face off in a 50-mile clash of champions.

It was a great idea—and a total joke, of course. No elite runner would take the risk; it wasn't just career suicide, it was *suicide* suicide. Just to get to the starting line, they'd have to slip past bandits, hike through the badlands, keep an eagle eye on every sip of water and every bite of food. If they got hurt, they were dead; not right away, maybe, but inevitably. They could be days from the nearest road and hours from fresh water, with no chance for a rescue chopper to thread its way between those tight rock walls.

No matter: Caballo had already begun working on his plan. That's the only reason he was in Creel. He'd left his hut at the bottom of the canyons and trekked into a town he loathed because he'd heard there was a PC with a dial-up connection in the back of a Creel candy shop. He'd learned some computer basics, gotten an e-mail account, and had begun sending messages to the outside world. And that's where I came in; the only reason "the gringo Indio" had gotten interested when I ambushed him back at the hotel was because I told him I was a writer. Maybe an article about his race would actually attract some racers.

"So who are you inviting?" I asked.

"Just one guy so far," he said. "I only want runners with the right spirit, real champions. So I've been messaging Scott Jurek."

Scott Jurek? Seven-time Western States champ and three-peat

Ultrarunner of the Year Scott Jurek? Caballo had to be high out of his skull if he thought Scott Jurek was coming down here to race a bunch of nobodies in the middle of nowhere. Scott was the top ultra-runner in the country, maybe in the world, arguably of all time. When Scott Jurek wasn't racing, he was helping Brooks design their signature trail shoe, the Cascadia, or setting up sold-out running camps, or making decisions about what high-profile event he'd run next in Japan, Switzerland, Greece, or France. Scott Jurek was a business enterprise that lived and died by the health of Scott Jurek—which meant the last thing the company's chief asset needed to do was risk getting sick, shot, or defeated in some half-assed pickup race in a sniper-patrolled corner of the Mexican outback.

But somewhere, Caballo had read an interview with Jurek and felt an instant thrum of brotherhood. In his own way, Scott was nearly as mysterious as Caballo. While far lesser ultra stars like Dean Karnazes and Pam Reed were touting themselves on TV, writing self-glorifying memoirs, and (in Dean's case) promoting a sports drink by running bare-chested on a sky-cammed treadmill over Times Square, the greatest American ultrarunner of them all was virtually invisible. He seemed to be a pure racing animal, which explained two of his other peculiar habits: at the start of every race, he'd let out a bloodcurdling shriek, and after he won, he'd roll in the dirt like a hyperactive hound. Then he'd get up, brush himself off, and vanish back to Seattle until it was time for his war cry to echo through the dark again.

Now *that* was the kind of champion Caballo was looking for; not some showboat who'd use the Tarahumara to boost his own brand, but a true student of the sport who appreciated the artistry and effort in even the slowest runner's performance. Caballo didn't need any more proof of Scott Jurek's worthiness, but he got it anyway: asked at the end of the interview to list his idols, Jurek named the Tarahu-mara. "For inspiration," the article noted, "he repeats a saying of the Tarahumara Indians: 'When you run on the earth and run with the earth, you can run forever.' "

"See!" Caballo insisted. "He has a Rarámuri soul."

But hold on a sec. . . . "Even if Scott Jurek does agree to come, how about the Tarahumara?" I asked. "Will they go for it?"

"Maybe," Caballo shrugged. "The guy I want is Arnulfo Quimare."

This thing was never going to happen. I knew from personal experience that Arnulfo would barely even *talk* to an outsider, let alone hang with a whole gang of them for a week and guide them over the hidden trails of his homeland. I admired Caballo's taste and ambition, but I seriously questioned his grasp of reality. No American runners knew who he was, and most of the Tarahumara weren't sure *what* he was. Yet he was expecting them all to trust him?

"I'm pretty sure Manuel Luna will come," Caballo continued. "Maybe with his son."

"Marcelino?" I asked.

"Yeah," Caballo said. "He's good."

"He's awesome!"

I still had an after-image on my retina of the teenage Human Torch surging over that dirt trail as fast as a flame along a fuse. Well, in that case, who cared if Scott Jurek or any of the other hotshots showed up? Just the chance to run alongside Manuel and Marcelino and Caballo again would be worth it. The way Caballo and Marcelino ran, it was the closest a human could come to flying. I'd gotten just a taste of it out there on the trails of Creel, and I wanted more; it was like flapping your arms really hard and lifting a half inch off the ground—after that, how could you think of anything except trying again?

"I can do this," I told myself. Caballo had been in the same position I was in when he came down here; he was a guy in his forties with busted-up legs, and within a year, he was sky-walking across mountaintops. If it worked for him, why not me? If I really applied the techniques he'd taught me, could I get strong enough to run fifty miles through the Copper Canyons? The odds against his race coming off were roughly—actually, there were no odds. It wasn't going to happen. But if by some miracle he managed to set up a run with the top Tarahumara of their generation, I wanted to be there.

When we got back to Creel, Caballo and I shook hands.

"Thanks for the lessons," I said. "You taught me a lot."

"*Hasta luego, norawa,*" Caballo replied. Till the next time, buddy. And then he was off.

I watched him go. There was something terribly sad, yet terribly uplifting, about watching this prophet of the ancient art of distance running turning his back on everything except his dream, and heading back down to "the best place in the world to run."

Alone.

CHAPTER 18

~~~

"YOU EVER HEARD of Caballo Blanco?"

After I got back from Mexico, I called Don Allison, the longtime editor of *UltraRunning* magazine. Caballo had let slip two details about his past worth following up: he'd been a pro fighter of some kind, and he'd won a few ultraraces. Fighting is insanely difficult to fact-check, what with its tangled ganglion of disciplines and accrediting bodies, but in ultrarunning, all roads lead to Don Allison in Weymouth, Massachusetts. As the clearinghouse for every rumor, race result, and rising star in the sport, Don Allison knew everyone and everything, and that's what made the first syllable out of his mouth doubly disappointing:

"*Who?*"

"I think he also goes by Micah True," I said. "But I'm not sure if that's really his name or his dog's."

Silence.

"Hello?" I said.

"Yeah, hang on," Allison finally responded. "I was just looking for something. So is he for real?"

"You mean, is he serious?"

"No, is he *real*? Does he really exist?"

"Yeah, he's real. I found him down in Mexico."

"Okay," Allison said. "Then is he crazy?"

"No, he's—" Now it was my turn to pause. "I don't *think* so."

"Because a guy by that name sent me a couple of articles. That's what I was looking for. I got to tell you, they were just unprintable."

Now that's saying something. *UltraRunning* is less like a magazine and more like those chatty family letters some people send instead of Christmas cards. Maybe 80 percent of every issue is made up of lists of names and times, the results of races no one ever heard of in places few but ultrarunners could ever find. Besides race reports, every issue has a few essays volunteered by runners opining on their latest obsessions, like "Using the Scale to Determine Your Optimum Hydration Needs" or "Headlamp and Flashlight Combinations." Needless to say, you've got to work hard to earn a rejection slip from *UltraRunning*, which made me afraid to even ask what Caballo, isolated in his hut like the Unabomber, had manifestoed about.

"Was he, like, threatening or something?"

"Nah," Allison said. "It just wasn't about running. It was more like a lecture on brotherhood and karma and greedy gringos."

"Did it mention this race he's planning?"

"Yeah, it talked about some race with the Tarahumara. But as far as I can see, he's the only one in it. Him, and about three Indians."

Coach Joe Vigil had never heard of Caballo, either. I'd hoped that maybe they'd met on that epic day in Leadville, or later on down in the Barrancas. But right after the Leadville race, Coach Vigil's life had taken a sudden and dramatic turn. It started with a phone call: a young woman was on the line, asking if Coach Vigil could help her qualify for the Olympics. She'd been pretty talented in college, but she'd gotten so sick of running that she'd given it up and was thinking of opening a bakery café instead. Unless Coach Vigil thought she should keep trying . . . ?

Vigil is a master motivator, so he knew just what to say: Forget it. Go make mochaccinos. Deena Kastor (then Drossin) sounded like a sweet kid, but she had no business even thinking about working with Vigil. She was a California beach girl who was used to running out her front door and along the Santa Monica trails under a warm Pacific sun. What Vigil had going was real Spartan warrior stuff—a survival-of-the-fittest program that combined a killer workload with the freezing, windswept Colorado mountains.

"I tried to discourage her because Alamosa is not a California town," Vigil would later say. "It's a little secluded, it's in the mountains, and it gets cold—sometimes thirty degrees below zero. Only the toughest people survive there in terms of running." When Deena showed up anyway, Vigil was kind enough to reward her persistence by testing her basic fitness and training potential. The results did nothing to change Vigil's mind: she was mediocre.

But the more Coach Vigil pushed her away, the more intrigued Deena became. Posted on the wall of Vigil's office was a magic formula for fast running that, as far as Deena could tell, had absolutely nothing to do with running: it was stuff like "Practice abundance by giving back," and "Improve personal relationships," and "Show integrity to your value system." Vigil's dietary advice was just as bare of sports or science. His nutrition strategy for an Olympic marathon hopeful was this: "Eat as though you were a poor person."

Vigil was building his own mini Tarahumara world. Until he could wrap up his commitments and decamp to the Copper Canyons, he would do his best to re-create the Copper Canyons in Colorado. If Deena even wanted to think about training under Vigil, she had better be ready to train like the Tarahumara. That meant living lean and building her soul as much as her strength.

Deena got it, and couldn't wait to start. Coach Vigil believed you had to become a strong person before you could become a strong runner. So how could she lose? Grudgingly, Coach Vigil decided to give her a chance. In 1996, he began putting her through his Tarahumara-tinged training system. Within a year, the aspiring baker was on her way to becoming one of the greatest distance runners in American history.

She crushed the field to win the national cross-country championships, and went on to break the U.S. record in distances from three miles to the marathon. At the 2004 Athens Games, Deena outlasted the world-record holder, Paula Radcliffe, to win the bronze, the first Olympic medal for an American marathoner in twenty years. Ask Joe Vigil about Deena's accomplishments, though, and near the top of the list will always be the Humanitarian Athlete of the Year award she won in 2002.

Bit by bit, Coach Vigil was being drawn deeper into American distance running and further from his Copper Canyon plans. Before the 2004 Games, he was asked to establish a training camp for Olympic hopefuls high in the California mountains at Mammoth

Lakes. It was a ton of work for a seventy-five-year-old man, and Vigil paid for it: a year before the Olympics, he suffered a heart attack and needed a triple bypass. His last chance to learn from the Tarahumara, Vigil realized, was gone for good.

That left only one researcher in the world who was still pursuing the secret art of Tarahumara running: Caballo Blanco, whose findings were archived only in his muscle memory.

When my article came out in *Runner's World*, it sparked a good bit of interest in the Tarahumara, but something less than a stampede of elite trail-runners eager to sign up for Caballo's race. Something less than one, to be exact.

That may have been partly my fault; I found it impossible to describe him truthfully without using the word "cadaverous," or mentioning that the Tarahumara called him "kind of strange." No matter how psyched you might have been about the race, consequently, you'd have to think twice about putting your life in the hands of a mysterious loner with a fake name whose closest friends lived in caves and ate mice and still considered him the iffy one.

It was no help, either, that it was so hard to find out where and when the race might actually take place. Caballo had gotten his Web site up, but swapping messages with him was like waiting for a note in a bottle to drift up on the beach. To check e-mail, Caballo had to run more than thirty miles over a mountain and wade through a river to the tiny town of Urique, where he'd cajoled a schoolteacher into letting him use the school's creaking PC and its single dial-up line. He could make the sixty-some-mile round trip only in good weather; otherwise he risked slipping to his death off a rain-slicked cliff or getting stranded between raging creeks. Phone service had just reached Urique in 2002, so maintenance was spotty at best; a trail-weary Caballo could arrive in Urique only to find the line had been down for days. Once, he missed checking messages because he'd been attacked by wild dogs and had to abort his trip to go in search of rabies shots.

Just seeing "Caballo Blanco" pop up in my in-box was always a huge relief. As nonchalant as he acted about the risks, Caballo was leading an extremely dangerous life. Every time he set out for a run, it could be his last; he liked to believe the drug assassins wrote him off as a harmless "gringo Indio," but who knew how the drug assassins felt? Plus, there were his strange fainting spells: every once in a while, Caballo would suddenly pass out cold. Random blackouts are risky enough when you live in a place with 911, but out there in the lonely vastness of the Barrancas, an unconscious Caballo would never be spotted—or missed, for that matter. He once had a close call when he fainted shortly after running to a village. When he came to, he found a thick bandage on the back of his head and blood caked in his hair. If he'd gone down just half an hour earlier, he'd have been sprawled somewhere in the wilderness with a cracked skull.

Even if he survived the snipers and his own treacherous blood pressure, death was still lurking at his feet; all it would take was one misjudged *chingoncito* on one of those dental-floss Tarahumara trails, and the only thing left of Caballo would be the echo of his screams as he disappeared into the gorge.

Nothing stopped him. Running seemed to be the only sensual pleasure in his life, and as such, he savored it less like a workout and more like a gourmet meal. Even when his hut was nearly demolished by a landslide, Caballo snuck in a run before getting the roof back over his head.

But come spring, disaster struck. I got this email:

> *hey amigo, am in Urique after an eventful run and hobble down. I fucked my left ankle for the first time in many years! I'm not used to running with thick soles anymore. thats what I get for bragging, and wearing shoes while trying to save my light sandals for running faster and racing! Was 10 miles from Urique en La Sierra and knew that snap was not good, had to painfully crawl down into Urique because I had no choice but to get here, and my left foot looks like elephantitis!*

Crap. I had a sick suspicion his accident was my fault. Just before we'd said good-bye in Creel, I noticed we had the same size feet, so I fished a pair of new Nike trail shoes out of my backpack and gave them to Caballo as a thank-you gift. He'd knotted the laces and slung them over his shoulder, figuring they might come in handy in a pinch if his sandals fell apart. He was too polite to point the finger in his accident report, but I was pretty sure he was referring to my shoes when he mentioned he'd been wobbling around on thick soles when he crunched his ankle.

By this point, I was cringing with guilt. I was screwing Caballo in every direction. First, I'd accidentally set a time bomb by giving him those sneaks, and then I'd written an article that made his eccentricities a little too public for PR purposes. Caballo was killing himself to make this thing happen, and now, after months of effort, the only one who might show up was me: the lousy, half-lame runner bringing him the most grief.

Caballo had been able to blind himself to the truth in the pleasure of his rambling runs, but as he lay hurt and helpless in Urique, reality came crashing down. You can't live the way he did without looking like a freak, and now he was paying the price: no one would take him seriously. He wasn't even sure if he could persuade the Tarahumara to trust him, and they were just about the only people in the world who knew him anymore. So what was the point? Why was he chasing a dream everyone else thought was a joke?

If he hadn't busted his ankle, he'd have waited a long time for his answer. But as it was, he was still recovering in Urique when he received a message from God. The only god he'd been praying to, at least.

CHAPTER 19

I always start these events with very lofty goals,
like I'm going to do something special. And after a point
of body deterioration, the goals get evaluated down to
basically where I am now—where the best I can hope for is
to avoid throwing up on my shoes.

—Nuclear engineer and ultrarunner EPHRAIM ROMESBERG,
sixty-five miles into the Badwater Ultramarathon

A FEW DAYS EARLIER, in the tiny Seattle apartment he shared with his wife and a mountain of trophies, America's greatest ultrarunner was also confronting the limits of his own body.

That body still looked great; it was plenty fine enough to turn women's heads whenever Scott Jurek and his willowy blonde wife, Leah, were pedaling around their Capitol Hill neighborhood, hitting the bookstores and coffee shops and their favorite vegan Thai restaurants, a beautiful young hipster couple on the mountain bikes they owned instead of a car. Scott was tall and supplely muscled, with soulful brown eyes and a boy-band smile. He hadn't cut his hair since Leah gave him a buzz cut before his first Western States victory, leaving him six years later with a headful of Greek god curls that rippled when he ran.

How the gangly geek known as "Jerker" became an ultra star still baffles those who knew him growing up back in Proctor, Minnesota. "We harassed the crap out of him," said Dusty Olson, Proctor's star jock when he and Scott were teenagers. During cross-country runs,

Dusty and his buddies would pelt Scott with mud and take off. "He could never catch up," Dusty said. "No one could understand why he was so slow, because Jerker trained harder than anyone."

Not that Scott had much time for training. When he was in grade school, his mother contracted multiple sclerosis. It was up to Scott, as the oldest of three kids, to nurse his mother after school, clean the house, and haul logs for the woodstove while his father was at work. Years later, ultrarunning vets would sniff at Scott's starting-line screams and flying kung-fu leaps into aid stations. But when you've spent your childhood working like a deckhand and watching your mother sink into a nightmare of pain, maybe you never get over the joy of leaving everything behind and running for the hills.

After his mother had to be moved to a nursing home, Scott found himself alone with empty afternoons and a troubled heart. Luckily, just when Scott needed a friend, Dusty needed a sidekick. They were an odd couple, but oddly well-suited; Dusty was hungry for adventure, Scott for escape. Dusty's taste for competition was insatiable; soon after he won both the junior nationals for Nordic skiing *and* the regional cross-country championship, he convinced Scott to join him in the Minnesota Voyageur Trail Ultra 50-Mile Footrace. "Yeah, I conned him into it," Dusty said. Scott had never run half that distance but revered Dusty too much to say no.

In the middle of the race, Dusty's shoe came off in the mud. Before he could get it back on, Scott was gone. He tore through the woods to finish his first ultra in second place, beating Dusty by more than five minutes. "What the heck is going *on*?" Dusty wondered. That night, his phone rang relentlessly. "All the guys were making fun of me, going, 'You loser! You got dropped by the Jerker!' "

Scott was just as surprised. *So all that misery was leading somewhere after all*, he realized. All the hopelessness of nursing a mother who would never get better, all the frustration of chasing taunting jerks he could never catch—it had quietly bloomed into an ability to push harder and harder as things looked worse and worse. Coach Vigil would have been touched; Scott asked for nothing from his endurance, and got more than he could have hoped for.

Strictly by accident, Scott stumbled upon the most advanced weapon in the ultrarunner's arsenal: instead of cringing from fatigue, you embrace it. You refuse to let it go. You get to know it so well, you're not afraid of it anymore. Lisa Smith-Batchen, the amazingly sunny and pixie-tailed ultrarunner from Idaho who trained through blizzards to win a six-day race in the Sahara, talks about exhaustion as if it's a playful pet. "I love the Beast," she says. "I actually look forward to the Beast showing up, because every time he does, I handle him better. I get him more under control." Once the Beast arrives, Lisa knows what she has to deal with and can get down to work. And isn't that the reason she's running through the desert in the first place—to put her training to work? To have a friendly little tussle with the Beast and show it who's boss? You can't hate the Beast and expect to beat it; the only way to truly conquer something, as every great philosopher and geneticist will tell you, is to love it.

Scott would never again linger in Dusty's shadow, or any other runner's. "Anybody who has seen him running fast on mountainous terrain in the last miles of a hundred-miler will be a changed person," an awestruck trail runner declared on Letsrun.com, the number one message board for all things running, after watching Scott shatter the record at Western States. Scott was a hero for a very different reason among back-of-the-packers too slow to see him in action. After winning a hundred-mile race, Scott would be desperate for a hot shower and cool sheets. But instead of leaving, he'd wrap himself in a sleeping bag and stand vigil by the finish line. When day broke the next morning, Scott would still be there, cheering hoarsely, letting that last, persistent runner know he wasn't alone.

By the time Scott turned thirty-one, he was virtually unbeatable. Every June another pack of gunslingers arrived at Western States aiming to take his title, and every year they found him wrapped in his sleeping bag by the time they had finished. "But so what?" Scott wondered. Now that he'd created this Ferrari of a body, what was he supposed to do? Keep racing the stopwatch and the gunslingers until they finally began to beat him? Running wasn't about winning. He'd known that ever since his lonely days as the Jerker, back when he was panting far behind Dusty with mud on his face. The true beauty of running was . . . was . . .

Well, Scott wasn't sure anymore. But by the time he'd sealed his seventh Western States victory in 2005, he knew where to start looking.

Two weeks after Western States, Scott came down from the mountains and made the long drive across the Mojave Desert to the starting line of the infamous Badwater Ultramarathon. When Ann Trason raced two ultras in one month, she at least stuck to planet Earth; Scott would be running his second on the surface of the sun.

Death Valley is the perfect flesh-grilling device, the Foreman Grill in Mother Nature's cupboard. It's a big, shimmering sea of salt ringed by mountains that bottle up the heat and force it right back down on your skull. The average air temperature hovers around 125 degrees, but once the sun rises and begins broiling the desert floor, the ground beneath Scott's feet would hit a nice, toasty 200 degrees—exactly the temperature you need to slow roast a prime rib. Plus, the air is so dry that by the time you feel thirsty, you could be as good as dead; sweat is sucked so quickly from your body, you can be dangerously dehydrated before it even registers in your throat. Try to conserve water, and you could be a dead man walking.

But every July, ninety runners from around the world spend up to sixty straight hours running down the sizzling black ribbon of Highway 190, making sure to stay on the white lines so the soles of their running shoes don't melt. At mile 17, they'll pass Furnace Creek, site of the hottest temperature ever recorded in the United States (134 degrees). From there, it only gets worse: they still have to climb three mountains and deal with hallucinations, rebellious stomachs, and at least one long night of running in the dark before they reach the finish. *If* they reach the finish: Lisa Smith-Batchen is the only American to ever win the six-day Marathon of the Sands across the Sahara, but even she had to be pulled from Badwater in 1999 and given an emergency IV to stop her dessicated kidneys from shutting down.

"This is the landscape of catastrophe," one Death Valley chronicler wrote. It's a bizarre and sort of Transylvanian experience to be running a race right through the heart of a killing field where lost hikers claw at their blackened tongues before dying of thirst, as Dr. Ben Jones can tell you firsthand. Dr. Jones was running Badwater in 1991 when he was hastily recruited to examine the body of a trekker discovered in the sands.

"I am the only one of which I am aware who has ever performed an autopsy during a race," he remarked. Not that he was any stranger to the morbid; "Badwater Ben" was also known for having his crew haul a coffin full of ice water out on the highway to help him cool off. When slower runners caught up, they were jolted to find the most experienced athlete in the field lying by the side of the road in a casket, eyes closed and arms folded over his chest.

What was Scott thinking? He was raised on cross-country skis in Minnesota. What did he know about melting shoes and ice coffins? Even the Badwater race director, Chris Kostman, knew Scott was out of his element: "This race was thirty-five miles further than his longest previous race," Kostman would comment, "and twice as far as he'd ever run on pavement, not to mention significantly hotter than he'd ever experienced."

Kostman didn't know the half of it. Scott had been so focused that year on sharpening his trail skills for Western States, he hadn't run more than ten miles at a time on asphalt. As for heat acclimation . . . well, it didn't rain *every* day in Seattle, but it might as well have. Death Valley was in the midst of one of its hottest summers in history, with temperatures hovering at around 130 degrees. The coolest part of the coolest day was still way hotter than it got in Seattle all summer.

A runner's only hope of surviving Badwater was to have an experienced crew monitoring his vitals and supplying digestible calories and electrolyte drinks. One of Scott's top competitors that year had brought a nutritionist and four custom-equipped vans to leapfrog his progress down the course. Scott, on the other hand, had his wife, two Seattle buddies, and Dusty, assuming Dusty recovered from the hangover he still had when he rocked up just before the race began.

Scott's competition was going to be as fierce as the heat. He was up against Mike Sweeney, the two-time champion of the sweltering H.U.R.T. 100 in Hawaii, and Ferg Hawke, the supremely prepared Canadian who'd finished a close second at Badwater the year before. Two-time Badwater champ Pam Reed was back, and so was Mr. Badwater himself: Marshall Ulrich, the ultrarunner who'd had his toenails removed. Marshall had not only won Badwater four times, he'd also run the course four times *nonstop*. Once, just for the hell of it, Marshall ran all the way across Death Valley by himself, pushing his food and water in a little bike-wheeled cart. And if Marshall was anything besides tough, it was canny; one of his favorite strategies was to have his crew gradually cover his van's taillights after dark with electrical tape. Runners trying to catch him at night would give up, believing Marshall was disappearing off into the distance when he was only a half mile away.

A few seconds before 10 a.m., someone punched a boom-box button. Hands covered hearts as the national anthem crackled. Just standing there in the full glare of the morning sun was unbearable for everyone but the true Badwater vets, whose savvy showed in their shorts: Pam and Ferg and Mike Sweeney, in silky shorts and muscle tees, looked totally unconcerned about the sun blazing overhead. Scott, on the other hand, could have been entering a biohazard site: he was covered chin to toe in a white sun suit, looking every bit the Minnesota yokel, with his long hair knotted inside a doofy French Foreign Legion cap.

GO! Scott leaped off the line like Braveheart. But for once, his bellow sounded weak and plaintive; it was swallowed in the awesome vastness of the Mojave like an echo from the bottom of a well. Mike Sweeney also had his own way of shutting Scott up: just in case Wonderboy had any plans to hang on Sweeney's shoulder and then get frisky in the final miles, Sweeney was going to open an unbeatable lead right from the start. He could do it, too; in a sport not known for aggression, Sweeney was one of the true tough guys. In his twenties, he had been an Acapulco cliff diver ("I'd pound on the top of my head to toughen it up"), and then became a bar pilot in San Francisco Bay, commanding a crew of seamen who guided massive freight ships. While Scott was enjoying cool, pine-scented breezes in the mountains all summer, Sweeney was fighting a ship's wheel through gale-force wind and jogging in a superheated sauna for up to two hours a day.

Mike Sweeney was leading the field when he came through Furnace Creek shortly before high noon. The thermometer had hit 126 degrees, but Sweeney was unfazed and kept increasing his lead. By mile 72, he had a solid ten miles over Ferg Hawke in second. Sweeney's crew was operating beautifully. As pacers, he had three elite ultrarunners, including a fellow H.U.R.T. 100 champion, Luis Escobar. As nutritionist, he had the perfectly named Sunny Blende, a beautiful endurance-sports specialist who not only monitored his calories, but hoisted her top and flashed her breasts whenever she felt Sweeney needed perking up.

Team Jerker wasn't quite as well oiled. One of Scott's pacers was fanning him with a sweatshirt, unaware that Scott was too exhausted to complain that the zipper was slashing his back. Scott's wife and his best friend, meanwhile, were at each other's throats. Dusty was annoyed by the way Leah kept trying to motivate Scott by giving him fake pacing splits, while Leah wasn't too pleased with Dusty's habit of calling her husband a fucking pussy.

By mile 60, Scott was vomiting and shaky. His hands dropped to his knees, then his knees dropped to the pavement. He collapsed by the side of the road, lying in his own sweat and spittle. Leah and his friends didn't bother trying to help him up; they knew there was no voice in the world more persuasive than the one inside Scott's own mind.

Scott lay there, thinking about how hopeless it all was. He wasn't even halfway done, and Sweeney was already too far ahead for him to see. Ferg Hawke was halfway up to the Father Crowley lookout, and Scott hadn't even started the climb yet. And the wind! It was like running into the blast of a jet engine. A couple of miles back, Scott had tried to cool off by sinking his entire head and torso into a giant cooler full of ice and holding himself underwater until his lungs were screaming. As soon as he got out, he was roasting again.

There's no way, Scott told himself. *You're done. You'd have to do something totally sick to win this thing now.*

Sick like what?

Like starting all over again. Like pretending you just woke up from a great night's sleep and the race hasn't even started yet. You'd have to run the next eighty miles as fast as you've ever run eighty miles in your life.

No chance, Jerker.

Yeah. I know.

For ten minutes, Scott lay like a corpse. Then he got up and did it, shattering the Badwater record with a time of 24:36.

King of the trails, king of the road. That 2005 doubleheader was one of the greatest performances in ultraracing history, and it couldn't have come at a better moment: just when Scott was becoming the greatest star in ultrarunning, ultrarunning was getting sexy. There was Dean Karnazes, shucking his shirt for magazine covers and telling David Letterman how he ordered pizzas on his cell phone in the middle of a 250-mile run. And check out Pam Reed; when Dean announced he was preparing for a 300-mile run, Pam went straight out and ran 301, landing her own Letterman appearance, and a book contract, and one of the greatest magazine headlines ever written: DESPERATE HOUSEWIFE STALKS MALE SUPERMODEL IN SPORTS DEATH MARCH.

Soooooo—where was the Scott Jurek memoir? The marketing campaign? The bare-chested treadmill run above Times Square, à la Karnazes? "If you're talking about hundred-mile races, or longer, on trails, there's no one in history who comes close to him. If you want to say he's the greatest all-time ultrarunner, a case could be made for it," came the judgment from *UltraRunning* editor Don Allison. "He's got the talent to put him up against anyone."

So where was he?

Long gone. Instead of promoting himself after his glorious summer, Scott and Leah immediately vanished into the deep woods to celebrate in solitude. Scott could give a crap about talk shows; he didn't even own a TV. He'd read Dean's book and Pam's book and all the magazine articles, and they turned his stomach. "Stunts," he muttered; they were taking this beautiful sport, this great gift of flight, and turning it into a freak show.

When he and Leah finally got back to their tiny apartment, Scott found another one of those crazy e-mails waiting for him. He'd been getting them on and off for about two years from some guy who kept signing off with different names: Caballo Loco . . . Caballo Confuso . . . Caballo Blanco. Something about a race, could he come, power to the people, blah blah blah. . . . Usually, Scott gave them a quick scan and clicked them into the trash, but this time, one word caught his eye: *Chingón.*

Whoa. Wasn't that a Spanish F-bomb? Scott didn't know much Spanish, but he recognized curse words when he saw them. Was this crazy Horse guy badmouthing him? Scott read the message again, more carefully this time:

> *I've been telling the Raramuri that my Apache friend Ramon Chingon says he's going to beat everybody. The tarahumara are more or less good runners compared to the Apaches, the Quimares a little more than less. But the question is, who's more chingon than Ramon?*

Deciphering Caballo-speak wasn't easy, but as best Scott could make out, it seemed that he—Scott—was supposed to be Ramón Chingón, the Mean Mutha who was going to come down and whomp Tarahumara butt. So this guy he'd never even met was trying to whip up a grudge match between the Tarahumara and their ancient Apache enemies, and he wanted Scott to play the role of masked villain? *Psycho-o-o-o-o . . .*

Scott fingered the delete button, then paused. On the other hand . . . wasn't that exactly what Scott had set out to do? Find the best runners and the toughest courses in the world and conquer them all? Someday no one, not even ultrarunners, would remember the names Pam Reed or Dean Karnazes. But if Scott was as good as he thought he was—if he was as good as he *dared* to be—then he'd run like no one ever had. Scott wasn't settling for best in the world; he was out to be the best of all time.

But like every champion, he was up against the Curse of Ali: he could beat everyone alive and still lose to guys who were dead (or at least, long retired). Every heavyweight boxer has to hear: "Yeah, you're good, but you'd never a' beat Ali in his prime." Likewise, no matter how many records Scott set, there would always be one unanswered question: what would have happened if he'd been in Leadville in 1994? Could he have whipped Juan Herrera and Team Tarahumara, or would they have run him down like a deer, just like they did the Bruja?

The heroes of the past are untouchable, protected forever by the fortress door of time—unless some mysterious stranger magically turns up with a key. Maybe Scott, thanks to this Caballo character, was the one athlete who could turn back the clock and test himself against the immortals.

Who's more chingón *than Ramón?*

CHAPTER 20

NINE MONTHS LATER, I found myself back on the Mexican border with a ticking clock and zero margin for error. It was Saturday evening, February 25, 2006, and I had twenty-four hours to find Caballo again.

As soon as he got a reply from Scott Jurek, Caballo began setting up a trapeze act of logistics. He only had a tiny window of opportunity, since the race couldn't take place during the fall harvest, the winter rainy season, or the blistering heat of summer, when many of the Tarahumara migrate toward cooler caves higher in the canyons. Caballo also had to avoid Christmas, Easter Week, the Fiesta Guadalupana and at least a half-dozen traditional wedding weekends.

Caballo finally figured he could wedge the race in on Sunday, March 5. Then the real tricky work began: because he'd barely have enough time to Paul Revere from village to village to announce the race logistics, he had to figure out exactly where and when the Tarahumara runners should meet up with us on the hike to the race-course. If he miscalculated, it was over; it was already a tremendous long shot that any Tarahumara would show up, and if they got to the meeting spot and we were a no-show, they'd be gone.

Caballo made his best-guess estimates, then set off into the canyons to spread the word, as he messaged me a few weeks later:

> *Ran 30 some miles out to Tarahumara country and back today, like*
> *the messenger that I am. The message fueled me more than the bag of*

pinole in my pocket. Was lucky enough to see both Manuel Luna and Felipe Quimare on the same loop, the same day. When I spoke to each of them, I could sense excitement even in the Geronimo like solemnness that is the face of Manuel.

But while things were looking up for Caballo, my end of the operation was maddeningly difficult. Once word hit the grapevine that Jurek might be going toe-to-toe with the Tarahumara, other ultra aces suddenly wanted a piece of the action. But there was no telling how many would really show up—and that included the star attraction himself.

In true Jurek fashion, Scott had told almost no one what he was up to, so word of his plans only began to spread a little more than a month before the race. He'd even kept me guessing, and I was pretty much his point man; Scott e-mailed me a few times with travel questions, but as crunch time approached, he dropped off the radar. Two weeks before race day, I was startled to see a posting on the *Runner's World* message board from a runner in Texas who'd gotten a jolt of his own that morning when he arrived at the starting line of the Austin Marathon and found himself standing next to America's greatest (and contender for most reclusive) ultrarunner.

Austin? Last I'd heard, Scott was supposed to be two thousand miles away at that very moment, crossing Baja with his wife to catch the Chihuahua-Pacific train to Creel. And what was the deal with the urban marathon—why was Scott flying across the country for a junior varsity road race, when he was supposed to be fine-tuning for the showdown of a lifetime on trails? He was up to something, no doubt about it; and as usual, whatever strategy he was developing remained locked in his own head.

So, until the moment I arrived in El Paso, Texas, that Saturday, I had no idea if I was leading a platoon or hucking solo. I checked into the airport Hilton, made arrangements for a ride across the border at five the next morning, then doubled back to the airport. I was pretty sure I was wasting my time, but there was a chance I'd be picking up Jenn "Mookie" Shelton and Billy "Bonehead" Barnett, a pair of twenty-one-year-old hotshots who'd been electrifying the East Coast ultra circuit, at least whenever they weren't otherwise occupied surfing, partying, or posting bail for simple assault (Jenn), disorderly conduct (Billy), or public indecency (both, for a burst of trail-side passion that resulted in an arrest and community service).

Jenn and Billy had only started running two years before, but Billy was already winning some of the toughest 50ks on the East Coast, while "the young and beautiful Jenn Shelton," as the ultrarace blogger Joey Anderson called her, had just clocked one of the fastest 100-mile times in the country. "If this young lady could swing a tennis racket as well as she runs," Anderson wrote, "she would be one of the richest women in sports with all the sponsors she would attract."

I'd spoken to Jenn once on the phone, and while she and Billy were wildly eager to join the trek into the Copper Canyons, I didn't see any way they'd pull it off. She and the Bonehead had no money, no credit cards, and no time off from school: they were both still in college and Caballo's race was smack in the middle of midterms, meaning they'd flunk the semester if they skipped out. But two days before my flight to El Paso, I suddenly got this frantic e-mail:

> *Wait for us! we can get in by 8:10 pm.*
> *El Paso is texas, right?*

After that—silence. On the slim chance that Jenn and Billy had actually found the right city and finagled their way onto a flight, I headed over to the airport for a look around. I'd never met them, but their outlaw reputation created a pretty vivid mental image. When I got to baggage claim, I immediately locked in on a couple who looked like teenage runaways hitchhiking to Lollapalooza.

"Jenn?" I asked.

"Right on!"

Jenn was wearing flip-flops, surf shorts, and a tie-dyed T-shirt. Her summer-wheat hair was in braids, giving her the look of a blonder, lesser-known Longstocking. She was pretty and petite enough to pass for a figure skater, an image she'd tried in the past to scruff up by shaving her head down to stubble and getting a big, black vampire bat tattooed on her right forearm, only discovering later that it was a dead ringer for the Bacardi rum logo. "Whatever," Jenn said with a shrug. "Truth in advertising."

Billy shared Jenn's raw good looks and beach-bum wardrobe. He had a tribal tattoo across the back of his neck and thick sideburns that blended into shaggy, sun-streaked hair. With his flowery board shorts and ripped surfer's build, he looked—to Jenn, at least—"like some little yeti who raided your underwear drawer."

"I can't believe you guys made it," I said. "But there's been a change of plans. Scott Jurek isn't going to be meeting us in Mexico."

"Oh, fuck me," Jenn said. "I knew this was too good to be true."

"He came here instead." On my way to the airport, I'd spotted two guys jogging across the parking lot. They were too far away for me to see their faces, but their smooth-glide strides gave them away. After quick introductions, they'd headed to the bar while I continued to the airport.

"Scott's here?"

"Yup. I just saw him on the way over. He's back at the hotel bar with Luis Escobar."

"Scott *drinks?*"

"Looks that way."

"Suh-*weet!!*"

Jenn and Billy grabbed their gear—a Nike shopping bag with a chiropractic stick jutting out the top and a duffel with the tail of a sleeping bag stuck in the zipper—and we began heading across the parking lot.

"So what's Scott like?" Jenn asked. Ultrarunning, like rap music, was split by geography; as East Coast playas, Jenn and Billy had done most of their racing close to home and hadn't yet crossed paths (or swords) with many of the West Coast elites. To them—to just about all ultrarunners, actually—Scott was as much of a mythic figure as the Tarahumara.

"I only caught a glimpse of him myself," I said. "Pretty tough guy to read, I can tell you that much."

Right there, I should have shut my stupid mouth. But who can predict when the trivial will become tragic? How could I have known that a friendly gesture, like giving Caballo my running shoes, would nearly cost him his life? Likewise, I never suspected that the next ten words out of my mouth would snowball into disaster:

"Maybe," I suggested, "you can get him drunk and loosen him up."

CHAPTER 21

"PREPARE TO MEET your god," I said as we entered the hotel bar. "Sucking down a cold one."

Scott was on a stool, sipping a Fat Tire Ale. Billy dropped his duffel and stuck out his hand, while Jenn hung behind me. She'd barely let Billy get a word in the whole way across the parking lot, but now, in Scott's presence, she was starstruck. At least I thought she was, till I saw the look in her eye. She wasn't bashful; she was sizing him up. Scott might be hunting the Tarahumara, but he'd better watch who was hunting him.

"Is this all of us?" Scott asked.

I looked around the bar and did a head count. Jenn and Billy were ordering beers. Beside them was Eric Orton, an adventure-sports coach from Wyoming and longtime student of the Tarahumara who'd made me his personal disaster reconstruction project; over the past nine months, we'd been in weekly contact, sometimes daily, as Eric attempted to transform me from a splintery wreck into an unbreakable ultramarathon man. He was the one guy I'd been sure would turn up; even though he'd be leaving his wife behind with their newborn daughter in the middle of a fierce Wyoming winter, there was no way he'd be sitting at home while I was putting his art to the test. I'd flat-out told him he was wrong and there was no way I could run fifty miles; now, we'd both see if he was right.

Sandwiching Scott were Luis Escobar and his father, Joe Ramírez.

Luis was not only an ultrastud who'd won the H.U.R.T. 100 and raced Badwater, but also one of the top race photographers in the sport (his artistry aided, of course, by the fact that his legs could take him places no other shooters could reach). Just by chance, Luis had recently called Scott to make sure they'd be seeing each other at Coyote Fourplay, a semi-secret, invitation-only free-for-all described as "a four-day orgy of idiocy involving severed coyote heads, poisoned snacks, panties in trees, and one hundred twenty miles of trails you'll wish you'd missed."

Fourplay is held at the end of February every year in the back-woods of Oxnard, California, and it exists to give a small band of ultrarunners a chance to whip each other's butts and then glue said butts to toilet seats. Every day, the Fourplayers race anywhere from thirty to fifty miles on trails marked by mummified coyote skulls and women's underwear. Every night, they face off with bowling tourna-ments and talent shows and endless guerrilla pranks, like replacing ProBars with frozen cat food and gluing the wrappers back shut. Fourplay was a battle royal for amateurs who loved to run hard and play rough; it wasn't really for pros who had to worry about their rac-ing schedules and sponsorship commitments. Naturally, Scott never missed it.

Until 2006, that is. "Sorry, something came up," Scott told Luis. When Luis heard what it was, his heart skipped a beat. No one had ever gotten photos of Tarahumara runners in full flight on their home turf, and for good reason: the Tarahumara run for fun, and having white devils around wasn't any fun. Their races were sponta-neous and secretive and absolutely hidden from outside eyes. But if Caballo pulled this thing off, then a few lucky devils would get the chance to cross over to the Tarahumara side. For the first time, they'd all be Running People together.

Luis's dad, Joe, has the chiseled-oak face, gray ponytail, and turquoise rings of a Native American sage, but he's actually a former migrant worker who, in his hard-scrapping sixty-plus years, made himself into a California highway patrolman, then a chef, and finally an artist with a flair for the colors and culture of his native Mexico. When Joe heard his kid was heading into the homeland to see their ancestral heroes in action, he set his jaw and insisted he was going, too. The hike alone could, quite literally, kill him, but Joe wasn't worried. Even more than the ultrastuds around him, this son of the picking fields was a survivor.

"How about that barefoot guy?" I asked. "Is he still coming?"

A few months before, someone who called himself "Barefoot Ted" began blitzing Caballo with a torrent of messages. He seemed to be the Bruce Wayne of barefoot running, the wealthy heir of a California amusement-park fortune who devoted himself to battling the worst crime ever committed against the human foot: the invention of the running shoe. Barefoot Ted believed we could abolish foot injuries by throwing away our Nikes, and he was willing to prove it on himself: he ran the Los Angeles and Santa Clarita marathons in his bare feet and finished fast enough to qualify for the elite Boston Marathon. He was rumored to train by running barefoot in the San Gabriel Mountains, and by pulling his wife and daughter through the streets of Burbank in a rickshaw. Now, he was coming to Mexico to commune with the Tarahumara and explore whether the key to their amazing resilience was their nearly bare feet.

"He left a message that he'd be getting here later," Luis said.

"I guess that's everyone, then. Caballo is going to be psyched."

"So what's the story with this guy?" Scott asked.

I shrugged. "I don't really know much. I only met him once."

Scott's eyes narrowed. Billy and Jenn turned from the bar and cocked their heads, suddenly more interested in me than the beers they were ordering. The atmosphere of the whole group instantly changed. Seconds ago, everyone was drinking and chatting, but now, it was quiet and a little tense.

"What?" I asked.

"I thought you were really good buddies," Scott said.

"Buddies? Not even close," I said. "He's a total mystery. I don't even know where he lives. I don't even know his real name."

"So how do you know he's legit?" Joe Ramírez asked. "Shit, he may not even know any Tarahumara."

"They know him," I said. "All I can tell you is what I wrote. He's kind of strange, he's a hell of a runner, and he's been down there for a long time. That's all I found out about him."

Everyone sat for a sec and drank that in, myself included. So why were we trusting Caballo? I'd gotten so carried away with training for the race, I'd forgotten that the real challenge was surviving the trip. I had no clue who Caballo really was, or where he was leading us. He could be totally demented or merrily inept, and the result would be the same: out there in the Barrancas, we'd be cooked.

"So!" Jenn blurted. "What are you guys up for tonight? I promised Billy some big-ass margaritas."

If the rest of the crew had hit a crossroad of doubt, they'd put it behind them. Scott and Luis and Eric and Joe all agreed to pile into the hotel courtesy van with Jenn and Billy and head downtown for drinks. Not me, though. We had a lot of hard miles ahead, and I wanted all the rest I could get. Unlike the rest of them, I'd been down there before. I knew what we were heading into.

Sometime in the middle of the night, I was jerked awake by shouting nearby. Very nearby—like, in my room. Then, a *BANG* shook the bathroom.

"Billy, get up!" someone yelled.

"Leemee here. I'm fine."

"You've got to get up!"

I snapped on a light, and saw Eric Orton, the adventure-sports coach, standing in the doorway. "The kids," he said, shaking his head. "I don't know, man."

"Is everyone all right?"

"I don't know, man."

I sat up, still groggy, and went to the door of the bathroom. Billy was sprawled in the tub with his eyes closed. Pink vomit was splattered all over his shirt . . . and the toilet . . . and the floor. Jenn had lost her clothes and found a shiner; she was wearing only shorts and a purple bra, and her left eye was swelling shut. She had Billy by the arm and was trying to haul him to his feet.

"Can you help me lift him?" Jenn asked.

"What happened to your eye?"

"Whaddaya mean?"

"JUST LEAVE ME HERE!" Billy was shouting. He cackled like an archvillain, then passed out cold.

Jesus. I squatted over him in the tub and looked for nonsticky places to get a grip. I got him under the arms, but couldn't find any soft flesh to grab hold of; Billy was so muscular, trying to hoist him was like lifting a side of lean beef. I finally managed to drag him out of the tub and into the sitting room. Eric and I had planned to share a room, but when Jenn and Billy showed up with no reservation or, it seemed, any money for a room, we said they could crash with us.

And crash they did. As soon as Eric yanked out the fold-out sofa, Jenn dropped like a sack of laundry. I stretched Billy out beside her with his head hanging over the edge. I got a wastebasket under his face just before another pink river gushed out. He was still retching when I hit the lights.

Back in the adjoining bedroom, Eric filled me in. They'd gone to a Tex-Mex place, and while everyone else was eating, Jenn and Billy had had a drinking contest with fishbowl-sized margaritas. At some point, Billy wandered off in search of a bathroom and never returned. Jenn, meanwhile, entertained herself by snatching Scott's cell phone while he was saying good night to his wife and shouting, "Help! I'm surrounded by penises!"

Luckily, that's when Barefoot Ted turned up. When he got to the hotel and heard that his traveling companions were out drinking, he commandeered the courtesy van and convinced the driver to shuttle him around till he found them. At the first stop, the driver spotted Billy asleep in the parking lot. The driver hauled Billy into the van while Barefoot Ted gathered the others. Whatever Billy was lacking in pep, Jenn made up for; during the ride back to the hotel, she did backflips over the seats until the driver slammed on the brakes and threatened to throw her out if she didn't sit the hell down.

The driver's jurisdiction, however, only extended as far as the van door. When he pulled up in front of the hotel, Jenn burst loose. She ran into the hotel, skidded across the lobby, and crashed into a giant fountain full of water plants, smashing her face against the marble and blackening her eye. She emerged soaking wet, waving fists full of foliage overhead like a Kentucky Derby winner.

"Miss! Miss!" the appalled desk clerk pleaded, before remembering that pleading doesn't work on drunks in fountains. "Get her under control," she warned the others, "or you're all out of here."

Gotcha. Luis and Barefoot Ted smothered Jenn in a tackle, then wrestled her into an elevator. Jenn kept wriggling, trying to break free while Scott and Eric were dragging Billy aboard. "Let me *gooooo!*" the hotel staff could hear Jenn wailing as the doors slid shut. "I'll be good! I promiiiiiiiissse. . . ."

"Damn," I said. I checked my watch. "We're going to have to haul their drunk asses out of here in five hours."

"I'll carry Billy," Eric said. "Jenn is all yours."

Sometime after 3 a.m., my phone rang.

"Mr. McDougall?"

"Hmm?"

"This is Terry at the front desk. Your little friend could use some help getting upstairs. Again."

"Huh? No, that's not her this time," I said, reaching for the light. "She's right—" I looked around. No Jenn. "Okay. Be right down."

When I got to the lobby, I found Jenn in her bra and shorts. She gave me a delighted smile, as if to say, "What a coincidence!" Beside her was a big ol' boy with cowboy boots and a rodeo belt buckle. He glanced at Jenn's black eye, then at me, then back to her black eye as he tried to decide whether to kick my ass.

Apparently, she'd woken up to use the toilet, but wandered right past the bathroom and ended up out in the hall. After relieving herself next to the soda machines, she heard music and started to explore. A wedding party was going on down the hall.

"HEY!!!" everyone shouted when Jenn poked her head in.

"HEY YA!" Jenn shouted back, and boogied in to get herself a drink. She butt-grinded with the groom, downed a beer, and fended off the guys who assumed that the wobbling, half-dressed hottie who magically appeared at 3 a.m. was their personal party favor. Jenn eventually meandered on, finally winding up in the lobby.

"Sweetie, you'd better not drink like that where you're going," the desk clerk called as Jenn wobbled toward the elevator. "They'll rape you and leave you for dead." The clerk knew what she was talking about; our first stop on the way to the canyons was Juárez, a border town so lawless that hundreds of young women Jenn's age had been murdered and dumped in the desert over the previous few years; five hundred other people were killed in one year alone. Any doubts about who ran the show in Juárez were cleared up when dozens of police commanders quit or were killed after drug lords nailed a list of their names on telephone poles.

"'Kay," Jenn said, waving good-bye. "Sorry about the plants."

I helped her back into the sofa bed, then double-locked the door to prevent any further escapes. I checked the time. Damn, 3:30. We had to be out the door in ninety minutes, or there was no chance of meeting Caballo. At that moment, he was making his way out of the canyons and up to the town of Creel. From there, he'd guide us down into the Barrancas. Two days later, we all had to be at a certain spot on a trail in the Batopilas mountain range, where the Tarahumara would be watching for us. The big problem was the bus schedule to Creel; if we got a late start tomorrow, there was no telling when we'd arrive. I knew Caballo wouldn't wait; for him, a choice between missing us or standing up the Tarahumara wasn't a choice at all.

"Look, you guys are going to have to go ahead," I told Eric when I got back into the bedroom. "Luis's dad speaks Spanish, so he can get you to Creel. I'll follow with those two as soon as they can walk."

"How are we going to find Caballo?"

"You'll recognize him. He's one of a kind."

Eric thought about it. "You sure you don't want me to drill sergeant those two with a bucket of ice water?"

"Tempting," I said. "But at this point, I like them better asleep."

About an hour later, we heard noises in the bathroom. "Hopeless," I muttered, getting up to see who was puking. Instead, I found Billy sudsing up in the shower and Jenn brushing her teeth.

"Good morning," Jenn said. "What happened to my eye?"

Half an hour later, the six of us were back in the hotel van and hissing through the damp morning streets of El Paso, heading toward the Mexican border. We'd have to cross over to Juárez, then hopscotch from bus to bus across the Chihuahua desert to the edge of the Barrancas. Even with luck on our side, we were facing at least fifteen straight hours on creaking Mexican buses before we got to Creel.

"The man who gets me a Mountain Dew can have my body," Jenn croaked, her eyes closed and face pressed against the cool of the van window. "And Billy's."

"If they race the way they party, the Tarahumara don't have a chance," Eric muttered. "Where'd you find these two?"

CHAPTER 22

JENN AND BILLY met in the summer of 2002, after Billy had
finished his freshman year at Virginia Commonwealth University
and returned home to lifeguard on Virginia Beach. One morning, he
arrived at his stand to discover that the Luck of the Bonehead had
struck again. His new partner was a Corona commercial come to life,
a beauty who earned top marks in all the Bonehead scoring categories: she was a surfer, a secret bookworm, and a hard-core partyer
whose ancient Mitsubishi had a life-size silhouette of gonzo writer
Hunter S. Thompson aiming a .44 Magnum stenciled on the hood.

But almost instantly, Jenn began to bug him. She fixated on Billy's
University of North Carolina baseball cap and wouldn't let up.
"Dude!" Jenn said. "I need that lid!" She'd gone to UNC for a year
before dropping out and moving to San Francisco to write poetry, so
if there was any karmic justice on this beach, then *she* should be
sporting the Tar Heels gear, not some pretty-boy surfer like him who
only wore it to keep the pretty-boy bangs out of his eyes. . . .

"Fine!" Billy erupted. "It's yours."

"Sweet!"

"*If*," Billy continued, "you run down the beach, bare-ass."

Jenn scoffed. "Dude, you are so on. Right after work."

Billy shook his head. "Nope. Right now."

Moments later, hoots and cheers rocked the boardwalk as Jenn burst out of a porta-potty, her lifeguard suit crumpled on the ground behind her. *Yeah, baby!* She made it to the next stand a block away, turned around, and came charging back toward the throngs of moms and kids she was supposed to be protecting from, among other things, full-frontal nudity by college dropouts goin' wild. Amazingly, Jenn didn't get canned (that came later, for shorting out the engine of her lifeguard captain's truck by sticking a live crab under the hood).

During quieter moments, Jenn and Billy talked big waves and books. Jenn revered the Beat poets so much, she was planning to study creative writing at the Jack Kerouac School of Disembodied Poetics if she ever dropped back into college and got a degree first. Then she picked up Lance Armstrong's *It's Not About the Bike* and fell in love with a new kind of warrior poet.

Lance wasn't just some brute on a bike, she realized; he was a philosopher, a latter-day Beat, a Dharma Bum sailing the asphalt seas in search of inspiration and Pure Experience. She'd known Armstrong had bounced back from cancer, but she had no idea just how close to the grave he'd actually been. By the time Armstrong had gone under the knife, tumors were spreading throughout his brain, lungs, and testicles. After chemotherapy, he was too weak to walk but had to make an urgent decision: should he cash in an insurance policy worth $1.5 million, or turn it down and try rebuilding himself into an endurance athlete? Take the payout, and he'd be set for life. Turn it down and relapse, and he's dead meat; he'd have no money, no health insurance, no chance of seeing age thirty.

"Fuck surfing," Billy blurted. Living on the edge wasn't about danger, he realized. It was about curiosity; audacious curiosity, like the kind Lance had when he was chalked off for good and still decided to see if he could build a wasted body into a world-beater. The way Kerouac did, when he set off on the road and then wrote about it in a mad, carefree burst he never thought would see the light of print. Looking at it that way, Jenn and Billy could trace a direct line of descent from a Beatnik writer to a champion cyclist to a pair of Pabst Blue Ribbon–chugging Virginia Beach lifeguards. They were expected to accomplish nothing, so they could try anything. Audacity beckoned.

"You ever heard of the Mountain Masochist?" Billy asked Jenn.
"Nope. Who's he?"

"It's a race, you crackhead. Fifty miles in the mountains."

Neither of them had even run a marathon before. They'd been beach kids all their lives, so they'd barely seen mountains, let alone run them. They wouldn't even be able to train properly; the tallest thing around Virginia Beach was a sand dune. Fifty mountain miles was *waaaay* over their heads.

"Dude, that's totally it," Jenn said. "I'm in."

They needed some serious help, so Jenn looked where she always did when she needed guidance. And as usual, her favorite chain-smoking alcoholics came through in the clutch. First, she and Billy dug into *The Dharma Bums* and began memorizing Jack Kerouac's description of hiking the Cascadia mountains.

"Try the meditation of the trail, just walk along looking at the trail at your feet and don't look about and just fall into a trance as the ground zips by," Kerouac wrote. "Trails are like that: you're floating along in a Shakespearean Arden paradise and expect to see nymphs and fluteboys, then suddenly you're struggling in a hot broiling sun of hell in dust and nettles and poison oak . . . just like life."

"Our whole approach to trail-running came from *Dharma Bums*," Billy told me later. As for inspiration, that's where Charles Bukowski stepped up: "If you're going to try, go all the way," the original Barfly wrote. "There is no other feeling like that. / you will be alone with the gods / and the nights will flame with fire. . . . you will ride life straight to / perfect laughter, it's / the only good fight there is."

Soon after, surf fishermen noticed weird goings-on each evening as the sun set on the Atlantic. Chants would echo across the dunes— "*Visionnnnns! O-O-O-O-O-mens! HallucinAAAAAtions!*"—followed by the appearance of some kind of loping, howling, four-legged man-beast. As it got closer, they could see it was actually two people, running shoulder-to-shoulder. One was a slim young woman with a "Gay Pride" bandanna on her head and a vampire bat tattooed on her arm, while the other, as best they could make out, seemed to be a welterweight werewolf under a rising moon.

Before setting out for their sunset runs, Jenn and Billy would snap a tape of Allen Ginsberg reading "Howl" into their Walkman. When running stopped being as fun as surfing, they had agreed, they'd quit. So to get that same surging glide, that same feeling of being lifted up and swept along, they ran to the rhythm of Beat poetry.

"Miracles! Ecstasies! Gone down the American river!" they'd shout, padding along the water's edge.

"New loves! Mad generation! Down on the rocks of Time!"

At the Old Dominion 100 a few months later, aid-station volunteers at the halfway mark heard screams echoing through the woods. Moments later, a girl in pigtails burst from the trees. She flipped up in a handstand, jumped back to her feet, and began shadowboxing.

"This all you got, Old Dominion?" she shouted, throwing punches in the air. As the sole member of Jenn's support crew, Billy was waiting with her favorite midrace meal: Mountain Dew and a cheese pizza. Jenn stopped bobbing and weaving and tore into a slice.

The aid-station volunteers stared in disbelief. "Hon," one of them warned her. "You'd better take it easy. Hundreds aren't halfway done till you hit the last twenty miles."

"Okay," Jenn said. Then she wiped her greasy mouth on her sports bra, burped up some Dew, and bounded off.

"You've got to get her to slow down," one of the aid-station volunteers told Billy. "She's going three hours faster than the course record." Tackling one hundred miles in the mountains wasn't like running some city marathon; get in trouble out there in the dark, and you'll be lucky to get back out again.

Billy shrugged. After a year of romance with Jenn, he'd learned she was capable of absolutely anything except moderation. Even when she wanted to rein herself in, whatever was building inside her—passion, inspiration, aggravation, hilarity—inevitably came fire-hosing out. After all, this was a woman who joined the UNC rugby team and set a standard considered previously unachievable throughout the sport's one-hundred-seventy-year history: Too Wild for Rugby Parties. "She'd get so nuts, guys on the men's team would wrestle her down and carry her back to her room," Jessie Polini, her best friend at UNC, said. Jenn always went full speed ahead, only dealing with stone walls after she hit them.

This time, the stone wall arrived with a vengeance at the seventy-five-mile mark. It was now six in the evening. An entire arc of the sun had passed since Jenn had started running at five that morning, and she still had a marathon to go. There was no shadowboxing this time as Jenn wobbled into the aid station. She stood in front of the food table, stupid with fatigue, too tired to eat and too fuzzy-headed to decide what to do instead. All she knew was if she sat down, she wouldn't get back up.

"Let's go, Mook!" someone shouted.

Billy had just arrived and was pulling off his jacket. Underneath, he had on surf shorts and a rock band T-shirt with the sleeves torn off. Some marathoners are thrilled when a friend paces them through the last two or three miles; Billy was jumping in for the full marathon. Jenn felt her spirits rising. The Bonehead. What a guy.

"You want some more pizza?" Billy asked.

"Ugh. No way."

"All right. Ready?"

"Right on."

The two of them set off down the trail. Jenn ran silently, still feeling awful and debating whether to return to the aid station and quit. Billy coaxed her along just by being there. Jenn struggled through one mile, then another, and something strange began to happen: her despair was replaced by elation, by the feeling that damn, how cool it was to be wandering this amazing wilderness under a burning sunset, feeling free and naked and fast, the forest breeze cooling their sweating skin.

By 10:30 that night, Jenn and Billy had passed every other runner in the woods except one. Jenn didn't just finish; she was the second runner overall and the fastest woman to ever run the course, breaking the old record by three hours (to this day, her 17:34 record still stands). When the national rankings came out a few months later, Jenn discovered she was one of the top three hundred-mile runners in the United States. Soon, she'd set a world best: her 14:57 at the Rocky Raccoon 100 was—and remains—the fastest hundred miles on dirt trails ever recorded by any woman, anywhere.

That fall, a photo appeared in *UltraRunning* magazine. It shows Jenn finishing a 30-mile race somewhere in the backwoods of Virginia. There's nothing amazing about her performance (third place), or her getup (basic black shorts, basic black sports bra), or even the camera work (dimly lit, crudely cropped). Jenn isn't battling a rival to the bitter end, or striding across a mountaintop with the steel-jawed majesty of a Nike model, or gasping toward glory with a grimace of heartbreaking determination. All she's doing is . . . running. Running, and smiling.

But that smile is strangely stirring. You can tell she's having an absolute blast, as if there's nothing on earth she'd rather be doing and nowhere on earth she'd rather be doing it than here, on this lost trail in the middle of the Appalachian wilderness. Even though she's just run four miles farther than a marathon, she looks light-footed and carefree, her eyes twinkling, her ponytail swinging around her head like a shirt in the fist of a triumphant Brazilian soccer player. Her naked delight is unmistakable; it forces a smile to her lips that's so honest and unguarded, you feel she's lost in the grip of artistic inspiration.

Maybe she is. Whenever an art form loses its fire, when it gets weakened by intellectual inbreeding and first principles fade into stale tradition, a radical fringe eventually appears to blow it up and rebuild from the rubble. Young Gun ultrarunners were like Lost Generation writers in the '20s, Beat poets in the '50s, and rock musicians in the '60s: they were poor and ignored and free from all expectations and inhibitions. They were body artists, playing with the palette of human endurance.

"So why not marathons?" I asked Jenn when I called to interview her about the Young Guns. "Do you think you could qualify for the Olympic Trials?"

"Dude, seriously," she'd said. "The qualifying standard is 2:48. Anyone can make it." Jenn could run a sub-three-hour marathon while wearing a string bikini and chugging a beer at mile 23—and she would, just five days after running a 50-mile trail race in the Blue Ridge Mountains.

"But then what?" Jenn went on. "I hate all this hype about the marathon. Where's the mystery? I know a girl who's training for the Trials, and she's got every single workout planned for the next three years! She's doing speedwork on the track like, every other day. I couldn't take it, man. I was supposed to run with her once at six in the morning, and I called her up at two a.m. to tell her I was shitfaced on margaritas and *puh-robably* not gonna make it."

Jenn didn't have a coach or a training program; she didn't even own a watch. She just rolled out of bed every morning, downed a veggie burger, and ran as far and as fast as she felt like, which usually turned out to be about twenty miles. Then she hopped on the skateboard she'd bought instead of a parking pass and kicked off to class at Old Dominion, where she'd recently dropped back into school and was making straight As.

"I never really discussed this with anyone because it sounds pretentious, but I started running ultras to become a better person," Jenn told me. "I thought if you could run one hundred miles, you'd be in this Zen state. You'd be the fucking Buddha, bringing peace and a smile to the world. It didn't work in my case—I'm the same old punk-ass as before—but there's always that hope that it will turn you into the person you want to be, a better, more peaceful person.

"When I'm out on a long run," she continued, "the only thing in life that matters is finishing the run. For once, my brain isn't going *blehblehbleh* all the time. Everything quiets down, and the only thing going on is pure flow. It's just me and the movement and the motion. That's what I love—just being a barbarian, running through the woods."

Listening to Jenn was like communing with the Ghost of Caballo Blanco. "It's weird how much you sound like a guy I met in Mexico," I told her. "I'm heading down there in a few weeks for a race he's putting on with the Tarahumara."

"No way!"

"Scott Jurek may be there, too."

"You. Are. *Shitting me!*" the budding Buddha exclaimed. "Really? Can me and my friend go? Oh no. Shit! We've got midterms that week. I'm going to have to pull a fast one on him. Give me till tomorrow, okay?"

The next morning, as promised, I got a message from Jenn:

> *My mom thinks you're a serial killer who's going to murder us in the desert. Totally worth the risk. So where do we meet you guys?*

CHAPTER 23

WE WHEEZED into Creel well after nightfall, the bus shuddering to a stop with a hiss from the brakes like a sigh of relief. Outside the window, I spotted Caballo's ghostly old straw hat bobbing toward us through the dark.

I couldn't believe how smoothly we'd crossed the Chihuahua desert. Ordinarily, the odds of getting across the border and catching four buses in a row without one of them breaking down or chugging in a half-day late were on a par with beating a Tijuana slot machine. On just about any trip through Chihuahua, someone is sure to have to console you with the local motto: "Nothing works out according to plan, but it always works out." But this plan, so far, was turning out to be foolproof, booze-proof, and cartel-proof.

Of course, that was before Caballo met Barefoot Ted.

"CABALLO BLANCO! That's YOU, RIGHT?"

Before I could make my way off the bus in Creel, I could hear a voice outside booming away like a siege gun. "YOU'RE Caballo! THAT IS SO COOL! You can call me MONO! THE MONKEY! That's ME, the MONKEY. That's my spirit animal—"

When I stepped through the door, I found Caballo staring in appalled disbelief at Barefoot Ted. As the rest of us had discovered during the long bus ride, Barefoot Ted talked the way Charlie Parker played the sax: he'd pick up on any cue and cut loose with a truly astonishing torrent of improvisation, seeming to breathe in through his nose while maintaining an endless flow of sound out of his mouth. In our first thirty seconds in Creel, Caballo got blasted with more conversation than he'd heard in a year. I felt a twinge of sympathy, but only a twinge. We'd been listening to The Mixed-Up Files of Barefoot Ted for the past fifteen hours. Now it was Caballo's turn.

". . . the Tarahumara have been VERY inspirational for me. The first time I read that the Tarahumara could run a one-hundred-mile race in sandals, that realization was so shocking and SUBVERSIVE, so counterintuitive to what I had assumed was NECESSARY for a human being to go that distance, I remember thinking *What in the HELL? How in the HELL is this possible?* That was the first thing, the first CHINK IN THE WALL, that *MAYYYBEE* modern shoe companies don't have all the answers. . . ."

You didn't even have to hear Barefoot Ted to appreciate his cocktail shaker of a mind; just seeing him was enough. His outfit was a combination of Tibetan Warrior Monk and skateboard chic: denim kickboxing pants with a drawstring waist, a skintight white tank top, Japanese bathhouse slippers, a brass skeleton amulet dangling to the middle of his chest, and a red bandanna knotted around his neck. With his shaved head, cinder-block build, and dark eyes that danced around seeking attention as much as his voice, he looked like Uncle Fester in good fighting trim.

"Yeah. Okay, man," Caballo muttered, easing past Ted to greet the rest of us. We grabbed our backpacks and followed Caballo across Creel's one main street toward lodging he'd arranged on the edge of town. We were all starving and exhausted after the long trip, shivering in the high-mesa cold and longing for nothing except a warm bed and a hot bowl of Mamá's frijoles—all of us except Ted, that is, who believed the first order of business was continuing the life story he'd begun telling Caballo the second they met.

Caballo's teeth were on edge, but he decided not to interrupt. He had some terrible news, and he hadn't figured out yet how to break it without all of us turning around and getting right back on the bus.

"My life is a controlled explosion," Barefoot Ted likes to say. He lives in Burbank, in a small compound that resembles Tom Hanks's kid-gone-wild apartment in *Big*. The grounds are full of gumball-colored

Spyder sports cars, carousel horses, Victorian high-wheel bicycles, vintage Jeeps, circus posters, a saltwater swimming pool, and a hot tub patrolled by an endangered California desert tortoise. Instead of a garage, there are two giant circus tents. Wandering in and out of the single-story bungalow are an assortment of dogs and cats, plus a goose, a tame sparrow, thirty-six homing pigeons, and a handful of odd Asian chickens with claws covered in fur-like feathers.

"I forget that heavy Heidegger word, but it's the one that means I'm an expression of this place," Ted says, although the place isn't his at all. It belongs to his cousin Dan, a self-taught mechanical genius who single-handedly created the world's leading carousel-restoration business. "Dita Von Teese strips on one of our horses," Ted says. "Christina Aguilera brought one on tour with her." While Dan was going through a bad divorce a few years ago, Ted decided that what his cousin needed most was more Ted, so he showed up at Dan's door with his wife, daughter, and menagerie and never left. "Dan spends all day fighting with big, cold, mean, mechanical things and emerges with grease dripping off his fingers like blood off the talons of a bird of prey," Ted says. "That's why we're indispensable. He'd be a sociopath if he didn't have me around to argue with."

Ted made himself useful by setting up a little online store for carousel trinkets, which he ran from a Mac in one of Dan's spare bedrooms. It didn't pay much, but it left Ted a lot of time to train for fifty-mile rides on his six-foot-tall Victorian bike and to cross-train by hauling his wife and daughter around in a rickshaw. Caballo had gotten totally the wrong impression of Ted's wealth, mostly because Ted's e-mails tended to be full of schemes better suited to an early Microsoft investor. While the rest of us were pricing economy flights to El Paso, for instance, Ted was asking about landing strips in the Mexican outback for a private bush plane. Not that Ted has a plane; he barely has a car. He sputters around in a '66 VW Beetle in such coughing decline, he can't take it more than twenty-five miles from home. But that's just fine by Ted; in fact, it's all part of the master plan. "That way, I never have to travel very far," he explains. "I'm a pauper by choice, and I find it extremely liberating."

During his student days at the Art Center College of Design in Pasadena, Ted had a major crush on a classmate, Jenny Shimizu.

While hanging out at her apartment one evening, he met two of Jenny's new friends: Chase Chen, a young artist from China, and Chase's sister, Joan. Neither of the Chen siblings spoke much English, so Ted anointed himself their personal cultural ambassador. The friendship worked out great for everyone: Ted had a captive audience for his symphonic stream-of-consciousness, the Chens were exposed to a flood of new vocabulary, and Jenny got a little breathing room from Ted's wooing. Within a few years, three of the foursome would be international names: Joan Chen became a Hollywood star and one of *People* magazine's "50 Most Beautiful People." Chase became a critically acclaimed portrait painter and the most highly paid Asian artist of his generation. Jenny Shimizu became a model and one of the planet's best-known lesbians ("a homohousehold name," as *The Pink Paper* declared) for her affairs with Madonna and Angelina Jolie (a career trajectory that, despite the tattoo on Jenny's right biceps of a hot babe straddling a Snap-on tool, Ted never saw coming).

As for Ted, well . . .

He did manage to crack the Top 30 in the world for breath-holding. "I got up to five minutes and fifteen seconds," Ted says. "Spent the whole summer practicing in the pool." But breath-holding, alas, is a fickle mistress, and it wasn't long before Ted was knocked out of the rankings by other competitors even more dedicated to the art of inhaling less than the rest of us. You have to feel a pang of sympathy for the poor guy, burbling away with dreams of glory at the bottom of his cousin's swimming pool, while just about everyone he knew was painting masterpieces, bedding superstars, and getting close-ups from Bernardo Bertolucci.

And the worst part? Ted holding his breath was actually Ted at his best. In a way, that's even what attracted Lisa, the woman who'd become his wife. They were roommates in the group house, but because Lisa was a bouncer at a heavy-metal bar and only got home at 3 a.m., her exposure to Ted was limited to the dry-land version of the bottom of the pool: after work, she'd come home to find Ted sitting quietly at the kitchen table, eating rice and beans with his nose buried in French philosophy. His stamina and intelligence were already legendary among his roommates; Ted could paint all morning, skateboard all afternoon, and memorize Japanese verbs all night. He'd fix Lisa a hot plate of beans, and then, with his manic motor finally running down, he'd stop performing and let her talk. Every once in a while, he'd chip in a sensitive insight, then encourage her to go on. Few ever saw this Ted. That was their great loss—and his.

But Chase Chen got it. His artist's eye also spotted the quiet intensity in the aftermaths of Hurricane Ted. Chase's specialty, after all, was "the dramatic dance between sunlight and shadow," and brother, was dramatic dancing ever Ted to a tee. What fascinated Chase wasn't action, but anticipation; not the ballerina's leap, but the instant before takeoff when her strength is coiled and anything is possible. He could see the same thing during Ted's quiet moments, the same simmering power and unlimited possibility, and that's when Chase reached for his sketch pad. For years, Chase would use Ted as a model; some of his finest works, in fact, are portraits of Ted, Lisa, and their incandescently lovely daughter, Ona. Chase was so entranced by the world as reflected by Ted that he released an entire book with nothing but portraits of Ted and his family: Ted and Ona cooped up in the old Beetle . . . Ona buried in a book . . . Lisa glancing over her shoulder at Ona, the living product of her father's sunlight and shadow.

By the time Ted was pushing forty, though, his four decades of dramatic dancing had gotten him no further than cameos in another man's masterpiece and a spare room in his cousin's bungalow. But just when it seemed he'd crossed that bridge between great potential and squandered talent, something wonderful happened:

He got a backache.

In 2003, Ted decided to celebrate his fortieth birthday with his own endurance event, "The Anachronistic Ironman." It would be a full Ironman triathlon—2.4-mile ocean swim, 112-mile bike ride, and 26.2-mile run—except, for reasons only clear to Ted, all the gear had to date from the 1890s. He was already two-thirds of the way there; he was strong enough to handle the swim in full-length woollies, and he'd become an ace on his high-wheel bike. But the run—the run was murdering him.

"Every time I ran for an hour, I had *excruciating* lower-back pain," Ted says. "It was so discouraging. I couldn't even imagine being able to run a marathon." And the worst was yet to come: if he couldn't handle six miles in bouncy modern running shoes, then he was in for a world of hurt when he went hard-core Victorian. Running shoes have only been around about as long as the space shuttle; before that, your dad wore flat rubber gym shoes and your granddad was in leather ballet slippers. For millions of years, humans ran without arch support, pronation control, or gel-filled pods under their heels. How the hell they managed, Ted had no idea. But first things first; he was less than six months out from his birthday, so Priority No. 1 was finding some way, *any* way, to cover twenty-six miles on foot. Once he figured that out, he could worry later about transitioning into the cowhide widow-makers.

"If I make up my mind, I will find a way," Ted says. "So I started doing research." First, he got checked by a chiropractor and an orthopedic surgeon, and both said there was really nothing wrong with him. Running was just an inherently dangerous sport, they told him, and one of the dangers was the way impact shock shoots up your legs and into your spine. But the docs did have some good news: if Ted insisted on running, he could probably be cured with a credit card. Top-of-the-line running shoes and some spongy heel pads, they said, should cushion his legs enough to get him through a marathon.

Ted spent a fortune he really didn't have on the most expensive shoes he could find, and was crushed to discover that they didn't help. But instead of blaming the docs, he blamed the shoes: he must need even more cushioning than thirty years of Nike air-injection R&D had come up with. So he gulped hard and sent three hundred dollars to Switzerland for a pair of Kangoo Jumps, the springiest shoes in the world. Kangoos are basically Rollerblades as designed by Wile E. Coyote: instead of wheels, each boot sits atop a full-length steel-spring suspension that lets you boing along like you're in a Moon bounce.

When the box arrived, six weeks later, Ted was almost quivering with excitement. He took a few tentative bounces . . . fantastic! It was like walking with Mick Jagger's mouth strapped to the bottom of each foot. *Oh, this was going to be the answer,* Ted thought as he began bouncing down the street. By the time he got to the corner, he was clutching his back and cursing. "The sensation I got after an hour in running shoes, I got almost instantly from these Kangoo boots," Ted says. "My worldview of what I needed was shattered."

Furious and frustrated, he yanked them off his feet. He couldn't wait to shove the stupid Kangoos back in the box and mail them back to Switzerland with instructions for further shoving. He stalked home barefoot, so pissed off and disappointed that it took him nearly the entire walk to notice what was happening: his back didn't hurt. Didn't hurt a bit.

Heyyy . . . Ted thought. *Maybe I can speed walk the marathon in bare feet.* Bare feet certainly qualified as 1890s sportswear.

So every day, Ted put on his running shoes and walked over to Hansen Dam, an oasis of scrub brush and lakes he calls "L.A.'s last wilderness." Once there, he pulled off his shoes and hiked barefoot along the bridle paths. "I was totally amazed at how enjoyable it was," he recalled. "The shoes would cause so much pain, and as soon as I took them off, it was like my feet were fish jumping back into water after being held captive. Finally, I just left the shoes at home."

But why did his back feel better with *less* cushioning, instead of more? He went online in search of answers, and the result was like parting the foliage in a rain forest and discovering a secret tribe of the Amazon. Ted stumbled across an international community of barefoot runners, complete with their own ancient wisdom and tribal nicknames and led by their great bearded sage, "Barefoot Ken Bob" Saxton. And luckily, this was one tribe that loved to write.

Ted pored over years' worth of Barefoot Ken Bob's archives. He discovered that Leonardo da Vinci considered the human foot, with its fantastic weight-suspension system comprising one quarter of all the bones in the human body, "a masterpiece of engineering and a work of art." He learned about Abebe Bikila—the Ethiopian marathoner who ran barefoot over the cobblestones of Rome to win the 1960 Olympic marathon—and about Charlie Robbins, M.D., a lone voice in the medical wilderness who ran barefoot and argued that marathons won't hurt you, but shoes sure as shooting will.

Most of all, Ted was transfixed by Barefoot Ken Bob's "Naked Toe Manifesto." It gave Ted chills, the way it seemed directed personally at him. "Many of you may be suffering from chronic running related injuries," Barefoot Ken Bob begins:

Shoes block pain, not impact!
Pain teaches us to run comfortably!
From the moment you start going barefoot, you will change the way
you run.

"That was my *Eureka!* moment," Ted recalled. Suddenly, it all made sense. So that's why those stinkin' Kangoo Jumps made his back ache! All that cushioning underfoot let him run with big, sloppy strides, which twisted and tweaked his lower back. When he went barefoot, his form instantly tightened; his back straightened and his legs stayed squarely under his hips.

"No wonder your feet are so sensitive," Ted mused. "They're self-correcting devices. Covering your feet with cushioned shoes is like turning off your smoke alarms."

On his first barefoot run, Ted went five miles and felt . . . nothing. Not a twinge. He bumped it up to an hour, then two. Within months, Ted had transformed himself from an aching, fearful non-runner into a barefoot marathoner with such speed that he was able to accomplish something that 99.9 percent of all runners never will: he qualified for the Boston Marathon.

Intoxicated with his startling new talent, Ted kept pushing further. He went on to run the Mother Road 100—one hundred miles of asphalt on the original Route 66—and the Leona Divide fifty-miler, and the Angeles Crest 100-Mile Endurance Run through the rugged San Gabriel Mountains. Whenever he hit gravel and broken glass, he yanked on rubber foot gloves called the Vibram FiveFingers and kept going. Soon, he wasn't just some runner; he was one of the best barefoot runners in America and a sought-after authority on stride technique and ancient footwear. One newspaper even ran an article on foot health headlined WHAT WOULD BAREFOOT TED DO?

Ted's evolution was complete. He'd emerged from the watery depths, learned to run, and captured the only quarry he desired—not fortune, just fame.

"Stop!"

Caballo was talking to all of us, not just Ted. He brought us to an abrupt halt in the middle of a wobbly footbridge over a sewage ditch.

"I need you all to swear a blood oath," he said. "So put up your right hands and repeat after me."

Eric looked over at me. "What's this all about?"

"Beats me."

"You've got to make the oath right here, before we cross over to the other side," Caballo insisted. "Back there is the way out. This is the way in. If you're in, you've got to swear it."

We shrugged, dropped our packs, and lifted our hands.

"If I get hurt, lost, or die," Caballo began.

"If I get hurt, lost, or die," we chanted.

"It's my own damn fault."

"It's my own damn fault!"

"Uh . . . amen."

"AMEN!"

Caballo led us over to the tiny house where he and I had eaten the day we met. We all squeezed into Mamá's living room as her daughter jammed two tables together. Luis and his dad ducked across the street and returned with two big bags of beer. Jenn and Billy took a few sips of Tecate and began to perk up. We all raised our beers and clinked cans with Caballo. Then he turned to me and got down to business. Suddenly, the oath on the bridge made sense.

"You remember Manuel Luna's son?"

"Marcelino?" Of course I remembered the Human Torch. I'd been mentally signing Nike contracts on his behalf ever since I'd seen him at the Tarahumara school. "Is he coming?"

"No," Caballo said. "He's dead. Someone beat him to death. They murdered him out on the trail. He was stabbed in the neck and under the arm and his head was bashed in."

"Who . . . what happened?" I stammered.

"There's all kind of drug shit going on these days," Caballo said. "Maybe Marcelino saw something he wasn't supposed to see. Maybe they were trying to get him to carry weed out of the canyon and he said no. No one really knows. Manuel is just heartbroken, man. He stayed over at my house when he came to tell the *federales*. But they're not going to do anything. There's no law down here."

I sat, stunned. I remembered the drug runners in the shiny red Deathmobile we'd seen on the way to the Tarahumara school the year before. I pictured stealthy Tarahumara tipping it over the edge of a cliff at night, the drug runners clawing frantically at their seat belts, the truck bouncing down the canyon and exploding in a giant fireball. I had no idea if the men in the Deathmobile had been involved. All I knew was I wanted to kill somebody.

Caballo was still talking. He had already absorbed Marcelino's death and was back to obsessing over his race. "I know Manuel Luna won't come, but I'm hoping Arnulfo will show up. And maybe Silvino." Over the winter, Caballo managed to put together a nice pot of prizes; not only was he kicking in his own money, but he'd also been contacted out of the blue by Michael French, a Texas triathlete who'd made a fortune from his IT company. French was intrigued by my *Runner's World* article, and while he couldn't make it to the race himself, he offered to put up cash and corn for the top finishers.

"Excuse me," I said. "Did you say Arnulfo is coming?"

"Yeah," Caballo nodded.

He had to be joking. Arnulfo? He wouldn't even *talk* to me, let alone join me for a run. If he wouldn't go for a jog with a guy who'd come to pay homage right at his doorstep, why would he travel across the mountains to run with a pack of gringos he'd never seen before? And Silvino; I'd met Silvino the last time I was down here. We'd run into him by chance in Creel, right after I'd gone running with Caballo. He was in his pickup and wearing his jeans, the spoils from the marathon he'd won in California. Where did Caballo get the idea that Silvino would bother coming to his race? Silvino couldn't even be induced to run another marathon for the chance of another big payday. I'd learned enough about the Tarahumara, and those two runners in particular, to know there was no way the Quimare clan had any intention of turning up.

"Victorian athletics were *fascinating*!" Oblivious to the fact that it suddenly seemed very unlikely that any Tarahumara runners were going to appear, Ted was prattling on. "That was the first English Channel crossing. Have you ever ridden a high-wheel bike? The engineering is so *ingenious. . . .*"

God, what a disaster. Caballo was rubbing his head; it was pushing midnight, and just being around humans was giving him a headache. Jenn and Billy had a platoon of dead Tecate cans in front of them and were falling asleep on the table. I was miserable, and I could tell Eric and Luis were picking up on the tension and getting concerned. But not Scott; he just sat back, amused. He caught everything and seemed worried by nothing.

"Look, I got to sleep," Caballo said. He led us over to a collection of neat, ancient cabins on the edge of town. The rooms were sparse as cells, but spotlessly clean and toasty from potbellied stoves crackling with pine branches. Caballo mumbled something and disappeared. The rest of us divided up into pairs. Eric and I grabbed one room, Jenn and Billy headed to another.

"All right!" Ted said, clapping his hands. "Who gets me?"

Silence.

"Okay," Scott said. "But you've got to let me sleep."

We shut our doors and sank into deep piles of wool blankets. Silence fell over Creel, until the last thing Scott heard was Barefoot Ted's voice in the dark.

"Okay, brain," Ted muttered. "Relax. Time to quiet down."

TAPTAPTAPPITYTAP.

Dawn broke with frost on the window and a rapping at our door.

"Hey," a voice outside whispered. "You guys up?"

I padded over to the door, shivering, wondering what the hell the Party Kids had done this time. Luis and Scott were outside, blowing into their cupped hands. It was so early, the sky was still a milky coffee color. The roosters hadn't even started crowing.

"Want to sneak in a run?" Scott asked. "Caballo said we're on the road by eight, so we've got to hit it now."

"Uh, yeah. Okay," I said. "Caballo took me on a great trail last time. Let me see if I can find him and—"

A window flew open in the cabin beside us. Jenn's head popped out. "You guys going for a run? I'm in! Billy," she called back over her shoulder. "Get your ass up, dude!"

I yanked on some shorts and a polypro top. Eric yawned and reached for running shoes. "Man, these guys are hard-core," he said. "Where's Caballo?"

"No idea. I'm going to look for him."

I walked to the end of the row of adjoining cabins, guessing Caballo would be as far from us as he could get. I rapped on the door of the very last cabin. Nothing. It was a pretty stout door, though, so just to be sure, I gave it a good hammering with the side of my fist.

"WHAT!!!" a voice roared. The curtains ripped open and Caballo's face appeared. His eyes were red and puffy.

"Sorry," I said. "You catch a cold or something?"

"No, man," he said wearily. "I was just getting to sleep." Barely twelve hours into this operation, Caballo was already so stressed that he'd spent the entire night tossing and turning with an anxiety headache. Being in Creel was enough to put him on edge in the first place. It's actually a pleasant little town, but it represents the two things Caballo despises most: bullshit and bullies. It's named for Enrique Creel, a land-raping kingpin of such dastardly magnificence that the Mexican Revolution was essentially thrown in his honor. Enrique not only engineered the land grab that ousted thousands of Chihuahua peasants from their farms, but personally made sure that any feisty farmers ended up in jail by moonlighting as the head of a spy network for the Mexican dictator Porfirio Díaz.

Enrique slithered into exile in El Paso when Pancho Villa's rebels came thundering after him (leaving behind a son who had to be ransomed from the revolutionaries for a million dollars), but once Mexico went through its inevitable correction and reverted back to contented corruption, Enrique returned in all his scheming glory. In a fitting tribute to the region's greatest human virus, Enrique Creel's namesake was now the launching area for every pestilence afflicting the Copper Canyons: strip-mining, clear-cut logging, drug ranching, and big-bus tourism. Spending time there drove Caballo nuts; for him, it was like staying at a bed-and-breakfast on a working slave plantation.

Most of all, though, he wasn't used to being responsible for anyone besides the guy inside his own sandals. Now that he'd had a look at us, his chest was squeezing tight with apprehension. He'd spent ten years building up the trust of the Tarahumara, and it could come crashing down in ten minutes. Caballo envisioned Barefoot Ted and Jenn yapping into the ears of the uncomprehending Tarahumara . . . Luis and his dad flashing cameras in their eyes . . . Eric and me pestering them with questions. What a nightmare.

"No, man, I ain't going for a run," he groaned. He snapped the curtains shut.

Soon, the seven of us—Scott, Luis, Eric, Jenn, Billy, Barefoot Ted, and I—were on the pine-needled trail that Caballo had taken me on before. We came out of the tree canopy just as the sun was breaking over the giant standing stones, making us squint as the world turned to gold. Mist and glittering droplets swirled around us.

"Gorgeous," Luis said.

"I've never seen a place like this," Billy said. "Caballo's got the right idea. I'd love to live here, just living cheap and running trails."

"He's brainwashed you already!" Luis hooted. "The Cult of the White Horse."

"It's not him," Billy protested. "It's this place."

"My Little Pony," Jenn smirked. "You kinda look like Caballo."

In the midst of this banter, Scott was busy watching Barefoot Ted. The trail was snaking through a rock field, but even though we had to hop from boulder to boulder, Ted wasn't slowing down a bit.

"Dude, what are those things on your feet?" Jenn asked.

"Vibram FiveFingers," Ted said. "Aren't they great? I'm their first sponsored athlete!"

Yes, it was true; Ted had become America's first professional barefoot runner of the modern era. FiveFingers were designed as a deck shoe for yacht racers; the idea was to give better grip on slippery surfaces while maintaining the feeling of shoelessness. You had to look closely just to spot them; they conformed so perfectly around his soles and each toe, it looked as if Ted had dipped the bottoms of his feet in greenish ink. Shortly before the Copper Canyon trip, he'd come across a photo of the FiveFingers on the Web and immediately grabbed the phone. Somehow, he connived his way through the thicket of switchboard operators and secretaries and got on the line with the CEO of Vibram USA, who turned out to be none other than . . .

Tony Post! The onetime Rockport exec who'd sponsored the Tarahumara at Leadville!

Tony heard Ted out, but was extremely doubtful. Not that he didn't love the idea of relying on foot strength instead of super cushioning and motion control; once, Tony even ran the Boston Marathon in a pair of Rockport dress shoes to demonstrate that comfort and good construction were all you needed, not all that Shox/anti-pronation/gel-support jazz. But at least Rockport dress shoes had arches and a cushioned sole; the FiveFingers were nothing but a sliver of rubber with a velcro strap. Still, Tony was intrigued and decided to try it out for himself. "I went for an easy little one-mile jog," he says. "I ended up doing seven. I'd never thought of the FiveFinger as a running shoe, but after that, I never thought of anything *else* as a running shoe." When he got home, he wrote a check to cover Barefoot Ted's trip to the Boston Marathon.

We'd run six miles along the mesa top and were heading back into Creel when, in the distance, a thin black shadow broke from the trees and started moving toward us.

"Is that Caballo?" Scott asked.

Jenn and Billy peered, then shot toward him like hounds off the leash. Barefoot Ted and Luis went after them. Scott stayed with us, but his racehorse instincts were making him itchy. He glanced apologetically at Eric and me. "You mind if I . . . ?" he asked.

"No problem," I said. "Run 'em down."

"Cool." By the time the "-ool" was out of his mouth, he was a good half-dozen yards away, his hair bouncing like streamers on a kid's handlebars.

"Shit," I muttered. Watching Scott surge off suddenly reminded me of Marcelino. Scott would have gotten such a kick out of that kid. Jenn and Billy, too; they would have loved mixing it up with their teenage Tarahumara triplet. I could even imagine what Manuel Luna was feeling. No, that wasn't true; I was just trying hard not to. Evil had followed the Tarahumara here, to the bottom of the earth where there was no place left to run. Even while mourning his magnificent son, Manuel had to be wondering which of his children would be next.

"You need a break?" Eric asked. "How are you doing?"

"No, I'm good. Something on my mind."

Caballo was approaching; after meeting the others, he'd kept on running toward Eric and me while the others took a breather and posed for Luis's camera. It was a good thing Caballo had changed his mind and decided to come for a run; for the first time since we'd gotten off the bus, he was smiling. The sparkling sunrise and the old familiar pleasure of feeling his body warm from the inside out seemed to have eased his anxiety. And man, was it great to see him in action again! Just watching him, I felt my back straightening and my feet quickening, as if someone had just switched on the *Chariots of Fire* soundtrack.

Apparently, the admiration was sort of mutual. "Look at you!" Caballo shouted. "You're a whole new bear." A while back, Caballo had decided on a spirit animal for me; while he was a sleek white horse, I was *Oso*—the lumbering bear. But at least he took the sting out of it with his reaction to the way I looked now, a year since I'd gasped and winced pathetically behind him.

"You're nothing like the guy I had up here before," Caballo said.

"Thanks to the man here," I said, jerking my thumb toward Eric. Nine months of Eric's Tarahumara-style training had worked wonders: I was twenty-five pounds lighter and running with ease on a trail that had killed me before. Despite all the miles I'd put in—up to eighty a week—I still felt light and loose and eager for more. Most of all, for the first time in a decade I wasn't nursing some kind of injury. "This guy is a miracle worker."

"Must be," Caballo grinned. "I saw what he had to work with. So what's the secret?"

"It's a pretty wild story—," I began, but by then we'd reached Scott and the others, who were listening to Barefoot Ted hold court. "Tell you later," I promised Caballo.

Barefoot Ted had slipped off his FiveFingers and was demonstrating the perfect shoeless foot strike. "Barefoot running really appealed to my artistic eye," Ted was saying. "This concept of bricolage—that less is more, the best solution is the most elegant. Why add something if you're born with everything you need?"

"You better add something to your feet when we cross the canyons," Caballo said. "You brought some other shoes, right?"

"Sure," Ted said. "I've got my flip-flops."

Caballo smiled, waiting for Barefoot Ted to smile back and show he was joking. Barefoot Ted didn't, and wasn't.

"You don't have shoes?" Caballo said. "You're going into the Barrancas *in flip-flops?*"

"Don't worry about me. I hiked the San Gabriels in bare feet. People kept looking at me like, 'Is this guy out of his *mind*,' and I'd say—"

"These ain't no San Gay-Bree-All Mountains!" Caballo spat,

mocking the California range with all the gringo butchery he could muster. "The cactus thorns out here are razor blades. You get one in your foot, we're all fucked. Those trails are dangerous enough without carrying you on our backs."

"Whoa, whoa, you guys," Scott said, getting a shoulder in and pushing them both back a step. "Caballo, Ted's probably been hearing 'Ted, go put some shoes on!' for years. But if he knows what he's doing, he knows what he's doing."

"He don't know *shit* about the Barrancas."

"I know this," Ted shot back. "If someone gets in trouble out there, I guarantee you it won't be me!"

"Yeah?" Caballo snarled. "We'll see, amigo." He turned and stalked down the trail.

"Hooo *mama*!" Jenn said. "Who's the troublemaker now, Ted?"

We followed Caballo toward the cabins, while Barefoot Ted loudly and persistently continued arguing his case to us, Caballo's back, and the awakening town of Creel. I glanced at my watch; I was tempted to tell Barefoot Ted to just shut up and buy a cheap pair of sneaks to keep Caballo happy, but there wasn't time. Only one bus a day made the ten-hour trip down into the canyons, and it would be pulling out before any shops opened.

Back at the cabins, we began jamming clothes into our backpacks. I told the others where they could scare up some breakfast, then I went to check Caballo's cabin. He wasn't there. Neither was his pack.

"Maybe he's cooling off on his own," I told myself. Maybe. But I had a sick feeling that he'd decided to hell with us and was gone for good. After a long night of worrying whether he'd made a colossal mistake, I was pretty sure he'd gotten his answer.

I decided not to tell anyone and hope for the best. One way or the other, we'd know in about thirty minutes if this operation was dead or hanging on life support. I shouldered my pack and walked back across the footbridge over the sewage ditch where we'd taken our oath the night before. I found the rest of the crew in a little restaurant down the block from the bus stop, loading up on bean and chicken burritos. I wolfed down two, then packed a few in my pack for later. When we got to the bus, it had already rumbled to life and was ready to go. The driver was tossing the last bags onto the roof rack, and signaled for ours.

"*Espera*," I said. Hang on a sec. Caballo wasn't anywhere in sight. I shoved my head inside the bus and scanned the full rows of seats. No Caballo. Damn. I got out to break the news to everyone else, but they'd all disappeared. I walked around the back, and found Scott climbing the rungs to the roof.

"C'mon up, Oso!" Caballo was on top of the bus, catching bags for the driver. Jenn and Billy were already beside him, lounging in a cushy pile of baggage. "You'll never get a ride like this again."

No wonder the Tarahumara thought Caballo was a ghost. There was no telling what this guy would do, or where he'd turn up. "Forget it," I said. "I've seen this road. I'm getting in the crash-ready position inside between the two fattest guys I can find."

Barefoot Ted grabbed the rungs behind Scott.

"Hey," I said. "Why don't you ride inside with me?"

"No, thanks. I'm going roof surfing."

"Look," I said, spelling it out. "Maybe you should give Caballo a little space. Push him too far, and this race is over."

"Nah, we're cool," Ted said. "He just needs to get to know me."

Yeah. That's exactly what he needs. The driver was settling behind the wheel, so Eric and I hustled aboard and squeezed into the back row. The bus misfired, stalled, then grumbled back to life. Soon, we were winding through the forest, heading toward the old mining town of La Bufa and from there, to the end of the road in the canyon-bottom village of Batopilas. After that, we'd strike out on foot.

"I'm waiting to hear a scream and see Barefoot Ted getting heaved off the roof," Eric said.

"You ain't kidding." Caballo's last words before storming off were still ringing in my ears: *We'll see, amigo!*

Caballo, as it turned out, had decided that before Barefoot Ted got us all in trouble, he was going to teach him a lesson. Unfortunately, it was a lesson that would have all of us running for our lives.

＞

CHAPTER 25

BAREFOOT TED was right, of course.

Lost in all the fireworks between Ted and Caballo was an important point: running shoes may be the most destructive force to ever
hit the human foot. Barefoot Ted, in his own weird way, was becoming the Neil Armstrong of twenty-first-century distance running, an
ace test pilot whose small steps could have tremendous benefit for
the rest of mankind. If that seems like excessive stature to load on
Barefoot Ted's shoulders, consider these words by Dr. Daniel Lieberman, a professor of biological anthropology at Harvard University:

"A lot of foot and knee injuries that are currently plaguing us are
actually caused by people running with shoes that actually make our
feet weak, cause us to over-pronate, give us knee problems. Until
1972, when the modern athletic shoe was invented by Nike, people
ran in very thin-soled shoes, had strong feet, and had much lower
incidence of knee injuries."

And the cost of those injuries? Fatal disease in epidemic proportions. "Humans really are obligatorily required to do aerobic exercise
in order to stay healthy, and I think that has deep roots in our evolutionary history," Dr. Lieberman said in 2008. "If there's any magic
bullet to make human beings healthy, it's to run."

Magic bullet? The last time a scientist with Dr. Lieberman's credentials used that term, he'd just created penicillin. Dr. Lieberman
knew it, and meant it. If running shoes never existed, he was saying,

more people would be running. If more people ran, fewer would be dying of degenerative heart disease, sudden cardiac arrest, hypertension, blocked arteries, diabetes, and most other deadly ailments of the Western world.

That's a staggering amount of guilt to lay at Nike's feet. But the most remarkable part? There's a good chance that Nike already knew it.

In April 2001, two Nike reps were watching the Stanford University track team practice. Part of a Nike rep's job is getting feedback from its sponsored runners about which shoes they prefer, but that was proving difficult at the moment because the Stanford runners all seemed to prefer . . . nothing.

"Vin, what's up with the barefooting?" they called to Stanford head coach Vin Lananna. "Didn't we send you enough shoes?"

Coach Lananna walked over to explain. "I can't prove this," he explained, "but I believe when my runners train barefoot, they run faster and suffer fewer injuries."

Faster *and* fewer injuries? Coming from anyone else, the Nike guys would have politely uh-huhed and ignored it, but this was one coach whose ideas they took seriously. Like Joe Vigil, Lananna was rarely mentioned without the word "visionary" or "innovator" popping up. In just ten years at Stanford, Lananna's track and cross-country teams had won five NCAA team championships and twenty-two individual titles, and Lananna himself had been named NCAA Cross Country Coach of the Year. Lananna had already sent three runners to the Olympics and was busy grooming more with his Nike-sponsored "Farm Team," a post-college club for the best of the very best. Needless to say, the Nike reps were a little chagrined to hear that Lananna felt the best shoes Nike had to offer for training were not as good as no shoes at all.

"We've shielded our feet from their natural position by providing more and more support," Lananna insisted. That's why he made sure his runners always did part of their workouts in bare feet on the track's infield. "I know as a shoe company, it's not the greatest thing to have a sponsored team not use your product, but people went thousands of years without shoes. I think you try to do all these corrective things with shoes and you overcompensate. You fix things that don't need fixing. If you strengthen the foot by going barefoot, I think you reduce the risk of Achilles and knee and plantar fascia problems."

"Risk" isn't quite the right term; it's more like "dead certainty." Every year, anywhere from 65 to 80 percent of all runners suffer an injury. That's nearly *every* runner, every single year. No matter who you are, no matter how much you run, your odds of getting hurt are the same. It doesn't matter if you're male or female, fast or slow, pudgy or ripped as a racehorse, your feet are still in the danger zone.

Maybe you'll beat the odds if you stretch like a swami? Nope. In a 1993 study of Dutch athletes published in *The American Journal of Sports Medicine*, one group of runners was taught how to warm up and stretch while a second group received no "injury prevention" coaching. Their injury rates? Identical. Stretching came out even worse in a follow-up study performed the following year at the University of Hawaii; it found that runners who stretched were 33 percent *more* likely to get hurt.

Lucky for us, though, we live in a golden age of technology. Running-shoe companies have had a quarter century to perfect their designs, so logically, the injury rate must be in free fall by now. After all, Adidas has come up with a $250 shoe with a microprocessor in the sole that instantly adjusts cushioning for every stride. Asics spent three million dollars and eight years—three more than it took the Manhattan Project to create the first atomic bomb—to invent the awe-inspiring Kinsei, a shoe that boasts "multi-angled forefoot gel pods," a "midfoot thrust enhancer," and an "infinitely adaptable heel component that isolates and absorbs impact to reduce pronation and aid in forward propulsion." That's big bucks for sneaks you'll have to toss in the garbage in ninety days, but at least you'll never limp again.

Right?

Sorry.

"Since the first real studies were done in the late '70's, Achilles complaints have actually *increased* by about 10 percent, while plantar fasciitis has remained the same," says Dr. Stephen Pribut, a running-injury specialist and past president of the American Academy of Podiatric Sports Medicine. "The technological advancements over the past thirty years have been amazing," adds Dr. Irene Davis, the director of the Running Injury Clinic at the University of Delaware.

"We've seen tremendous innovations in motion control and cushion-ing. And yet the remedies don't seem to defeat the ailments."

In fact, there's no evidence that running shoes are any help at all in injury prevention. In a 2008 research paper for the *British Journal of Sports Medicine*, Dr. Craig Richards, a researcher at the University of Newcastle in Australia, revealed that there are *no* evidence-based studies—not one—that demonstrate that running shoes make you less prone to injury.

It was an astonishing revelation that had been hidden in plain sight for thirty-five years. Dr. Richards was so stunned that a twenty-billion-dollar industry seemed to be based on nothing but empty promises and wishful thinking that he even issued a challenge:

Is any running shoe company prepared to claim that wearing their distance running shoes will decrease your risk of suffering musculoskeletal running injuries?

Is any shoe manufacturer prepared to claim that wearing their running shoes will improve your distance running performance?

If you are prepared to make these claims, where is your peer reviewed data to back it up?

Dr. Richards waited, and even tried contacting the major shoe companies for their data. In response, he got silence.

So if running shoes don't make you go faster and don't stop you from getting hurt, then what, exactly, are you paying for? What are the benefits of all those microchips, "thrust enhancers," air cushions, torsion devices, and roll bars? Well, if you have a pair of Kinseis in your closet, brace yourself for some bad news. And like all bad news, it comes in threes:

PAINFUL TRUTH No. 1: The Best Shoes Are the Worst

RUNNERS wearing top-of-the-line shoes are 123 percent *more likely* to get injured than runners in cheap shoes, according to a study led by Bernard Marti, M.D., a preventative-medicine specialist at

Switzerland's University of Bern. Dr. Marti's research team analyzed 4,358 runners in the Bern Grand-Prix, a 9.6-mile road race. All the runners filled out an extensive questionnaire that detailed their training habits and footwear for the previous year; as it turned out, 45 percent had been hurt during that time.

But what surprised Dr. Marti, as he pointed out in *The American Journal of Sports Medicine* in 1989, was the fact that the most common variable among the casualties wasn't training surface, running speed, weekly mileage, or "competitive training motivation." It wasn't even body weight, or a history of previous injury: it was the price of the shoe. Runners in shoes that cost more than $95 were more than twice as likely to get hurt as runners in shoes that cost less than $40. Follow-up studies found similar results, like the 1991 report in *Medicine & Science in Sports & Exercise* that found that "Wearers of expensive running shoes that are promoted as having additional features that protect (e.g., more cushioning, 'pronation correction') are injured significantly more frequently than runners wearing inexpensive shoes (costing less than $40)."

What a cruel joke: for double the price, you get double the pain.

Sharp-eyed as ever, Coach Vin Lananna had already spotted the same phenomenon himself back in the early '80s. "I once ordered high-end shoes for the team, and within two weeks, we had more plantar fasciitis and Achilles problems than I'd ever seen. So I sent them back and told them, 'Send me my cheap shoes,' " Lananna says. "Ever since then, I've always ordered the low-end shoes. It's not because I'm cheap. It's because I'm in the business of making athletes run fast and stay healthy."

PAINFUL TRUTH No. 2: Feet Like a Good Beating

AS FAR back as 1988, Dr. Barry Bates, the head of the University of Oregon's Biomechanics/Sports Medicine Laboratory, gathered data that suggested that beat-up running shoes are safer than newer ones. In the *Journal of Orthopaedic & Sports Physical Therapy*, Dr. Bates and his colleagues reported that as shoes wore down and their cushioning thinned, runners gained more foot control.

So how do foot control and a flapping old sole add up to injury-free legs? Because of one magic ingredient: fear. Contrary to what pillowy-sounding names like the Adidas MegaBounce would have you believe, all that cushioning does nothing to reduce impact. Logically, that should be obvious—the impact on your legs from running can be up to twelve times your body weight, so it's preposterous to believe a half inch of rubber is going to make a bit of difference against, in my case, 2,760 pounds of earthbound beef. You can cover an egg with an oven mitt before rapping it with a hammer, but that egg ain't coming out alive.

When E. C. Frederick, then the director of Nike Sports Research Lab, arrived at the 1986 meeting of the American Society of Biomechanics, he was packing a bombshell. "When subjects were tested with soft versus hard shoes," he said, "no difference in impact force was found." No difference! "And curiously," he added, "the second, propulsive peak in the vertical ground reaction force was actually *higher* with soft shoes."

The puzzling conclusion: the more cushioned the shoe, the less protection it provides.

Researchers at the University of Oregon's Biomechanics/Sports Medicine Laboratory were verifying the same finding. As running shoes got worn down and their cushioning hardened, the Oregon researchers revealed in a 1988 study for the *Journal of Orthopaedic & Sports Physical Therapy*, runners' feet stabilized and became less wobbly. It would take about ten years before scientists came up with an explanation for why the old shoes that sports companies were telling you to throw away were better than the new ones they were urging you to buy. At McGill University in Montreal, Steven Robbins, M.D., and Edward Waked, Ph.D., performed a series of tests on gymnasts. They found that the thicker the landing mat, the harder the gymnasts stuck their landings. Instinctively, the gymnasts were searching for stability. When they sensed a soft surface underfoot, they slapped down hard to ensure balance.

Runners do the same thing, Robbins and Waked found: just the way your arms automatically fly up when you slip on ice, your legs and feet instinctively come down hard when they sense something squishy underfoot. When you run in cushioned shoes, your feet are pushing *through* the soles in search of a hard, stable platform.

"We conclude that balance and vertical impact are closely

related," the McGill docs wrote. "According to our findings, currently available sports shoes . . . are too soft and thick, and should be redesigned if they are to protect humans performing sports."

Until reading this study, I'd been mystified by an experience I'd had at the Running Injury Clinic. I'd run back and forth over a force plate while alternating between bare feet, a superthin shoe, and the well-cushioned Nike Pegasus. Whenever I changed shoes, the impact levels changed as well—but not the way I'd expected. My impact forces were lightest in bare feet, and heaviest in the Pegs. My running form also varied: when I changed footwear, I instinctively changed my footfall. "You're much more of a heel striker in the Pegasus," Dr. Irene Davis concluded.

David Smyntek decided to test the impact theory with a unique experiment of his own. As both a runner and a physical therapist specializing in acute rehabilitation, Smyntek was wary when the people telling him he had to buy new shoes were the same people who sold them. He'd been warned forever by *Runner's World* and his local running store that he had to replace his shoes every three hundred to five hundred miles, but how was it that Arthur Newton, one of the greatest ultrarunners of all time, saw no reason to replace his thin rubber sneakers until he'd put at least four thousand miles on them? Newton not only won the 55-mile Comrades race five times in the 1930s, but his legs were still springy enough to break the record for the 100-mile Bath-to-London run at age fifty-one.

So Smyntek decided to see if he could out-Newton Newton. "When my shoes wear down on one side," he wondered, "what if I just wear them on the wrong feet?" Thus began the Crazy Foot Experiment: when his shoes got thin on the outside edge, Dave swapped the right for the left and kept running. "You have to understand the man," says Ken Learman, one of Dave's fellow therapists. "Dave is not the average individual. He's curious, smart, the kind of guy you can't BS real easy. He'll say, 'Hey, if it's supposed to be this way, let's see if it really is.' "

For the next ten years, David ran five miles a day, every day. Once he realized he could run comfortably in wrong-footed shoes, he started questioning why he needed running shoes in the first place. If he wasn't using them the way they were designed, Dave reasoned, maybe that design wasn't such a big deal after all. From then on, he only bought cheap dime-store sneaks.

"Here he is, running more than most people, with the wrong shoe on the wrong foot and not having any problems," Ken Learman says. "That experiment taught us all something. Taught us that when it comes to running shoes, all that glitters isn't gold."

FINAL PAINFUL TRUTH: Even Alan Webb Says "Human Beings
Are Designed to Run Without Shoes"

BEFORE Alan Webb became America's greatest miler, he was a flat-footed frosh with awful form. But his high school coach saw potential, and began rebuilding Alan from—no exaggeration—the ground up.

"I had injury problems early on, and it became apparent that my biomechanics could cause injury," Webb told me. "So we did foot-strengthening drills and special walks in bare feet." Bit by bit, Webb watched his feet transform before his eyes. "I was a size twelve and flat-footed, and now I'm a nine or ten. As the muscles in my feet got stronger, my arch got higher." Because of the barefoot drills, Webb also cut down on his injuries, allowing him to handle the kind of heavy training that would lead to his U.S. record for the mile and the fastest 1,500-meter time in the world for the year 2007.

"Barefoot running has been one of my training philosophies for years," said Gerard Hartmann, Ph.D., the Irish physical therapist who serves as the Great and Powerful Oz for the world's finest distance runners. Paula Radcliffe never runs a marathon without seeing Dr. Hartmann first, and titans like Haile Gebrselassie and Khalid Khannouchi have trusted their feet to his hands. For decades, Dr. Hartmann has been watching the explosion of orthotics and ever-more-structured running shoes with dismay.

"The deconditioned musculature of the foot is the greatest issue leading to injury, and we've allowed our feet to become badly deconditioned over the past twenty-five years," Dr. Hartmann said. "Pronation has become this very bad word, but it's just the natural movement of the foot. The foot is *supposed* to pronate."

To see pronation in action, kick off your shoes and run down the driveway. On a hard surface, your feet will briefly unlearn the habits they picked up in shoes and automatically shift to self-defense mode: you'll find yourself landing on the outside edge of your foot, then gently rolling from little toe over to big until your foot is flat. That's pronation—just a mild, shock-absorbing twist that allows your arch to compress.

But back in the '70s, the most respected voice in running began expressing some doubts about all that foot twisting. Dr. George Sheehan was a cardiologist whose essays on the beauty of running had made him the philosopher-king of the marathon set, and he came up with the notion that excessive pronation might be the cause of runner's knee. He was both right and very, very wrong. You have to land on your heel to overpronate, and you can only land on your heel if it's cushioned. Nevertheless, the shoe companies were quick to respond to Dr. Sheehan's call to arms and came up with a nuclear response; they created monstrously wedged and superengineered shoes that wiped out virtually all pronation.

"But once you block a natural movement," Dr. Hartmann said, "you adversely affect the others. We've done studies, and only two to three percent of the population has real biomechanical problems. So who is getting all these orthotics? Every time we put someone in a corrective device, we're creating new problems by treating ones that don't exist." In a startling admission in 2008, *Runner's World* confessed that for years it had accidentally misled its readers by recommending corrective shoes for runners with plantar fasciitis: "But recent research has shown stability shoes are unlikely to relieve plantar fasciitis *and may even exacerbate the symptoms*" (italics mine).

"Just look at the architecture," Dr. Hartmann explained. Blueprint your feet, and you'll find a marvel that engineers have been trying to match for centuries. Your foot's centerpiece is the arch, the greatest weight-bearing design ever created. The beauty of any arch is the way it gets stronger under stress; the harder you push down, the tighter its parts mesh. No stonemason worth his trowel would ever stick a support *under* an arch; push up from underneath, and you weaken the whole structure. Buttressing the foot's arch from all sides is a high-tensile web of twenty-six bones, thirty-three joints, twelve rubbery tendons, and eighteen muscles, all stretching and flexing like an earthquake-resistant suspension bridge.

"Putting your feet in shoes is similar to putting them in a plaster cast," Dr. Hartmann said. "If I put your leg in plaster, we'll find forty to sixty percent atrophy of the musculature within six weeks. Something similar happens to your feet when they're encased in shoes." When shoes are doing the work, tendons stiffen and muscles shrivel. Feet live for a fight and thrive under pressure; let them laze around, as Alan Webb discovered, and they'll collapse. Work them out, and they'll arc up like a rainbow.

"I've worked with over a hundred of the best Kenyan runners, and one thing they have in common is marvelous elasticity in their feet," Dr. Hartmann continued. "That comes from never running in shoes until you're seventeen." To this day, Dr. Hartmann believes that the best injury-prevention advice he's ever heard came from a coach who advocated "running barefoot on dewy grass three times a week."

He's not the only medical professional preaching the Barefoot Doctrine. According to Dr. Paul W. Brand, chief of rehab at the U.S. Public Health Service Hospital in Carville, Louisiana, and a professor of surgery at Louisiana State University Medical School, we could wipe out every common foot ailment within a generation by kicking off our shoes. As far back as 1976, Dr. Brand was pointing out that nearly every case in his waiting room—corns, bunions, hammertoes, flat feet, fallen arches—was nearly nonexistent in countries where most people go barefoot.

"The barefoot walker receives a continuous stream of information about the ground and about his own relationship to it," Dr. Brand has said, "while a shod foot sleeps inside an unchanging environment."

Drumbeats for the barefoot uprising were growing. But instead of doctors leading the charge for a muscular foot, it was turning into a class war pitting podiatrists against their own patients. Barefoot advocates like Drs. Brand and Hartmann were still rare, while traditional podiatric thinking still saw human feet as Nature's Mistake, a work in progress that could always be improved by a little scalpel-sculpting and orthotic reshaping.

That born-broken mentality found its perfect expression in *The Runners' Repair Manual.* Written by Dr. Murray Weisenfeld, a leading sports podiatrist, it's one of the top-selling foot-care books of all time, and begins with this dire pronouncement:

"Man's foot was not originally designed for walking, much less running long distances."

So what, according to the *Manual*, was our foot designed for? Well, at first swimming ("The modern foot evolved out of the fin of some primordial fish and these fins pointed backward"). After that, climbing ("The grasping foot permitted the creature to squat on branches without falling out").

And then . . . ?

And then, according to the podiatric account of evolution, we got stuck. While the rest of our bodies adapted beautifully to solid earth, somehow the only part of our body that actually touched the earth got left behind. We developed brains and hands deft enough to perform intravascular surgery, yet our feet never made it past the Paleolithic era. "Man's foot is not yet completely adapted to the ground," the *Manual* laments. "Only a portion of the population has been endowed with well ground-adapted feet."

So who are these lucky few with well-evolved feet? Come to think of it, nobody: "Nature has not yet published her plan for the perfect modern runner's foot," Dr. Weisenfeld writes. "Until the perfect foot comes along, my experience has shown me that we've all got an excellent chance at having some kind of injury." Nature may not have published her blueprint, but that didn't stop some podiatrists from trying to come up with one of their own. And it was exactly that kind of thinking—the belief that four years of podiatric training could trump two million years of natural selection—that led to a catastrophic rash of operations in the '70s.

"Not too many years ago, runner's knee was treated by surgery," Dr. Weisenfeld acknowledges. "That didn't work too well, since you need that cushioning when you run." Once the patients came out from under the knife, they discovered that their nagging ache had turned into a life-changing mutilation; without cartilage in their knees, they'd never be able to run without pain again. Despite the podiatric profession's checkered history of attempting to one-up nature, *The Runners' Repair Manual* never recommends strengthening feet; instead, the treatment of choice is always tape, orthotics, or surgery.

It even took Dr. Irene Davis, whose credentials and open-mindedness are hard to beat, until 2007 to take barefooting seriously, and only then because one of her patients flat-out defied her. He was so frustrated by his chronic plantar fasciitis, he wanted to try blasting it away by running in thin-soled, slipperlike shoes. Dr. Davis told him he was nuts. He did it anyway.

"To her surprise," as *BioMechanics* magazine would later report, "the plantar fasciitis symptoms abated and the patient was able to run short distances in the shoes."

"This is how we often learn things, when patients don't listen to us," Dr. Davis graciously responded. "I think perhaps the widespread plantar fasciitis in this country is partly due to the fact that we really don't allow the muscles in our feet to do what they are designed to do." She was so impressed by her rebellious patient's recovery that she even began adding barefoot walks to her own workouts.

Nike doesn't earn $17 billion a year by letting the Barefoot Teds of the world set the trends. Soon after the two Nike reps returned from Stanford with news that the barefoot uprising had even spread to elite college track, Nike set to work to see if it could make a buck from the problem it had created.

Blaming the running injury epidemic on big, bad Nike seems too easy—but that's okay, because there's a lot to throw at them. The company was founded by Phil Knight, a University of Oregon runner who could sell anything, and Bill Bowerman, the University of Oregon coach who thought he knew everything. Before these two men got together, the modern running shoe didn't exist. Neither did most modern running injuries, according to Arthur Lydiard, one of the sport's greatest thinkers.

For a guy who told so many people how to run, Bowerman didn't do much of it himself. He only started to jog a little at age fifty, after spending time in New Zealand with Arthur Lydiard, the father of fitness running and the most influential distance-running coach of all time. Lydiard had begun the Auckland Joggers Club back in the late '50s to help rehab heart-attack victims. It was wildly controversial at the time; physicians were certain that Lydiard was mobilizing a mass suicide. But once the formerly ill men realized how great they felt after a few weeks of running, they began inviting their wives, kids, and parents to come along for the two-hour trail rambles.

By the time Bill Bowerman paid his first visit in 1962, Lydiard's Sunday morning group run was the biggest party in Auckland. Bowerman tried to join them, but was in such lousy shape that he had to be helped along by a seventy-three-year-old man who'd survived three coronaries. "God, the only thing that kept me alive was the hope that I would die," Bowerman said afterward.

But he came home a convert, and soon penned a best-selling book whose one-word title introduced a new word and obsession to the American public: *Jogging*. Between writing and coaching, Bowerman was busy ruining his nervous system and his wife's waffle iron by tinkering in the basement with molten rubber to invent a new kind of footwear. His experiments left Bowerman with a debilitating nerve condition, but also the most cushioned running shoe ever created. In a stroke of dark irony, Bowerman named it the Cortez—after the conquistador who plundered the New World for gold and unleashed a horrific smallpox epidemic.

Bowerman's deftest move was advocating a new style of running that was only possible in his new style of shoe. The Cortez allowed people to run in a way no human safely could before: by landing on their bony heels. Before the invention of a cushioned shoe, runners through the ages had identical form: Jesse Owens, Roger Bannister, Frank Shorter, and even Emil Zatopek all ran with backs straight, knees bent, feet scratching back under their hips. They had no choice: the only shock absorption came from the compression of their legs and their thick pad of midfoot fat. Fred Wilt verified as much in 1959 in his classic track text, *How They Train*, which detailed the techniques of more than eighty of the world's top runners. "The forward foot moves toward the track in a downward, backward, 'stroking' motion (not punching or pounding) and the outer edge of the ball of the foot makes first contact with the track," Wilt writes. "Running progression results from these forces pushing behind the center of gravity of the body. . . ."

In fact, when the biomedical designer Van Phillips created a state-of-the-art prosthetic for amputee runners in 1984, he didn't even bother equipping it with a heel. As a runner who lost his left leg below the knee in a water-skiing accident, Phillips understood that the heel was needed only for standing, not motion. Phillips's C-shaped "Cheetah foot" mimics the performance of an organic leg so effectively, it allowed the South African double amputee Oscar Pistorius to compete with the world's greatest sprinters.

But Bowerman had an idea: maybe you could grab a little extra distance if you stepped *ahead* of your center of gravity. Stick a chunk of rubber under the heel, he mused, and you could straighten your leg, land on your heel, and lengthen your stride. In *Jogging*, he compared the styles: with the time-tested "flat foot" strike, he acknowledged, "the wide surface area pillows the footstrike and is easy on the rest of the body." Nevertheless, he still believed a "heel-to-toe" stride would be "the least tiring over long distances." *If* you've got the shoe for it.

Bowerman's marketing was brilliant. "The same man created a market for a product and then created the product itself," as one Oregon financial columnist observed. "It's genius, the kind of stuff they study in business schools." Bowerman's partner, the runner-turned-entrepreneur Phil Knight, set up a manufacturing deal in Japan and was soon selling shoes faster than they could come off the assembly line. "With the Cortez's cushioning, we were in a monopoly position probably into the Olympic year, 1972," Knight would gloat. By the time other companies geared up to copy the new shoe, the Swoosh was a world power.

Delighted with the reaction to his amateur designs, Bowerman let his creativity take off. He contemplated a waterproof shoe made of fish skin, but let that one die on the drawing board. He did come out with the LD-1000 Trainer, a shoe with a sole so wide it was like running on pie plates. Bowerman figured it would kill pronation in its tracks, overlooking the fact that unless the runner's foot was perfectly straight, the flared heel would wrench his leg. "Instead of stabilizing, it accelerated pronation and hurt both feet and ankles," former Oregon runner Kenny Moore reported in his biography of Bowerman. The shoe that was supposed to give you a perfect stride, in other words, only worked if you already had one. When Bowerman realized he was causing injuries instead of preventing them, he had to backtrack and narrow the heel in later versions.

Back in New Zealand, meanwhile, an appalled Arthur Lydiard was watching the flashy exports flooding out of Oregon and wondering what in the world his friend was up to. Compared with Bowerman, Lydiard was by far the superior track mind; he'd coached many more Olympic champions and world-record holders, and he'd created a training program that remains the gold standard. Lydiard liked Bill Bowerman and respected him as a coach, but good God! What was this stuff he was selling?

Lydiard knew all this pronation stuff was just marketing gibberish. "If you told the average person of any age to take off his or her shoes and run down the hallway, you would almost always discover the foot action contains no hint of pronation or supination," Lydiard complained. "Those sideways flexings of the ankles begin only when people lace themselves into these running shoes because the construction of many of the shoes immediately alters the natural movement of the feet.

"We ran in canvas shoes," Lydiard went on. "We didn't get plantar fascia, we didn't pronate or supinate, we might have lost a bit of skin from the rough canvas when we were running marathons, but, generally speaking, we didn't have foot problems. Paying several hundred dollars for the latest in high-tech running shoes is no guarantee you'll avoid any of these injuries and can even guarantee that you will suffer from them in one form or another."

Eventually, even Bowerman was stricken by doubt. As Nike steamrolled along, churning out a bewildering variety of shoes and changing models every year for no reason besides having something else to sell, Bowerman felt his original mission of making an honest shoe had been eroded by a new ideology, which he summed up in two words: "Make money." Nike, he griped in a letter to a colleague, was "distributing a lot of crap." Even to one of Nike's founding partners, it seemed, the words of the social critic Eric Hoffer were ringing true: "Every great cause begins as a movement, becomes a business, and turns into a racket."

Bowerman had died by the time the barefoot uprising was taking hold in 2002, so Nike went back to Bowerman's old mentor to see if this shoeless stuff really had merit. "Of course!" Arthur Lydiard reportedly snorted. "You support an area, it gets weaker. Use it extensively, it gets stronger. . . . Run barefoot and you don't have all those troubles.

"Shoes that let your foot function like you're barefoot—they're the shoes for me," Lydiard concluded.

Nike followed up that blast with its own hard data. Jeff Pisciotta, the senior researcher at Nike Sports Research Lab, assembled twenty runners on a grassy field and filmed them running barefoot. When he zoomed in, he was startled by what he found: instead of each foot clomping down as it would in a shoe, it behaved like an animal with a mind of its own—stretching, grasping, seeking the ground with splayed toes, gliding in for a landing like a lake-bound swan.

"It's beautiful to watch," a still spellbound Pisciotta later told me. "That made us start thinking that when you put a shoe on, it starts to take over some of the control." He immediately deployed his team to gather film of every existing barefoot culture they could find. "We found pockets of people all over the globe who are still running barefoot, and what you find is that during propulsion and landing, they have far more range of motion in the foot and engage more of the toe. Their feet flex, spread, splay, and grip the surface, meaning you have less pronation and more distribution of pressure."

Faced with the almost inescapable conclusion that it had been selling lemons, Nike shifted into make-lemonade mode. Jeff Pisciotta became head of a top-secret and seemingly impossible project: finding a way to make a buck off a naked foot.

It took two years of work before Pisciotta was ready to unveil his masterpiece. It was presented to the world in TV ads that showed so many barefoot athletes—Kenyan marathoners padding along a dirt trail, swimmers curling their toes around a starting block, gymnasts and Brazilian capoeira dancers and rock climbers and wrestlers and karate masters and beach soccer players—that after a while, it was hard to remember who *does* wear shoes, or why.

Flashing over the images were motivational messages: "Your feet are your foundation. Wake them up! Make them strong! Connect with the ground. . . . Natural technology allows natural motion. . . . Power to your feet." Across the sole of a bare foot is scrawled "Performance Starts Here." Then comes the grand finale: as "Tiptoe Through the Tulips" crescendos in the background, we cut back to those Kenyans, whose bare feet are now sporting some kind of thin little shoe. It's the new Nike Free, a swooshed slipper even thinner than the old Cortez.

And its slogan?

"Run Barefoot."

CHAPTER 26

Baby, this town rips the bones from your back;
It's a death trap, it's a suicide rap . . .

—Bruce Springsteen, *"Born to Run"*

CABALLO BLANCO'S face was pink with pride, so I tried to think of something nice to say.

We'd just arrived in Batopilas, an ancient mining town tucked eight thousand feet below the lip of the canyon. It was founded four hundred years ago when Spanish explorers discovered silver ore in the stony river, and it hasn't changed much since then. It's still a tiny strip of houses hugging the riverbank, a place where burros are as common as cars and the first telephone was installed when the rest of the world was programming iPods.

Getting down there took a cast-iron stomach and supreme faith in your fellow man, the man in question being the one driving the bus. The only way into Batopilas is a dirt road that corkscrews along the sheer face of a cliff, dropping seven thousand feet in less than ten miles. As the bus strained around hairpin turns, we hung on tight and looked far below at the wrecks of cars whose drivers had miscalculated by a few inches. Two years later, Caballo would make his own contribution to the steel cemetery when the pickup truck he was driving caught the lip of the cliff and tumbled over. Caballo managed to dive out just in time and watched as the truck exploded far below. Later, chunks of the scorched carcass were scavenged as good-luck charms.

After the bus pulled over on the edge of town, we climbed down stiffly, our faces as war-painted with dust and sweat salt as Caballo's had been the first the time I met him. "There she is!" Caballo hollered. "That's my place."

We looked around, but the only thing in sight was the ancient ruin of an old mission across the river. Its roof was gone and its red-stone walls were collapsing into the ruddy canyon they'd been carved from, looking like a sand castle dissolving back into sand. It was perfect; Caballo had found the ideal home for a living ghost. I could only imagine how freaky it must be to pass here at night and see his monstrous shadow dancing around behind his campfire as he wandered the ruins like Quasimodo.

"Wow, that's really something, uh . . . else," I said.

"No, man," he said. "Over here." He pointed behind us, toward a faint goat trail disappearing into the cactus. Caballo began to climb, and we fell in behind him, grabbing at brush for balance as we slipped and scrabbled up the stony path.

"Damn, Caballo," Luis said. "This is the only driveway in the world that needs trail markers and an aid station at mile two."

After a hundred yards or so, we came through a thicket of wild lime trees and found a small, clay-walled hut. Caballo had built it by hauling up rocks from the river, making the round-trip over that treacherous path hundreds of times with river-slick stones in his hands. As a home, it suited Caballo even better than the ruined mission; here in his handmade fortress of solitude, he could see everything in the river valley and remain unseen.

We wandered inside, and saw Caballo had a small camp bed, a pile of trashed sports sandals, and three or four books about Crazy Horse and other Native Americans on a shelf next to a kerosene lamp. That was it; no electricity, no running water, no toilet. Out back, Caballo had cut away the cactus and smoothed a little place to kick back after a run, smoke something relaxing, and gaze off at the prehistoric wilderness. Whatever Barefoot Ted's heavy Heidegger word was, no one was ever more an expression of their place than Caballo was of his hut.

Caballo was anxious to get us fed and off his hands so he could catch up on sleep. The next few days were going to take everything we had, and none of us had gotten much rest since El Paso. He led us

back down his hidden driveway and up the road to a tiny shop operating from the front window of a house; you poked your head in and
if shopkeeper Mario had what you wanted, you got it. Upstairs,
Mario rented us a few small rooms with a cold-water shower at the
end of the hall.

Caballo wanted us to dump our bags and head off immediately for
food, but Barefoot Ted insisted on stripping down and padding off to
the shower to sluice away the road grime. He came out screaming.

"Jesus! The shower's got loose wires. I just got the shit shocked
out of me!"

Eric looked at me. "You think Caballo did it?"

"Justifiable homicide," I said. "No jury would convict." The Barefoot Ted–Caballo Blanco storm front hadn't improved a bit since
we'd left Creel. During one rest stop, Caballo climbed down from
the roof and squeezed his way into the back of the bus to escape.
"That guy doesn't know what silence is," Caballo fumed. "He's from
L.A., man; he thinks you've got to fill every space with noise."

After we'd gotten settled at Mario's, Caballo brought us to
another of his Mamás. We didn't even have to order; as soon as we
arrived, Doña Mila began pulling out whatever she had in the fridge.
Soon, platters were being handed around of guacamole, frijoles,
sliced cactus and tomatoes doused in tangy vinegar, Spanish rice, and
a fragrant beef stew thickened with chicken liver.

"Pack it in," Caballo had said. "You're going to need it tomorrow." He was taking us on a little warm-up hike, Caballo said. Just a
jaunt up a nearby mountain to give us a taste of the terrain we'd be
tackling on the trek to the racecourse. He kept saying it was no big
deal, but then he'd warn us we'd better pound down the food and get
right to bed. I became even more apprehensive after a white-haired
old American ambled in and joined us.

"How's the giddyup, Hoss?" he greeted Caballo. His name was
Bob Francis. He had first wandered down to Batopilas in the '6os,
and part of him had never left. Even though he had kids and grandkids back in San Diego, Bob still spent most of the year wandering
the canyons around Batopilas, sometimes guiding trekkers, sometimes just visiting Patricio Luna, a Tarahumara friend who was
Manuel Luna's uncle. They met thirty years before, when Bob got

lost in the canyons. Patricio found him, fed him, and brought him back to his family's cave for the night.

Because of his long friendship with Patricio, Bob is one of the only Americans to have ever attended a Tarahumara *tesgüinada*—the marathon drinking party that precedes and occasionally prevents the ball races. Even Caballo hasn't reached that level of trust with the Tarahumara, and after listening to Bob's stories, he wasn't sure he wanted to.

"All of a sudden, Tarahumara I've been friends with for years, guys I knew as shy, gentle amigos, are in my face, butting against me with their chests, spitting insults at me, ready to fight," Bob said. "Meanwhile, their wives are in the bushes with other men, and their grown-up daughters are wrestling naked. They keep the kids away from these deals; you can imagine why."

Anything goes at a *tesgüinada*, Bob explained, because everything is blamed on the peyote, moonshine tequila, and *tesgüino*, the potent corn beer. As wild as these parties get, they actually serve a noble and sober purpose: they act as a pressure valve to vent explosive emotions. Just like the rest of us, the Tarahumara have secret desires and grievances, but in a society where everyone relies on one another and there are no police to get between them, there has to be a way to satisfy lusts and grudges. What better than a booze-fest? Everyone gets ripped, goes wild, and then, chastened by bruises and hangovers, they dust themselves off and get on with their lives.

"I could have been married or murdered twenty times before the night was over," Bob said. "But I was smart enough to put down the gourd and get myself out of there before the real shenanigans started." If one outsider knew the Barrancas as well as Caballo, it was Bob, which was why, even though he was liquored up and in a bit of a ranting mood, I paid careful attention when he got into it with Ted.

"Those fucking things are going to be dead tomorrow," Bob said, pointing at the FiveFingers on Ted's feet.

"I'm not going to wear them," Ted said.

"Now you're talking sense," Bob said.

"I'm going barefoot," Ted said.

Bob turned to Caballo. "He messing with us, Hoss?"

Caballo just smiled.

———

Early the next morning, Caballo came for us as dawn was breaking over the canyon. "That's where we're headed tomorrow," Caballo said, pointing through the window of my room toward a mountain rearing in the distance. Between us and the mountain was a sea of rolling foothills so thickly overgrown that it was hard to see how a trail could punch through. "We'll run one of those little guys this morning."

"How much water do we need?" Scott asked.

"I only carry this," Caballo said, waving a sixteen-ounce plastic bottle. "There's a freshwater spring up top to refill."

"Food?"

"Nah," Caballo shrugged as he and Scott left to check on the others. "We'll be back by lunch."

"I'm bringing the big boy," Eric said to me, gurgling springwater into the bladder on his ninety-six-ounce hydration backpack. "I think you should, too."

"Really? Caballo says we're only going about ten miles."

"Can't hurt to carry the max when you go off-road," Eric said. "Even if you don't need it, it's training for when you do. And you never know—something happens, you could be out there longer than you think."

I put down my handheld bottle and reached for my hydration pack. "Bring iodine pills in case you need to purify water. And shove in some gels, too," Eric added. "On race day, you're going to need two hundred calories an hour. The trick is learning how to take in a little at a time, so you've got a steady drip of fuel without overwhelming your stomach. This'll be good practice."

We walked through Batopilas, past shopkeepers hand-sprinkling water on the stones to keep the dust down. Schoolkids in spotless white shirts, their black hair sleek with water, interrupted their chatter to politely wish us "*Buenos días.*"

"Gonna be a hot one," Caballo said, as we ducked into a storefront with no sign out front. "*¿Hay teléfono?*" he asked the woman who greeted us. Are the phones working?

"*Todavía no,*" she said, shaking her head in resignation. Not yet. Clarita had the only two public phones in all Batopilas, but service had been knocked out for the past three days, leaving shortwave radio the only form of communication. For the first time, it hit me how cut off we were; we had no way of knowing what was going on in the outside world, or letting the outside world know what was happening to us. We were putting a hell of a lot of trust in Caballo, and once again, I had to wonder why; as knowledgeable as Caballo was, it still seemed crazy to put our lives in the hands of a guy who didn't seem too concerned about his own.

But for the moment, the grumble of my stomach and the aroma of Clarita's breakfast managed to push those thoughts aside. Clarita served up big plates of huevos rancheros, the fried eggs smothered in homemade salsa and freshly chopped cilantro and sitting atop thick, hand-patted tortillas. The food was too delicious to wolf down, so we lingered, refilling our coffee a few times before getting up to go. Eric and I followed Scott's example and tucked an extra tortilla in our pockets for later.

Only after we finished did I realize that the Party Kids hadn't shown up. I checked my watch; it was already pushing 10 a.m.

"We're leaving them," Caballo said.

"I'll run back for them," Luis offered.

"No," Caballo said. "They could still be in bed. We've got to hit it if we're going to dodge the afternoon heat."

Maybe it was for the best; they could use a day to rehydrate and power up for the hike tomorrow. "No matter what, don't let them try to follow us," Caballo told Luis's father, who was staying behind. "They get lost out there, we'll never see them again. That's no joke."

Eric and I cinched tight our hydration packs, and I pulled a bandanna over my head. It was already steamy. Caballo slid through a gap in the retaining wall and began picking his way over the boulders to the edge of the river. Barefoot Ted pushed ahead to join him, showing off how nimbly he could hop from rock to rock in his bare feet. If Caballo was impressed, he wasn't showing it.

"YOU GUYS! HOLD UP!" Jenn and Billy were sprinting down the street behind us. Billy had his shirt in his hand, and Jenn's shoelaces were untied.

"You sure you want to come?" Scott asked when they panted up. "You haven't even eaten anything."

Jenn tore a PowerBar in two and gave half to Billy. They were each carrying a skinny water bottle that couldn't have held more than six swallows. "We're good," Billy said.

We followed the stony riverbank for a mile, then turned into a dry gully. Without a word, we all spontaneously broke into a trot. The gully was wide and sandy, leaving plenty of room for Scott and Barefoot Ted to flank Caballo and run three abreast.

"Check out their feet," said Eric. Even though Scott was in the Brooks trail shoe he'd helped design and Caballo was in sandals, they both skimmed their feet over the ground just the way Ted did in his bare feet, their foot strikes in perfect sync. It was like watching a team of Lipizzaner stallions circle the show ring.

After about a mile, Caballo veered onto a steep, rocky washout that climbed up into the mountain. Eric and I eased back to a walk, obeying the ultrarunner's creed: "If you can't see the top, walk." When you're running fifty miles, there's no dividend in bashing up the hills and then being winded on the way down; you only lose a few seconds if you walk, and then you can make them back up by flying downhill. Eric believes that's one reason ultrarunners don't get hurt and never seem to burn out: "They know how to train, not strain."

As we walked, we caught up with Barefoot Ted. He'd had to slow down to pick his way over the jagged, fist-sized stones. I squinted up at the trail ahead: we had at least another mile of crumbly rock to climb before the trail leveled and, hopefully, smoothed.

"Ted, where are your FiveFingers?" I asked.

"Don't need 'em," he said. "I made a deal with Caballo that if I handled this hike, he wouldn't get mad anymore if I went barefoot."

"He rigged the bet," I said. "This is like running up the side of a gravel pit."

"Humans didn't invent rough surfaces, Oso," Ted said. "We invented the *smooth* ones. Your foot is perfectly happy molding itself around rocks. All you've got to do is relax and let your foot flex. It's like a foot massage. Oh, hey!" he called after us as Eric and I pulled ahead. "Here's a great tip. Next time your feet are sore, walk on slippery stones in a cold creek. Unbelievable!"

Eric and I left Ted singing to himself as he hopped and trotted along. The glare off the stones was blinding and heat kept rising, making it feel as if we were climbing straight into the sun. In a way, we were; after two miles, I checked the altimeter on my watch and saw we'd climbed over a thousand feet. Soon, though, the trail plateaued and softened from stones to footworn dirt.

The others were a few hundred yards ahead, so Eric and I started to run to close the gap. Before we caught them, Barefoot Ted came whisking by. "Time for a drink," he said, waving his empty water bottle. "I'll wait for you guys at the spring."

The trail veered abruptly upward again, jagging back and forth in lightning-bolt switchbacks. Fifteen hundred feet . . . two thousand . . . We bent into the slope, feeling as though we only gained a few inches every step. After three hours and six miles of hard climbing, we hadn't hit the spring; we hadn't seen shade since we left the riverbank.

"See?" Eric said, waving the nozzle of his hydration pack. "Those guys have got to be parched."

"And starving," I added, ripping open a raw-food granola bar.

At thirty-five hundred feet, we found Caballo and the rest of the crew waiting in a hollow under a juniper tree. "Anyone need iodine pills?" I asked.

"Don't think so," Luis said. "Take a look."

Under the tree was a natural stone basin carved out by centuries of cool, trickling spring water. Except there was no water.

"We're in a drought," Caballo said. "I forgot about that."

But there was a chance another spring might be flowing a few hundred feet higher up the mountain. Caballo volunteered to run up and check. Jenn, Billy, and Luis were too thirsty to wait and went with him. Ted gave his bottle to Luis to fill up for him and sat to wait in the shade with us. I gave him a few sips from my pack, while Scott shared some pita and hummus.

"You don't use goos?" Eric asked.

"I like real food," Scott said. "It's just as portable and you get real calories, not just a fast burn." As a corporate-sponsored elite athlete, Scott had the worldwide buffet of nutrition at his fingertips, but after experimenting with the entire spectrum—everything from deer meat to Happy Meals to organic raw-food bars—he'd ended up with a diet a lot like the Tarahumara.

"Growing up in Minnesota, I used to be a total junk eater," he said. "Lunch used to be two McChickens and large fries." When he was a

Nordic skier and cross-country runner in high school, his coaches were always telling him he needed plenty of lean meat to rebuild his muscles after a tough workout, yet the more Scott researched traditional endurance athletes, the more vegetarians he found.

Like the Marathon Monks in Japan he'd just been reading about; they ran an ultramarathon *every day for seven years*, covering some twenty-five thousand miles on nothing but miso soup, tofu, and vegetables. And what about Percy Cerutty, the mad Australian genius who coached some of the greatest milers of all time? Cerutty believed food shouldn't even be cooked, let alone slaughtered; he put his athletes through triple sessions on a diet of raw oats, fruit, nuts, and cheese. Even Cliff Young, the sixty-three-year-old farmer who stunned Australia in 1983 by beating the best ultrarunners in the country in a 507-mile race from Sydney to Melbourne, did it all on beans, beer, and oatmeal ("I used to feed the calves by hand and they thought I was their mother," Young said. "I couldn't sleep too good those nights when I knew they would get slaughtered." He switched to grains and potatoes, and slept a whole lot better. Ran pretty good, too).

Scott wasn't sure why meatless diets worked for history's great runners, but he figured he'd trust the results first and figure out the science later. From that point on, no animal products would pass his lips—no eggs, no cheese, not even ice cream—and not much sugar or white flour, either. He stopped carrying Snickers and PowerBars during his long runs; instead, he loaded a fanny pack with rice burritos, pita stuffed with hummus and Kalamata olives, and home-baked bread smeared with adzuki beans and quinoa spread. When he sprained his ankle, he eschewed ibuprofen and relied instead on wolfsbane and whomping portions of garlic and ginger.

"Sure, I had my doubts," Scott said. "Everyone told me I'd get weaker, I wouldn't recover between workouts, I'd get stress fractures and anemia. But I found that I actually feel better, because I'm eating foods with more high-quality nutrients. And after I won Western States, I never looked back."

By basing his diet on fruits, vegetables, and whole grains, Scott is deriving maximum nutrition from the lowest possible number of calories, so his body isn't forced to carry or process any useless bulk.

And because carbohydrates clear the stomach faster than protein, it's easier to jam a lot of workout time into his day, since he doesn't have to sit around waiting for a meatball sub to settle. Vegetables, grains, and legumes contain all the amino acids necessary to build muscle from scratch. Like a Tarahumara runner, he's ready to go any distance, any time.

Unless, of course, he runs out of water.

"Not good, guys," Luis called as he trotted back down. "That one's dry, too." He was getting worried; he'd just tried to piss, and after four hours of sweating in 95-degree heat, it came out looking like convenience-store coffee. "I think we should run for it."

Scott and Caballo agreed. "If we open it up, we'll be down in an hour," Caballo said. "Oso," he asked me. "You okay?"

"Yeah, I'm fine," I said. "And we're still packing water."

"All right, let's do it," Barefoot Ted said.

We began running single file down the trail, Caballo and Scott up front. Barefoot Ted was amazing; he was speeding down the mountain hard on the heels of Luis and Scott, two of the best downhillers in the sport. With all that talent pushing up against each other, the pace was getting ferocious. "YEEEEEAAAHHH, BABY!" Jenn and Billy were hollering.

"Let's hang back," Eric said. "We're going to crash if we try to hang with them."

We settled into an easy lope, falling far behind as the others slashed back and forth down the switchbacks. Running downhill can trash your quads, not to mention snap your ankle, so the trick is to pretend you're running uphill: keep your feet spinning under your body like you're a lumberjack rolling a log, and control your speed by leaning back and shortening your stride.

By midafternoon, the heat had bottled up in the canyon until it was over 100 degrees. We'd lost sight of the others, so Eric and I took our time, running easily and sipping often from our quickly emptying hydration packs, feeling our way carefully down the confusing web of trails, unaware that an hour before, Jenn and Billy had vanished.

"Goat's blood is *good*," Billy kept insisting. "We can drink the blood, then eat the meat. Goat meat is *good*." He'd read a book by a guy whose trick for cheating death in the Arizona desert was to stone a wild horse to death and suck the blood from its throat. *Geronimo used to do that, too,* Billy thought. *Wait, it might've been Kit Carson....*

Drink the blood? Jenn, her throat so parched it hurt to talk, just stared at him. *He's losing it,* she thought. *We can barely walk, and Bonehead's talking about killing a goat we can't catch with a knife we don't have. He's in worse shape than I am. He's—*

Suddenly, her stomach clenched so badly she could barely breathe. She got it. Billy didn't sound crazy because of the heat. He sounded crazy because the only sane thing left to talk about was the one thing he wouldn't admit: there was no way out of this.

On a good day, no one in the world could have dropped Jenn and Billy on a measly six-mile trail run, but this was turning out to be a pretty bad day. The heat, their hangovers, and their empty stomachs had caught up with them before they'd made it halfway down the mountain. They lost sight of Caballo on one of the switchbacks, then they hit a fork in the trail. Next thing they knew, they were alone.

Disoriented, Jenn and Billy wandered off the mountain and into a stone maze that webbed in every direction. The rock walls were mirroring the heat so hideously, Jenn suspected she and Billy were just going whichever way looked a little shadier. Jenn felt dizzy, as if her mind were floating free of her body. They hadn't eaten since splitting that PowerBar six hours before, and hadn't had a sip of water since noon. Even if heat stroke didn't wipe them out, Jenn knew, they were still doomed: the 100-plus degree heat would drop, but keep on dropping. Come nightfall, they'd be shivering in the freezing dark in their surf shorts and T-shirts, dying of thirst and exposure in one of the most unreachable corners of Mexico.

What weird corpses they'd make, Jenn thought as they trudged along. Whoever found them would have to wonder how a pair of twenty-two-year-old lifeguards in surf baggies ended up at the bottom of a Mexican canyon, looking like they'd been tossed in from Baja by a rogue wave. Jenn had never been so thirsty in her life; she'd lost twelve pounds during a hundred-mile race before and still didn't feel as desperate as she did now.

"Look!"

"The Luck of the Bonehead!" Jenn marveled. Under a stone

ledge, Billy had spotted a pool of fresh water. They ran toward it, fumbling the tops off their water bottles, then stopped.

The water wasn't water. It was black mud and green scum, buzzing with flies and churned by wild goats and burros. Jenn bent down for a closer look. *Ugh!* The smell was nasty. They knew what one sip could do; come nightfall, they could be too weak with fever and diarrhea to walk, or infected with cholera or giardia or guinea worm disease, which has no cure except slowly pulling the three-foot-long worms out of the abscesses that erupt on your skin and eye sockets.

But they knew what would happen without that sip. Jenn had just read about those two best friends who'd gotten lost in a canyon in New Mexico and became so sun-crazed after a single day without water that one stabbed the other to death. She'd seen photos of hikers who'd been found in Death Valley with their mouths choked with dirt, their last moments alive spent trying to suck moisture from scorching sand. She and Billy could stay away from the puddle and die of thirst, or they could swallow a few gulps and risk dying from something else.

"Let's hold off," Billy said. "If we don't find our way out in one hour, we'll come back."

"Okay. This way?" she said, pointing away from Batopilas and straight toward a wilderness that stretched four hundred miles to the Sea of Cortez.

Billy shrugged. They'd been too rushed and groggy that morning to pay attention to where they were going, not that it would have mattered: everything looked exactly the same. As they walked, Jenn flashed back to the way she'd scoffed at her mother the night before she and Billy had left for El Paso. "Jenn," her mother had implored. "You don't know these people. How do you know they'll take care of you if something goes wrong?"

Dang, Jenn thought. *Mom nailed that one.*

"How long's it been?" she asked Billy.

"About ten minutes."

"I can't wait anymore. Let's go back."

"All right."

When they found the puddle again, Jenn was ready to drop to her knees and start slurping, but Billy held her back. He swirled aside the mold, covered the open mouth of his water bottle with his hand, then filled it from the bottom of the puddle, half hoping the water would be a little less bacteria-ridden beneath the muck. He handed his bottle to Jenn, then filled hers the same way.

"I always knew you'd kill me," Jenn said. They clinked their bottles, said "Cheers," and started to gulp, trying not to gag.

They drank their bottles dry, refilled them, and started walking west again into the wilderness. Before they'd gotten far, they noticed deep shadows were stretching farther across the canyon.

"We've got to get more water," Billy said. He hated the idea of backtracking, but their only chance of surviving through the night was getting to the puddle and hunkering down till dawn. Maybe if they chugged three bottles full of water, they'd be hydrated enough to climb up the mountain for a last look around before dark.

They turned and, once again, trudged back into the maze.

"Billy," Jenn said. "We're really in trouble."

Billy didn't answer. His head was killing him, and he couldn't shake a line from "Howl" that kept beating in time to the throbbing in his skull:

> . . . *who disappeared into the volcanoes of Mexico leaving behind nothing but the shadow of dungarees and the lava and ash of poetry. . . .*

Disappeared in Mexico, Billy thought. *Leaving nothing behind.*

"*Billy*," Jenn repeated. They'd put each other through some bad times in the past, she and the Bonehead, but they'd found a way to stop breaking each other's hearts and become best friends. She'd gotten Billy into this, and she felt worse for what was about to happen to him than what would happen to her.

"This is for real, Billy," Jenn said. Tears began trickling down her face. "We're going to die out here. We're going to die *today*."

"SHUT UP!" Billy screamed, so rattled by the sight of Jenn's tears that he erupted in a total non-Bonehead frenzy. "JUST SHUT UP!"

The outburst stunned both of them into silence. And in that silence, they heard a sound: rocks clattering somewhere behind them.

"HEY!" Jenn and Billy shouted together. "HEY! HEY! HEY!"

They began running before realizing that they didn't know what they were running toward. Caballo had warned them that if they faced one danger out there greater than being lost, it was being found.

Jenn and Billy froze, trying to peer into the shadows below the canyon's crest. Could it be the Tarahumara? A Tarahumara hunter would be invisible, Caballo had told them; he'd watch from a distance, and if he didn't like what he saw, he'd disappear back into the forest. What if it was drug cartel enforcers? Whoever it was, they had to risk it.

"HEY!" they shouted. "WHO'S THERE?"

They listened until the last echo of their voices died away. Then a shadow split from the canyon wall, and began moving toward them.

"You hear that?" Eric asked me.

It had taken us two hours to pick our way down the mountain. We'd kept losing the trail, and had to stop to backtrack and search our memories for landmarks before continuing. Wild goats had turned the mountain into a web of faint, crisscrossing trails, and with the sun fading below the canyon lip, it was getting hard to keep track of which direction we were going.

Finally, we spotted a dry creek bed down below that I was pretty sure led to the river. Just in time, too; I'd finished my water half an hour before and was already pasty mouthed. I broke into a jog, but Eric called me back. "Let's make sure," he said. He climbed back up the cliff to check our bearings.

"Looks good," he called. He started to climb down—and that's when he heard voices echoing from somewhere inside the gorges. He called me up, and together we began following the echoes. A few moments later, we found Jenn and Billy. Tears were still streaking Jenn's face. Eric gave them his water, while I handed them the last of my goos.

"You really drank out of that?" I asked, looking at the wild burro dung in the puddle and hoping they'd confused it with another one.

"Yeah," Jenn said. "We were just coming back for more."

I dug out my camera in case an infectious-disease specialist wanted to see exactly what had gotten into their bowels. Foul as it was, though, that puddle had saved their lives: if Jenn and Billy hadn't come back for another drink at precisely that moment, they'd still be walking deeper and deeper into no-man's-land, the canyon walls closing behind them.

"Can you run a little more?" I asked Jenn. "I think we're not that far from the village."

"Okay," Jenn said.

We set off at an easy trot, but as the water and goo revived them, Jenn and Billy set a pace I could barely keep up with. Once again, I was amazed at their ability to bounce back from the dead. Eric led us down the creek bed, then spotted a bend in the gorge he recognized. We doglegged left, and even with the light getting dim, I could see that the dust ahead of us had been tromped by feet. A mile and a half later, we emerged from the gorges to find Scott and Luis waiting anxiously for us on the outskirts of Batopilas.

We got four liters of water from a little grocery store and dumped in a handful of iodine pills. "I don't know if it will work," Eric said, "but maybe you can flush out whatever bacteria you swallowed." Jenn and Billy sat on the curb and began gulping. While they drank, Scott explained that no one had noticed that Jenn and Billy were missing until the rest of the group had gotten off the mountain. By then, everyone was so dangerously dehydrated that turning back to search would have put them all in danger. Caballo grabbed a bottle of water and went back on his own, urging the others to sit tight; the last thing he wanted was for all his gringos to go scattering into the canyons at nightfall.

About half an hour later, Caballo ran back into Batopilas, red-faced and drenched in sweat. He'd missed us in the branching gorges, and when he realized the hopelessness of his one-man search party, he'd returned to town for help. He looked at Eric and me—tired but still on our feet—and then at the two ace young ultrarunners, exhausted and distraught on the curb. I could tell what Caballo was thinking before he said it.

"What's your secret, man?" he asked Eric, nodding toward me. "How'd you fix this guy?"

CHAPTER 27

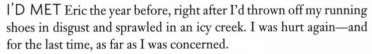

I'D MET Eric the year before, right after I'd thrown off my running shoes in disgust and sprawled in an icy creek. I was hurt again—and for the last time, as far as I was concerned.

As soon as I'd gotten home from the Barrancas, I'd started putting Caballo's lessons to work. I couldn't wait to lace up my shoes every afternoon and try to recapture the sensation I'd had in the hills of Creel, back when running behind Caballo made the miles feel so easy, light, smooth, and fast that I never wanted to stop. As I ran, I screened my mental film footage of Caballo in action, remembering the way he'd floated up the hills of Creel as if he were being abducted by aliens, somehow keeping everything relaxed except those bony elbows, which pumped for power like a Rock'em-Sock'em Robot. For all his gangliness, Caballo on a trail reminded me of Muhammad Ali in the ring: loose as wave-washed seaweed, with just a hint of ferocity ready to explode.

After two months, I'd built up to six miles a day with a ten-miler on the weekend. My form hadn't graduated to *Smooth* yet, but I was keeping the needle wavering pretty steadily between *Easy* and *Light*. I was getting a little anxious, though; no matter how gingerly I tried to take it, my legs were already starting to rebel; that little flamethrower in my right foot was shooting out sparks and the backs of both calves felt twangy, as if my Achilles tendons had been replaced with piano wire. I stocked up on stretching books and put in a dutiful half hour of loosening up before every run, but the long shadow of Dr. Torg's cortisone needle loomed over me.

By late spring, the time had come for a test. Thanks to a forest-ranger friend, I lucked into the perfect opportunity: a three-day, fifty-mile running trip through Idaho's River of No Return, two and a half million acres of the most untouched wilderness in the continental U.S. The setup was perfect: our supplies would be hauled by a mule packer, so all that I and the other four runners had to do was kick up fifteen miles of dirt a day from campsite to campsite.

"I really didn't know anything about the woods till I came to Idaho," Jenni Blake began, as she led us down a thin wisp of a dirt trail winding through the junipers. Watching her flow over the trail with such teenage strength, it was hard to believe that nearly twenty years had passed since her arrival; at thirty-eight, Jenni still has the blonde bangs, winsome blue eyes, and lean, tan limbs of a college frosh on summer break. Oddly, though, she's more of a carefree kid now than she was back then.

"I was bulimic in college and had a terrible self-image, until I found myself out here," Jenni said. She came as a summer volunteer, and was immediately loaded with a lumberjack saw and two weeks of food and pointed toward the backcountry to go clear trails. She nearly buckled under the weight of the backpack, but she kept her doubts to herself and set off, alone, into the woods.

At dawn, she'd pull on sneakers and nothing else, then set off for long runs through the woods, the rising sun warming her naked body. "I'd be out here for weeks at a time by myself," Jenni explained. "No one could see me, so I'd just go and go and go. It was the most fantastic feeling you can imagine." She didn't need a watch or a route; she judged her speed by the tickle of wind on her skin, and kept racing along the pine-needled trails until her legs and lungs begged her to head back to camp.

Jenni has been hard-core ever since, running long miles even when Idaho is blanketed by snow. Maybe she's self-medicating against deep-seated problems, but maybe (to paraphrase Bill Clinton) there was never anything wrong with Jenni that couldn't be fixed by what's right with Jenni.

Yet when I winced my way down the final downhill leg three days later, I could barely walk. I hobbled into the creek and sat there, simmering and wondering what was wrong with me. It had taken me three days to run the same distance as Caballo's racecourse, and I'd ended up with one Achilles tear, maybe two, and a pain in my heel that felt suspiciously like the vampire bite of running injuries: plantar fasciitis.

Once PF sinks its fangs into your heels, you're in danger of being infected for life. Check any running-related message board, and you're guaranteed to find a batch of beseeching threads from PF sufferers begging for a cure. Everyone is quick to suggest the same remedies—night splints, elastic socks, ultrasound, electroshock, cortisone, orthotics—but the messages keep coming because none of them really seems to work.

But how come Caballo could hammer descents longer than the Grand Canyon in crappy old sandals, while I couldn't manage a few easy months of miles without a major breakdown? Wilt Chamberlain, all seven feet one inch and 275 pounds of him, had no problem running a 50-mile ultra when he was sixty years old after his knees had survived a lifetime of basketball. Hell, a Norwegian sailor named Mensen Ernst barely even remembered what dry land felt like when he came ashore back in 1832, but he still managed to run all the way from Paris to Moscow to win a bet, averaging one hundred thirty miles a day for fourteen days, wearing God only knows what kind of clodhoppers on God only knows what kind of roads.

And Mensen was just cracking his knuckles before getting down to serious business: he then ran from Constantinople to Calcutta, trotting ninety miles a day for two straight months. Not that he didn't feel it; Mensen had to rest three whole days before beginning the 5,400-mile jog back home. So how come Mensen never got plantar fasciitis? He couldn't have, because his legs were in excellent shape a year later when dysentery killed him as he tried to run all the way to the source of the Nile.

Everywhere I looked, little pockets of superrunning savants seemed to emerge from the shadows. Just a few miles away from me in Maryland, thirteen-year-old Mackenzie Riford was happily running the JFK 50-miler with her mom ("It was fun!"), while Jack Kirk—a.k.a. "the Dipsea Demon"—was still running the hellacious Dipsea Trail Race at age ninety-six. The race begins with a 671-step cliffside climb, which means a man nearly half as old as America was climbing a fifty-story staircase before running off into the woods. "You don't stop running because you get old," said the Demon. "You get old because you stop running."

So what was I missing? I was in worse shape now than when I'd started; not only couldn't I race with the Tarahumara, I doubted my PF-inflamed feet could even get me to the starting line.

"You're like everyone else," Eric Orton told me. "You don't know what you're doing."

A few weeks after my Idaho debacle, I'd gone to interview Eric for a magazine assignment. As an adventure-sports coach in Jackson Hole, Wyoming, and the former fitness director for the University of Colorado Health Sciences Center, Eric's specialty is tearing endurance sports down to their integral movements and finding transferable skills. He'd study rock climbing to find shoulder techniques for kayakers, and apply Nordic skiing's smooth propulsion to mountain biking. What he's really looking for are basic engineering principles; he's convinced that the next great advance in fitness will come not from training or technology, but technique—the athlete who avoids injury will be the one who leaves the competition behind.

He'd read my article about Caballo and the Tarahumara and was intensely curious to hear more. "What the Tarahumara do is pure body art," he said. "No one else on the planet has made such a virtue out of self-propulsion." Eric had been fascinated with the Tarahumara since an athlete he'd trained for Leadville returned with amazing stories about fantastic Indians flying through the Druidic dusk in sandals and robes. Eric scoured libraries for books on the Tarahumara, but all he found were some anthropological texts from the '50s and an amateur account by a husband-and-wife team who'd traveled through Mexico in their camper. It was a mystifying gap in sports literature; distance running is the world's No. 1 participation sport, but almost nothing had been written about its No. 1 practitioners.

"Everyone thinks they know how to run, but it's really as nuanced as any other activity," Eric told me. "Ask most people and they'll say,

'People just run the way they run.' That's ridiculous. Does everyone just swim the way they swim?" For every other sport, lessons are fundamental; you don't go out and start slashing away with a golf club or sliding down a mountain on skis until someone takes you through the steps and teaches you proper form. If not, inefficiency is guaranteed and injury is inevitable.

"Running is the same way," Eric explained. "Learn it wrong, and you'll never know how good it can feel." He grilled me for details about the race I'd seen at the Tarahumara school. ("The little wooden ball," he mused. "The way they learn to run by kicking it; that can't be an accident.") Then he offered me a deal; he'd get me ready for Caballo's race, and in return, I'd vouch for him with Caballo.

"If this race comes off, we have to be there," Eric urged. "It'll be the greatest ultra of all time."

"I just don't think I'm built for running fifty miles," I said.

"*Everyone* is built for running," he said.

"Every time I up my miles, I break down."

"You won't this time."

"Should I get the orthotics?"

"Forget the orthotics."

I was dubious, but Eric's absolute confidence was winning me over. "I should probably cut weight first to make it easier on my legs."

"Your diet will change all by itself. Wait and see."

"How about yoga? That'll help, yeah?"

"Forget yoga. Every runner I know who does yoga gets hurt."

This was sounding better all the time. "You really think I can do it?"

"Here's the truth," Eric said. "You've got zero margin of error. But you can do it." I'd have to forget everything I knew about running and start over from the beginning.

"Get ready to go back in time," Eric said. "You're going tribal."

A few weeks later, a man with a right leg twisted below the knee limped toward me carrying a rope. He looped the rope around my waist and pulled it taut. "Go!" he shouted.

I bent against the rope, churning my legs as I dragged him forward. He released the rope, and I shot off. "Good," the man said. "Whenever you run, remember that feeling of straining against the rope. It'll keep your feet under your body, your hips driving straight ahead, and your heels out of the picture."

Eric had recommended I begin my tribal makeover by heading down to Virginia to apprentice myself to Ken Mierke, an exercise physiologist and world champion triathlete whose muscular dystrophy forced him to squeeze every possible bit of economy out of his running style. "I'm living proof of God's sense of humor," Ken likes to say. "I was an obese kid with a drop foot whose dad lived for sports. So as an overweight Jerry's Kid, I was way slower than everyone I ever played against. I learned to examine everything and find a better way."

In basketball Ken couldn't drive the lane, so he practiced three-pointers and a deadly hook shot. He couldn't chase a quarterback or shake a safety, but he studied body angles and lines of attack and became a formidable left tackle. He couldn't outsprint a cross-court volley, so in tennis he developed a ferocious serve and service return. "If I couldn't outrun you, I'd outthink you," he says. "I'd find your weakness and make it my strength."

Because of the withered calf muscles in his right leg, when he began to compete in triathalons Ken could only run with a heavy shoe he'd built from a Rollerblade boot and a leaf spring. That put him at a substantial weight disadvantage to the amputee athletes in the physically challenged division, so ramping up his energy efficiency to compensate for his seven-pound shoes could make a huge difference.

Ken got a stack of videos of Kenyan runners and ran through them frame by frame. After hours of viewing, he was struck by a revelation: the greatest marathoners in the world run like kindergartners. "Watch kids at a playground running around. Their feet land right under them, and they push back," Ken said. "Kenyans do the same thing. The way they ran barefoot growing up is astonishingly similar to how they run now—and astonishingly different from how Americans run." Grabbing a pad and pen, Ken went back through the tapes and jotted down all the components of a Kenyan stride. Then he went looking for guinea pigs.

Fortunately, Ken had already begun doing physiological testing

on triathletes as part of his kinesiology studies at Virginia Polytech-
nic, so that gave him access to a lot of athletes to experiment on.
Runners would have been resistant to having someone tinker with
their stride, but Ironmen are up for anything. "Triathletes are very
forward thinking," Ken explains. "It's a young sport, so it's not mired
in tradition. Back in 1988, triathletes started to use aero bars on their
bikes and cyclists mocked them mercilessly—until Greg Lemond
used one and won the Tour de France by eight seconds."

Ken's first test subject was Alan Melvin, a world-class Masters
triathlete in his sixties. First, Ken set a baseline by having Melvin run
four hundred meters full out. Then he clipped a small electric
metronome to his T-shirt.

"What's this for?"

"Set it for one hundred eighty beats a minute, then run to the
beat."

"Why?"

"Kenyans have superquick foot turnover," Ken said. "Quick, light
leg contractions are more economical than big, forceful ones."

"I don't get it," Alan said. "Don't I want a longer stride, not a
shorter one?"

"Let me ask you this," Ken replied. "You ever see one of those
barefoot guys in a 10K race?"

"Yeah. It's like they're running on hot coals."

"You ever *beat* one of those barefoot guys?"

Alan reflected. "Good point."

After practicing for five months, Alan came back for another
round of testing. He ran four one-mile repeats, and every lap of the
track was faster than his previous four hundred-meter best. "This
was someone who'd been running for forty years and was already Top
Ten in his age group," Ken pointed out. "This wasn't the improve-
ment of a beginner. In fact, as a sixty-two-year-old athlete, he should
have been declining."

Ken was working on himself, as well. He'd been such a weak runner that in his best triathlon to date, he'd come off the bike with a
ten-minute lead and still lost. Within a year of creating his new technique in 1997, Ken became unbeatable, winning the world disabled
championship the next two years in a row. Once word got out that
Ken had figured out a way to run that was not only fast but gentle on

the legs, other triathletes began hiring him as their coach. Ken went on to train eleven national champions and built up a roster of more than one hundred athletes.

Convinced that he'd rediscovered an ancient art, Ken named his style Evolution Running. Coincidentally, two other barefoot-style running methods were popping up around the same time. "Chi Running," based on the balance and minimalism of tai chi, began taking off in San Francisco, while Dr. Nicholas Romanov, a Russian exercise physiologist based in Florida, was teaching his POSE Method. The surge in minimalism did not arise through copying or cross-pollination; instead, it seemed to be testament to the urgent need for a response to the running-injury epidemic, and the pure mechanical logic of, as Barefoot Ted would call it, "the bricolage of barefooting"—the elegance of a less-is-more cure.

But a simple system isn't necessarily simple to learn, as I found out when Ken Mierke filmed me in action. My mind was registering easy, light, and smooth, but the video showed I was still bobbing up and down while bending forward like I was leaning into a hurricane. My ease with Caballo's style, Ken explained, had been my mistake.

"When I teach this technique and ask someone how it feels, if they say 'Great!,' I go 'Damn!' That means they didn't change a thing. The change should be awkward. You should go through a period where you're no longer good at doing it wrong and not yet good at doing it right. You're not only adapting your skills, but your tissues; you're activating muscles that have been dormant most of your life."

Eric had a foolproof system for teaching the same style.

"Imagine your kid is running into the street and you have to sprint after her in bare feet," Eric told me when I picked up my training with him after my time with Ken. "You'll automatically lock into perfect form—you'll be up on your forefeet, with your back erect, head steady, arms high, elbows driving, and feet touching down quickly on the forefoot and kicking back toward your butt."

Then, to embed that light, whispery foot strike into my muscle memory, Eric began programming workouts for me with lots of hill repeats. "You can't run uphill powerfully with poor biomechanics," Eric explained. "Just doesn't work. If you try landing on your heel with a straight leg, you'll tip over backward."

Eric also had me get a heart-rate monitor so I could correct the second-most common mistake of the running class—pace. Most of us are just as clueless about speed as we are about form. "Nearly all runners do their slow runs too fast, and their fast runs too slow," Ken Mierke says. "So they're just training their bodies to burn sugar, which is the last thing a distance runner wants. You've got enough fat stored to run to California, so the more you train your body to burn fat instead of sugar, the longer your limited sugar tank is going to last."

The way to activate your fat-burning furnace is by staying below your aerobic threshold—your hard-breathing point—during your endurance runs. Respecting that speed limit was a lot easier before the birth of cushioned shoes and paved roads; try blasting up a scree-covered trail in open-toed sandals sometime and you'll quickly lose the temptation to open the throttle. When your feet aren't artificially protected, you're forced to vary your pace and watch your speed: the instant you get recklessly fast and sloppy, the pain shooting up your shins will slow you down.

I was tempted to go the Full Caballo and chuck my running shoes for a pair of sandals, but Eric warned me that I was cruising for a stress fracture if I tried to suddenly go naked after keeping my feet immobilized for forty years. Since the No. 1 priority was getting me ready for fifty backcountry miles, I didn't have time to slowly build up foot strength before starting my serious training. I'd need to start off with some protection, so I experimented with a few low-slung models before settling on a classic I found on eBay: a pair of old-stock Nike Pegasus* from 2000, something of a throwback to the flat-footed feel of the old Cortez.

By week two, Eric was sending me off for two hours at a stretch,

---

*Nike's policy of yanking best-selling shoes from the shelves every ten months has inspired some truly operatic bursts of profanity on running message boards. The Nike Pegasus, for instance, debuted in 1981, achieved its sleek, waffled apotheosis in '83, and then—despite being the most popular running shoe of all time—was suddenly discontinued in '98, only to reappear as a whole new beast in 2000. Why so much surgery? Not to improve the shoe, as a former Nike shoe designer who worked on the original Pegasus told me, but to improve revenue; Nike's aim is to triple sales by enticing runners to buy two, three, five pairs at a time, stockpiling in case they never see their favorites again.

his only advice being to focus on form and keep the pace relaxed enough to occasionally breathe with my mouth shut. (Fifty years earlier, Arthur Lydiard offered an equal but opposite tip for managing heart rate and pace: "Only go as fast as you can while holding a conversation.") By week four, Eric was layering in speedwork: "The faster you can run comfortably," he taught me, "the less energy you'll need. Speed means less time on your feet." Barely eight weeks into his program, I was already running more miles per week—at a much faster pace—than I ever had in my life.

That's when I decided to cheat. Eric had promised that my eating would self-regulate once my mileage began climbing, but I was too doubtful to wait and see. I have a cyclist friend who dumps his water bottles before riding uphill; if twelve ounces slowed him down, it wasn't hard to calculate what thirty pounds of spare tire were doing to me. But if I was going to tinker with my diet a few months before a 50-mile race, I had to be careful to do it Tarahumara-style: I had to get strong while getting lean.

I tracked down Tony Ramirez, a horticulturist in the Mexican border town of Laredo who's been traveling into Tarahumara country for thirty years and now grows Tarahumara heritage corn and grinds his own pinole. "I'm a big fan of pinole. I love it," Tony told me. "It's an incomplete protein, but combined with beans, it's more nutritious than a T-bone steak. They usually mix with it with water and drink it, but I like it dry. It tastes like shredded popcorn.

"Do you know about phenols?" Tony added. "They're natural plant chemicals that combat disease. They basically boost your immune system." When Cornell University researchers did a comparison analysis of wheat, oats, corn, and rice to see which had the highest quantity of phenols, corn was the hands-down winner. And because it's a low-fat, whole-grain food, pinole can slash your risk of diabetes and a host of digestive-system cancers—in fact, of *all* cancers. According to Dr. Robert Weinberg, a professor of cancer research at MIT and discoverer of the first tumor-suppressor gene, one in every seven cancer deaths is caused by excess body fat. The math is stark: cut the fat, and cut your cancer risk.

So the Tarahumara Miracle, when it comes to cancer, isn't such a mystery after all. "Change your lifestyle, and you can reduce your risk of cancer by sixty to seventy percent," Dr. Weinberg has said. Colon, prostate, and breast cancer were almost unknown in Japan, he points out, until the Japanese began eating like Americans; within a few decades, their mortality rate from those three diseases skyrocketed. When the American Cancer Society compared lean and heavy people in 2003, the results were even grimmer than expected: heavier men and women were far more likely to die from at least ten different kinds of cancer.

The first step toward going cancer-free the Tarahumara way, consequently, is simple enough: Eat less. The second step is just as simple on paper, though tougher in practice: Eat better. Along with getting more exercise, says Dr. Weinberg, we need to build our diets around fruit and vegetables instead of red meat and processed carbs. The most compelling evidence comes from watching cancer cells fight for their own survival: when cancerous tumors are removed by surgery, they are *300 percent* more likely to grow back in patients with a "traditional Western diet" than they are in patients who eat lots of fruit and veggies, according to a 2007 report by *The Journal of the American Medical Association*. Why? Because stray cells left behind after surgery seem to be stimulated by animal proteins. Remove those foods from your diet, and those tumors may never appear in the first place. Eat like a poor person, as Coach Joe Vigil likes to say, and you'll only see your doctor on the golf course.

"Anything the Tarahumara eat, you can get very easily," Tony told me. "It's mostly pinto beans, squash, chili peppers, wild greens, pinole, and lots of *chia*. And pinole isn't as hard to get as you think." Nativeseeds.org sells it online, along with heritage seeds in case you want to grow your own corn and whiz up some homemade pinole in a coffee grinder. Protein is no problem; according to a 1979 study in *The American Journal of Clinical Nutrition*, the traditional Tarahumara diet exceeds the United Nations' recommended daily intake by more than 50 percent. As for bone-strengthening calcium, that gets worked into tortillas and pinole with the limestone the Tarahumara women use to soften the corn.

"How about beer?" I asked. "Any benefit to drinking like the Tarahumara?"

"Yes and no," Tony said. "Tarahumara *tesgüino* is very lightly fermented, so it's low in alcohol and high in nutrients." That makes

Tarahumara beer a rich food source—like a whole-grain smoothie—while ours is just sugar water. I could try home-brewing my own corn near-beer, but Tony had a better idea. "Grow some wild geranium," he suggested. "Or buy the extract online." *Geranium niveum* is the Tarahumara wonder drug; according to the *Journal of Agricultural and Food Chemistry*, it's as effective as red wine at neutralizing disease-causing free radicals. As one writer put it, wild geranium is "anti-everything—anti-inflammatory, antiviral, antibacterial, antioxidant."

I stocked up on pinole and *chia*, and even ordered some Tarahumara corn seeds to plant out back: cocopah and mayo yellow chapalote and pinole maiz. But realistically, I knew it was only a matter of time before I got sick of seeds and dried corn and started double-fisting burgers again. Luckily, I spoke to Dr. Ruth Heidrich first.

"Have you ever had salad for breakfast?" she asked me. Dr. Ruth is a six-time Ironman triathlete and, according to *Living Fit* magazine, one of the ten Fittest Women in America. She only became an athlete and a Ph.D. in health education, she told me, after she was diagnosed with breast cancer, twenty-four years ago. Exercise has been shown to cut the risk of breast cancer reoccurrence by up to 50 percent, so even with the sutures still in her chest from her mastectomy, Dr. Ruth began training for her first triathlon. She also started researching the diets of noncancerous cultures and became convinced that she needed to immediately transition from the standard American diet—or SAD, as she calls it—and eat more like the Tarahumara.

"I had a medical gun at my head," Dr. Ruth told me. "I was so scared, I'd have bargained with the devil. So by comparison, giving up meat wasn't that big a deal." She had a simple rule: if it came from plants, she ate it; if it came from animals, she didn't. Dr. Ruth had much more to lose than I did if she got it wrong, but almost immediately, she felt her strength increasing.

Her endurance increased so dramatically that within one year, she'd progressed from 10ks to marathons to the Ironman. "Even my cholesterol dropped from two hundred thirty to one hundred sixty in twenty-one days," she adds. Under her Tarahumara-style eating plan, lunch and dinner were built around fruit, beans, yams, whole grains, and vegetables, and breakfast was often salad.

"You get leafy greens in your body first thing in the morning and you'll lose a lot of weight," she urged me. Because a monster salad is loaded with nutrient-rich carbs and low in fat, I could stuff myself and not feel hungry—or queasy—when it came time to work out. Plus, greens are packed with water, so they're great for rehydrating after a night's sleep. And what better way to down your five vegetables a day than forking them all down at once?

So the next morning, I gave it a stab. I wandered around the kitchen with a mixing bowl, throwing in my daughter's half-eaten apple, some kidney beans of questionable vintage, a bunch of raw spinach, and a ton of broccoli, which I chopped into splinters, hoping to make it more like coleslaw. Dr. Ruth fancies up her salads with blackstrap molasses, but I figured I'd earned the extra fat and sugar, so I went upscale, dousing mine with gourmet poppy-seed dressing.

After two bites, I was a convert. A breakfast salad, I was happy to find, is also a sweet-topping delivery system, just like pancakes and syrup. It's far more refreshing than frozen waffles, and, best of all, I could cram myself till my eyes were green and still shoot out the door for a workout an hour later.

"The Tarahumara aren't great runners," Eric messaged me as we began my second month of those workouts. "They're great athletes, and those two things are very different." Runners are assembly-line workers; they become good at one thing—moving straight ahead at a steady speed—and repeat that motion until overuse fritzes out the machinery. Athletes are Tarzans. Tarzan swims and wrestles and jumps and swings on vines. He's strong and explosive. You never know what Tarzan will do next, which is why he never gets hurt.

"Your body needs to be shocked to become resilient," Eric explained. Follow the same daily routine, and your musculoskeletal system quickly figures out how to adapt and go on autopilot. But surprise it with new challenges—leap over a creek, commando-crawl under a log, sprint till your lungs are bursting—and scores of nerves and ancillary muscles are suddenly electrified into action.

For the Tarahumara, that's just daily life. The Tarahumara step into the unknown every time they leave the cave, because they never know how fast they'll have to sprint after a rabbit, how much firewood they'll have to haul home, how tricky the climbing will be during a winter storm. The first challenge they face as kids is surviving on the edge of a cliff; their first and lifelong way to play is the ball game, which is nothing if not an exercise in uncertainty. You can't drive a wooden ball over a jumble of rocks unless you're ready to lunge, lope, backpedal, sprint, and leap in and out of ditches.

Before the Tarahumara run long, they get strong. And if I wanted to stay healthy, Eric warned me, I'd better do likewise. So instead of stretching before a run, I got right to work. Lunges, pushups, jump squats, crunches; Eric had me powering through a half hour of raw strength drills every other day, with nearly all of them on a fitness ball to sharpen my balance and fire those supportive ancillary muscles. As soon as I finished, it was off to the hills. "There's no sleep-walking your way up a hill," Eric pointed out. Long climbs were an exercise in shock and awe, forcing me to focus on form and shift gears like a Tour de France cyclist. "Hills are speedwork in disguise," Frank Shorter used to say.

That was the year my hometown in Pennsylvania got a heat flash for Christmas. On New Year's Day, I pulled on shorts and a thermal top for a five-mile trail run, just an easy leg-stretcher on a rest day. I rambled through the woods for half an hour, then cut through a field of winter hay and headed for home. The warm sun and the aroma of sun-baked grass were so luxurious, I kept slowing down, dragging out that last half mile as long as I could.

When I got within one hundred yards of my house, I stopped, shucked my thermal shirt, and turned back for one last lap through the hay. I finished that one and started another, tossing my T-shirt aside as well. By lap four, my socks and running shoes were on the pile, my bare feet cushioned by dry grass and warm dirt. By lap six, I was fingering my waistband, but decided to keep the shorts out of consideration for my eighty-two-year-old neighbor. I'd finally recovered that feeling I'd had during my run with Caballo—the easy, light, smooth, fast sensation that I could outrun the sun and still be going by morning.

Like Caballo, the Tarahumara secret had begun working for me before I even understood it. Because I was eating lighter and hadn't been laid up once by injury, I was able to run more; because I was running more, I was sleeping great, feeling relaxed, and watching my resting heart rate drop. My personality had even changed: The grouchiness and temper I'd considered part of my Irish-Italian DNA had ebbed so much that my wife remarked, "Hey, if this comes from ultrarunning, I'll tie your shoes for you." I knew aerobic exercise was a powerful antidepressant, but I hadn't realized it could be so profoundly mood stabilizing and—I hate to use the word—meditative. If you don't have answers to your problems after a four-hour run, you ain't getting them.

I kept waiting for all the old ghosts of the past to come roaring out—the screaming Achilles, the ripped hamstring, the plantar fasciitis. I started carrying my cell phone on the longer runs, convinced that any day now, I'd end up a limping mess by the side of the road. Whenever I felt a twinge, I ran through my diagnostics:

Back straight? Check.

Knees bent and driving forward? Check.

Heels flicking back? . . . There's your problem. Once I made the adjustment, the hot spot always eased and disappeared. By the time Eric bumped me up to five-hour runs in the last month before the race, ghosts and cell phone were forgotten.

For the first time in my life, I was looking forward to superlong runs not with dread, but anticipation. How had Barefoot Ted put it? *Like fish slipping back into water.* Exactly. I felt like I was born to run.

And, according to three maverick scientists, I was.

CHAPTER 28

TWENTY YEARS EARLIER, in a tiny basement lab, a young scientist stared into a corpse and saw his destiny staring back.

At that moment, David Carrier was an undergraduate at the University of Utah. He was puzzling over a rabbit carcass, trying to figure out what the deal was with those bony things right over the butt. The bony things bugged him, because they weren't supposed to be there. David was the star student in Professor Dennis Bramble's evolutionary biology class, and he knew exactly what he was supposed to see whenever he cut into a mammal's abdomen. Those big belly muscles on the diaphragm? They need to anchor down on something strong, so they connect to the lumbar vertebra, just the way you'd lash a sail down to a boom. That's how it is for every mammal from a whale to a wombat—but not, apparently, for this rabbit; instead of grabbing hold of something sturdy, its belly muscles were connected to these flimsy chicken-wing-looking things.

David pushed one with his finger. Cool; it compressed like a Slinky, then sprang back out. But why, in all mammaldom, would a jackrabbit need a spring-loaded belly?

"That made me start thinking about what they do when they run, the way they arch their backs with every galloping stride," Carrier later told me. "When they push off with their hind legs, they extend the back, and as soon as they land on the front legs, the back bends dorsally." Lots of mammals jackknife their bodies the same way, he mused. Even whales and dolphins move their tails up and down, while a shark slashes from side to side. "Think of an inchworming cheetah movement," David says. "Classic example."

Good; this was good. David was getting somewhere. Big cats and little rabbits run the same way, but one has Slinkies stuck to its diaphragm and one doesn't. One is fast, but the other has to be faster, at least for a little while. And why? Simple economics: if mountain lions ran down all the rabbits, you'd have no more rabbits and, eventually, no more mountain lions. But jackrabbits are born with a big problem: unlike other running animals, they don't have reserve artillery. They don't have antlers or horns or hard-kicking hooves, and they don't travel in the protection of herds. For rabbits, it's all or nothing; either they dart their way to safety, or they're cat food.

Okay, David thought, maybe the Slinkies have something to do with speed. So what makes you fast? David began ticking off components. Let's see. You need an aerodynamic body. Awesome reflexes. Power-loaded haunches. High-volume capillaries. Fast-twitch muscle fiber. Small, nimble feet. Rubbery tendons that return elastic energy. Skinny muscles near the paws, beefy muscles near the joints . . .

Damn. It didn't take David long to figure out he was heading toward a dead end. A lot of factors contribute to speed, and jackrabbits share most of them with their hunters. Instead of finding out how they were different, he was finding out how they were alike. So he tried a trick Dr. Bramble had taught him: when you can't answer the question, flip it over. Forget what makes something go fast— what makes it slow down? After all, it didn't just matter how fast a rabbit could go, but how fast it could *keep* going until it found a hole to dive down.

Now that one was easy: other than a lasso around the leg, the quickest way to bring a fast-moving mammal to a halt is by cutting off its wind. No more air equals no more speed; try sprinting while holding your breath sometime and see how far you get. Your muscles needs oxygen to burn calories and convert them into energy, so the better you are at exchanging gases—sucking in oxygen, blowing out carbon dioxide—the longer you can sustain your top speed. That's why Tour de France cyclists keep getting caught with other people's blood in their veins; those illicit transfusions pack in extra red-blood cells, which carry lots of extra oxygen to their muscles.

Wait a second . . . that meant that for a jackrabbit to stay one hop ahead of those snapping jaws, it would need a little more air than the big mammal on its tail. David had a vision of a Victorian flying machine, one of those wacky but plausible contraptions rigged with pistons and steam valves and endless mazes of wheezing levers. Levers! Those Slinkies were beginning to make sense. They had to be levers that turbocharged the rabbit's lungs, pumping them in and out like a fireplace bellows.

David ran the numbers to see if his theory held up and . . . bingo! There it was, as elegant and niftily balanced as an Aesop's fable: Jackrabbits can hit forty-five miles per hour, but due to the extra energy needed to operate the levers (among other things), they can only sustain it for a half mile. Cougars, coyotes, and foxes, on the other hand, can go a lot farther but top out at forty miles per. The Slinkies balance the game, giving the otherwise defenseless jackrabbits exactly forty-five seconds to either live or die. Seek shelter quickly and live long, young Thumper; or get cocky about your speed and be dead in less than a minute.

"You know," he thought, "if you take away the levers, isn't it the same engineering for every other mammal?" Maybe that's why their diaphragms hooked on to the lumbar vertebra—not because the vertebra was sturdy and wouldn't move, but because it was stretchy and would. Because it *flexed*!

"It seemed obvious that when the animal pushed off and extended its back, it wasn't just for propulsion—it was also for respiration," David says. He imagined an antelope racing for its life across a dusty savannah, and behind it, a streaking blur. He focused on the blur, froze it in place, then clicked it forward a frame at a time:

Click—as the cheetah stretches long for a stride, its rib cage is pulled back, sucking air into the lungs and . . .

Click—now the front legs whip back until front and rear paws are touching. The cheetah's spine bends, squeezing the chest cavity and squishing the lungs empty of air and . . .

And there you had it—another Victorian breathing contraption, albeit with a little less turbo power.

David's heart was racing. Air! Our bodies were all about getting air! Flip the equation, as Dr. Bramble had taught him, and you have this: getting air may have determined the way we got our bodies.

God, it was so simple—and so mind-blowing. Because if David was right, he'd just solved the greatest mystery in human evolution. No one had ever figured out why early humans had separated themselves from all creation by taking their knuckles off the ground and standing up. It was to breathe! To open their throats, swell out their chests, and suck in air better than any other creature on the planet.

But that was just the beginning. Because the better you are at breathing, David quickly realized, the better you are at—

"*Running?* You're saying humans evolved to go running?"

Dr. Dennis Bramble listened with interest as David Carrier explained his theory. Then he casually took aim and blew it to smithereens. He tried to be gentle; David was a brilliant student with a truly original mind, but this time, Bramble suspected, he'd fallen victim to the most common mistake in science: the Handy Hammer Syndrome, in which the hammer in your hand makes everything look like a nail.

Dr. Bramble knew a little about David's life outside the classroom, and was aware that on sunny spring afternoons, David loved to bolt from the labs and go trail-running in the Wasatch Mountains, which lap right up to the back of the University of Utah campus. Dr. Bramble was a runner himself, so he understood the attraction, but you had to be careful with stuff like that; a biologist's biggest occupational hazard, second only to falling in love with your research assistants, was falling in love with your hobbies. You become your own test subject; you start seeing the world as a reflection of your own life, and your own life as a reference point for just about every phenomenon in the world.

"David," Dr. Bramble began. "Species evolve according to what they're good at, not what they're bad at. And as runners, humans aren't just bad—we're awful." You didn't even need to get into the biology; you could just look at cars and motorcycles. Four wheels are faster than two, because as soon as you go upright, you lose thrust, stability, and aerodynamics. Now transfer that design to animals. A tiger is ten feet long and shaped like a cruise missile. It's the drag racer of the jungle, while humans have to putter along with their skinny legs, tiny strides, and piss-poor wind resistance.

"Yeah, I get it," David said. Once we came up off our knuckles, everything went to hell. We lost raw speed and upper-body power—

Good kid, Bramble thought. *Learns quick.*

But David wasn't done. So why, David continued, would we give up strength *and* speed at the same time? That left us unable to run, unable to fight, unable to climb and hide in the tree canopy. We'd have been wiped out—*unless* we got something pretty amazing in exchange. Right?

That, Dr. Bramble had to admit, was a damn clever way to put the question. Cheetahs are fast but frail; they have to hunt by day to avoid nocturnal killers like lions and panthers, and they abandon their kills and run for cover when scrappy little thugs like hyenas show up. A gorilla, on the other hand, is strong enough to lift a four-thousand-pound SUV, but with a gorilla's land speed of twenty miles per hour, that same SUV could run it over in first gear. And then we have humans, who are part cheetah, part gorilla—we're slow *and* wimpy.

"So why would we evolve into a *weaker* creature, instead of a stronger one?" David persisted. "This was long before we could make weapons, so what was the genetic advantage?"

Dr. Bramble played the scenario out in his head. He imagined a tribe of primitive hominids, all squat, quick, and powerful, keeping their heads low for safety as they scrambled nimbly through the trees. One day, out pops a slow, skinny, sunken-chested son who's barely bigger than a woman and keeps making a tiger target out of himself by walking around in the open. He's too frail to fight, too slow to run away, too weak to attract a mate who'll bear him children. By all logic, he's marked for extinction—yet somehow, this dweeb becomes the father of all mankind, while his stronger, swifter brothers disappear into oblivion.

That hypothetical account was actually a pretty accurate description of the Neanderthal Riddle. Most people think Neanderthals were our ancestors, but they were actually a parallel species (or subspecies, some say) that competed with *Homo sapiens* for survival. "Competed," actually, is being kind; the Neanderthals had us beat any way you keep score. They were stronger, tougher, and probably smarter: they had burlier muscles, harder-to-break bones, better natural insulation against the cold, and, the fossil record suggests, a bigger brain. Neanderthals were fantastically gifted hunters and skilled weapon-makers, and may very well have acquired language before we did. They had a huge head start in the race for world domination; by the time the first *Homo sapiens* appeared in Europe, Neanderthals had already been cozily established there for nearly two hundred thousand years. If you had to choose between Neanderthals and Early Us in a Last Man Standing contest, you'd go Neanderthal all the way.

So—where are they?

Within ten thousand years of the arrival of *Homo sapiens* in Europe, the Neanderthals vanished. How it happened, no one knows. The only explanation is that some mysterious X Factor gave us—the weaker, dumber, skinnier creatures—a life-or-death edge over the Ice Age All-Stars. It wasn't strength. It wasn't weapons. It wasn't intelligence.

Could it have been running ability? Dr. Bramble wondered. Is David really onto something?

There was only one way to find out: go to the bones.

"At first I was very skeptical of David, for the same reason most morphologists would be," Dr. Bramble later told me. Morphology is basically the science of reverse engineering; it looks at how a body is assembled and tries to figure out how it's supposed to function. Morphologists know what to look for in a fast-moving machine, and in no way did the human body match the specs. All you had to do was look at our butts to figure that out. "In the whole history of vertebrates on Earth—*the whole history*—humans are the only running biped that's tailless," Bramble would later say. Running is just a controlled fall, so how do you steer and keep from smacking down on your face without a weighted rudder, like a kangaroo's tail?

"That's what led me, like others, to dismiss the idea that humans evolved as running animals," Bramble said. "And I would have bought into the story and remained a skeptic, if I hadn't also been trained in paleontology."

Dr. Bramble's secondary expertise in fossils allowed him to compare how the human blueprint had been modified over the millennia and check it against other designs. Right off the bat, he began finding things that didn't fit. "Instead of looking at the conventional list, like most morphologists, and ticking off the things I expected to see, I began focusing on the abnormalities," Bramble said. "In other words, what's there that shouldn't be there?" He began by splitting the animal kingdom into two categories: runners and walkers. Runners include horses and dogs; walkers are pigs and chimps. If humans were designed to walk most of the time and run only in emergencies, our mechanical parts should match up pretty closely to those of other walkers.

Common chimps were the perfect place to start. Not only are they a classic example of the walking animal, but they're also our closest living relative; after more than six million years of separate evolution, we still share 95 percent of our DNA sequence with chimps. But what we don't share, Bramble noted, is an Achilles tendon, which connects the calf to the heel: we've got one, chimps don't. We have very different feet: ours are arched, chimps' are flat. Our toes are short and straight, which helps running, while chimps' are long and splayed, much better for walking. And check out our butts: we've got a hefty gluteus maximus, chimps have virtually none. Dr. Bramble then focused on a little-known tendon behind the head known as the nuchal ligament. Chimps don't have a nuchal ligament. Neither do pigs. Know who does? Dogs. Horses. And humans.

Now this was perplexing. The nuchal ligament is useful only for stabilizing the head when an animal is moving fast; if you're a walker, you don't need one. Big butts are only necessary for running. (See for yourself: clutch your butt and walk around the room sometime. It'll stay soft and fleshy, and only tighten up when you start to run. Your butt's job is to prevent the momentum of your upper body from flipping you onto your face.) Likewise, the Achilles tendon serves no purpose at all in walking, which is why chimps don't have one. Neither did *Australopithecus*, our semi-simian four-million-year-old ancestor; evidence of an Achilles tendon only began to appear two million years later, in *Homo erectus*.

Dr. Bramble then took a closer look at the skulls and got a jolt. *Holy moly!* he thought. *There's something going on here.* The back of the *Australopithecus* skull was smooth, but when he checked *Homo erectus*, he found a shallow groove for a nuchal ligament. A mystifying but unmistakable time line was taking shape: as the human body changed over time, it adopted key features of a running animal.

Weird, Bramble thought. *How come we acquired all this specialized running stuff, and other walkers didn't?* For a walking animal, the Achilles would just be a liability. Moving on two legs is like walking on stilts; you plant your foot, pivot your body weight over the leg, and repeat. The last thing you'd want would be stretchy, wobbly tendons right at your base of support. All an Achilles tendon does is stretch like a rubber band—

A rubber band! Dr. Bramble felt twin surges of pride and embarrassment. Rubber bands . . . There he'd been, thumping his chest about not being like all those other morphologists who "tick off the things they expect to see," when all along, he'd been just as misguided by myopia; he hadn't even thought about the rubber-band factor. When David started talking about running, Dr. Bramble assumed he meant speed. But there are *two* kinds of great runners: sprinters and marathoners. Maybe human running was about going *far*, not fast. That would explain why our feet and legs are so dense with springy tendons—because springy tendons store and return energy, just like the rubber-band propellers on balsa-wood airplanes. The more you twist the rubber band, the farther the plane flies; likewise, the more you can stretch the tendons, the more free energy you get when that leg extends and swings back.

And if I were going to design a long-distance running machine, Dr. Bramble thought, that's exactly what I'd load it with—lots of rubber bands to maximize endurance. Running is really just jumping, springing from one foot to another. Tendons are irrelevant to walking, but great for energy-efficient jumping. So forget speed; maybe we were born to be the world's greatest marathoners.

"And you've got to ask yourself why only one species in the world has the urge to gather by the tens of thousands to run twenty-six miles in the heat for fun," Dr. Bramble mused. "Recreation has its reasons."

Together, Dr. Bramble and David Carrier began putting their World's Greatest Marathoner model to the test. Soon, evidence was turning up all over, even in places they weren't looking. One of their first big discoveries came by accident when David took a horse for a jog. "We wanted to videotape a horse to see how its gait coordinated with its breathing," Dr. Bramble says. "We needed someone to keep the gear from getting tangled, so David ran alongside it." When they played back the tape, something seemed strange, although Bramble couldn't figure out what it was. He had to rewind a few times before it hit him: even though David and the horse were moving at the same speed, David's legs were moving more slowly.

"It was astonishing," Dr. Bramble explains. "Even though the horse has long legs and four of them, David had a longer stride." David was in great shape for a scientist, but as a medium-height, medium-weight, middle-of-the-pack runner, he was perfectly average. That left only one explanation: as bizarre as it may seem, the average human has a longer stride than a horse. The horse looks like it's taking giant lunges forward, but its hooves swing back before touching the ground. The result: even though biomechanically smooth human runners have short strides, they still cover more distance per step than a horse, making them more efficient. With equal amounts of gas in the tank, in other words, a human can theoretically run farther than a horse.

But why settle for theory when you can put it to the test? Every October, a few dozen runners and riders face off in the 50-mile Man Against Horse Race in Prescott, Arizona. In 1999, a local runner named Paul Bonnet passed the lead horses on the steep climb up Mingus Mountain and never saw them again till after he'd crossed the finish line. The following year, Dennis Poolheco began a remarkable streak: he beat every man, woman, and steed for the next six years, until Paul Bonnet wrested the title back in 2006. It would take eight years before a horse finally caught up with those two and won again.

Discoveries like these, however, were just happy little extras for the two Utah scientists as they tunneled closer to their big breakthrough. As David had suspected on the day he peered into a rabbit's carcass and saw the history of life staring back at him, evolution seemed to be all about air; the more highly evolved the species, the better its carburetor. Take reptiles: David put lizards on a treadmill, and found they can't even run and breathe at the same time. The best they can manage is a quick scramble before stopping to pant.

Dr. Bramble, meanwhile, was working a little higher up the evolutionary ladder with big cats. He discovered that when many quadrupeds run, their internal organs slosh back and forth like water in a bathtub. Every time a cheetah's front feet hit the ground, its guts slam forward into the lungs, forcing out air. When it reaches out for the next stride, its innards slide rearward, sucking air back in. Adding that extra punch to their lung power, though, comes at a cost: it limits cheetahs to just one breath per stride.

Actually, Dr. Bramble was surprised to find that *all* running mammals are restricted to the same cycle of take-a-step, take-a-breath. In the entire world, he and David could only find one exception:

You.

"When quadrupeds run, they get stuck in a one-breath-per-locomotion cycle," Dr. Bramble said. "But the human runners we tested *never* went one to one. They could pick from a number of different ratios, and generally preferred two to one." The reason we're free to pant to our heart's content is the same reason you need a shower on a summer day: we're the only mammals that shed most of our heat by sweating. All the pelt-covered creatures in the world cool off primarily by breathing, which locks their entire heat-regulating system to their lungs. But humans, with our millions of sweat glands, are the best air-cooled engine that evolution has ever put on the market.

"That's the benefit of being a naked, sweating animal," David Carrier explains. "As long as we keep sweating, we can keep going." A team of Harvard scientists had once verified exactly that point by sticking a rectal thermometer in a cheetah and getting it to run on a treadmill. Once its temperature hit 105 degrees, the cheetah shut down and refused to run. That's the natural response for all running mammals; when they build up more heat in their bodies than they can puff out their mouths, they have to stop or die.

Fantastic! Springy legs, twiggy torsos, sweat glands, hairless skin, vertical bodies that retain less sun heat—no wonder we're the world's greatest marathoners. But so what? Natural selection is all about two things—eating and not getting eaten—and being able to run twenty miles ain't worth a damn if the deer disappears in the first twenty seconds and a tiger can catch you in ten. What good is endurance on a battlefield built on speed?

That's the question Dr. Bramble was mulling in the early '90s when he was on sabbatical and met Dr. Dan Lieberman during a visit to Harvard. At the time, Lieberman was working on the other end of the animal Olympics; he had a pig on a treadmill and was trying to figure out why it was such a lousy runner.

"Take a look at its head," Bramble pointed out. "It wobbles all over the place. Pigs don't have a nuchal ligament."

Lieberman's ears perked up. As an evolutionary anthropologist, he knew that nothing on our bodies has changed as much as the shape of our skulls, or says more about who we are. Even your break-fast burrito plays a role; Lieberman's investigations had revealed that as our diet shifted over the centuries from chewy stuff like raw roots and wild game and gave way to mushy cooked staples like spaghetti and ground beef, our faces began to shrink. Ben Franklin's face was chunkier than yours; Caesar's was bigger than his.

The Harvard and Utah scientists got along right from the start, mostly because of Lieberman's eyes: they didn't roll when Bramble briefed him on the Running Man theory. "No one in the scientific community was willing to take it seriously," Bramble said. "For every one paper on running, there were four thousand on walking. When-ever I'd bring it up at conferences, everyone would always say, 'Yeah, but we're slow.' They were focused on speed and couldn't understand how endurance could be an advantage."

Well, to be fair, Bramble hadn't really figured that one out yet, either. As biologists, he and David Carrier could decipher how the machine was designed, but they needed an anthropologist to deter-mine what that design could actually do. "I knew a lot about evolu-tion and a little about locomotion," Lieberman says. "Dennis knew a shitload about locomotion, but not so much about evolution."

As they traded stories and ideas, Bramble could tell that Lieber-man was his kind of lab partner. Lieberman was a scientist who believed that being hands-on meant being prepared to soak them in blood. For years, Lieberman had organized a Cro-Magnon barbecue on a Harvard Yard lawn as part of his human evolution class. To demonstrate the dexterity necessary to operate primitive tools, he'd get his students to butcher a goat with sharpened stones, then cook it in a pit. As soon as the aroma of roasting goat spread and the post-butchering libations began flowing, homework turned into a house party. "It eventually evolved into a kind of bacchanalian feast," Lieberman told the *Harvard University Gazette*.

But there was an even more important reason that Lieberman was the perfect guy to tackle the Running Man mystery: the solution seemed to be linked to his specialty, the head. Everyone knew that at some point in history, early humans got access to a big supply of protein, which allowed their brains to expand like a thirsty sponge in a bucket of water. Our brains kept growing until they were seven times larger than the brains of any comparable mammal. They also sucked up an ungodly number of calories; even though our brains account for only 2 percent of our body weight, they demand 20 percent of our energy, compared with just 9 percent for chimps.

Dr. Lieberman threw himself into Running Man research with his usual creative zeal. Soon, students dropping by Lieberman's office on the top floor of Harvard's Peabody Museum were startled to find a sweat-drenched one-armed man with an empty cream-cheese cup strapped to his head running on a treadmill. "We humans are weird," Lieberman said as he punched buttons on the control panel. "No other creature has been found with a neck like ours." He paused to shout a question to the man on the treadmill. "How much faster can you go, Willie?"

"Faster than this thing!" Willie called back, his steel left hand clanging against the treadmill rail. Willie Stewart lost his arm when he was eighteen after a steel cable he was carrying on a construction job got caught in a whirling turbine, but he recovered to become a champion triathlete and rugby player. In addition to the cream-cheese cup, which was being used to secure a gyroscope, Willie also had electrodes taped to his chest and legs. Dr. Lieberman had recruited him to test his theory that the human head, with its unique position directly on top of the neck, acts like the roof weights used to prevent skyscrapers from pitching in the wind. Our heads didn't just expand because we got better at running, Lieberman believed; we got better at running because our heads were expanding, thereby providing more ballast.

"Your head works with your arms to keep you from twisting and swaying in midstride," Dr. Lieberman said. The arms, meanwhile, also work as a counterbalance to keep the head aligned. "That's how bipeds solved the problem of how to stabilize a head with a movable neck. It's yet another feature of human evolution that only makes sense in terms of running."

But the big mystery continued to be food. Judging by the

Godzilla-like growth of our heads, Lieberman could pinpoint the exact moment when the caveman menu changed: it had to be two million years ago, when apelike *Australopithecus*—with his tiny brain, giant jaw, and billy-goat diet of tough, fibrous plants—evolved into *Homo erectus*, our slim, long-legged ancestor with the big head and small, tearing teeth perfectly suited for raw flesh and soft fruits. Only one thing could have sparked such a dramatic makeover: a diet no primate had ever eaten before, featuring a reliable supply of meat, with its high concentrations of calories, fat, and protein.

"So where the fuck did they get it?" Lieberman asks, with all the gusto of a man who's not squeamish about hacking into goats with a rock. "The bow and arrow is twenty thousand years old. The spearhead is two hundred thousand years old. But *Homo erectus* is around two *million* years old. That means that for most of our existence—*for nearly two million years!*—hominids were getting meat with their bare hands."

Lieberman began playing the possibilities out in his mind. "Maybe we pirated carcasses killed by other predators?" he asked himself. "Scooting in and grabbing them while the lion was sleeping?"

No; that would give us an appetite for meat but not dependable access. You'd have to get to a kill site before the vultures, who can strip an antelope in minutes and "chew bones like crackers," as Lieberman likes to say. Even then, you might only tear off a few mouthfuls before the lion opened a baleful eye or a pack of hyenas drove you away.

"Okay, maybe we didn't have spears. But we could have jumped on a boar and throttled it. Or clubbed it to death."

Are you kidding? With all that thrashing and goring, you'd get your feet crushed, your testicles torn, your ribs broken. You'd win, but you'd pay for it; break an ankle in the prehistoric wilderness while hunting for dinner, and you might become dinner yourself.

There's no telling how long Lieberman would have remained stumped if his dog hadn't finally given him the answer. One summer afternoon, Lieberman took Vashti, his mutty half border collie, for a five-mile jog around Fresh Pond. It was hot, and after a few miles, Vashti plopped down under a tree and refused to move. Lieberman got impatient; yeah, it was a little warm, but not *that* bad. . . .

As he waited for his panting dog to cool off, Lieberman's mind flashed back to his time doing fossil research in Africa. He recalled the shimmering waves across the sun-scorched savannah, the way the dry clay soaked up the heat and beamed it right back up through the soles of his boots. Ethnographers' reports he'd read years ago began flooding his mind; they told of African hunters who used to chase antelope across the savannahs, and Tarahumara Indians who would race after a deer "until its hooves fell off." Lieberman had always shrugged them off as tall tales, fables of a golden age of heroes who'd never really existed. But now, he started to wonder. . . .

So how long would it take to actually run an animal to death? he asked himself. Luckily, the Harvard bio labs have the best locomotive research in the world (as their willingness to insert a thermometer in a cheetah's butt should make clear), so all the data Lieberman needed was right at his fingertips. When he got back to his office, he began punching in numbers. *Let's see,* he began. A jogger in decent shape averages about three to four meters a second. A deer trots at almost the identical pace. But here's the kicker: when a deer wants to accelerate to four meters a second, it has to break into a heavy-breathing gallop, *while a human can go just as fast and still be in his jogging zone.* A deer is way faster at a sprint, but we're faster at a jog; so when Bambi is already edging into oxygen debt, we're barely breathing hard.

Lieberman kept looking, and found an even more telling comparison: the top galloping speed for most horses is 7.7 meters a second. They can hold that pace for about ten minutes, then have to slow to 5.8 meters a second. But an elite marathoner can jog for hours at 6 meters a second. The horse will erupt away from the starting line, as Dennis Poolheco had discovered in the Man Against Horse Race, but with enough patience and distance, you can slowly close the gap.

You don't even have to go fast, Lieberman realized. *All you have to do is keep the animal in sight, and within ten minutes, you're reeling him in.*

Lieberman began calculating temperatures, speed, and body weight. Soon, there it was before him: the solution to the Running Man mystery. To run an antelope to death, Lieberman determined, all you have to do is scare it into a gallop on a hot day. "If you keep just close enough for it to see you, it will keep sprinting away. After about ten or fifteen kilometers' worth of running, it will go into hyperthermia and collapse." Translation: if you can run six miles on a summer day, then you, my friend, are a lethal weapon in the animal kingdom. We can dump heat on the run, but animals can't pant while they gallop.

"We can run in conditions that no other animal can run in," Lieberman realized. "And it's not even hard. If a middle-aged professor can outrun a dog on a hot day, imagine what a pack of motivated hunter-gatherers could do to an overheated antelope."

It's easy to picture the scorn on the faces of those Masters of the Universe, the Neanderthals, as they watched these new Running Men puffing along behind bouncy little Bambis, or jogging all day under a hot sun to return with nothing but an armload of yams. The Running Men could get a load of meat by running, but they couldn't run with a belly load of meat, so most of the time they carbo-loaded on roots and fruits, saving the antelope chops for special, calorie-boosting occasions. Everyone scavenged together—Running Men, Running Women, Running Kids, and Grampies—but despite all that team activity, they were more likely to dine on grubs than wild game.

Bleh. Neanderthals wouldn't touch bugs and dirt food; they ate meat and only meat, and not gristly little antelopes, either. Neanderthals went Grade A all the way: bears, bison, and elk marbled with juicy fat, rhinos with livers rich in iron, mammoths with luscious, oily brains and bones dripping with lip-smacking marrow. Try chasing monsters like those, though, and they'll be chasing you. Instead, you've got to outsmart and outfight them. The Neanderthals would lure them into ambushes and launch a pincer attack, storming from all sides with eight-foot wooden lances. Hunting like that isn't for the meek; Neanderthals were known to suffer the kind of injuries you find on the rodeo circuit, neck and head trauma from getting thrown by bucking beasts, but they could count on their band of brothers to care for their wounds and bury their bodies. Unlike our true ancestors, those scampering Running Men, the Neanderthals were the mighty hunters we like to imagine we once were; they stood shoulder to shoulder in battle, a united front of brains and bravery, clever warriors armored with muscle but still refined enough to slow-cook their meat to tenderness in earth ovens and keep their women and children away from the danger.

Neanderthals ruled the world—till it started getting nice outside. About forty-five thousand years ago, the Long Winter ended and a hot front moved in. The forests shrank, leaving behind parched grasslands stretching to the horizon. The new climate was great for the Running Men; the antelope herds exploded and feasts of plump roots were pushing up all over the savannah.

The Neanderthals had it tougher; their long spears and canyon ambushes were useless against the fleet prairie creatures, and the big game they preferred was retreating deeper into the dwindling forests. Well, why didn't they just adopt the hunting strategy of the Running Men? They were smart and certainly strong enough, but that was the problem; they were *too* strong. Once temperatures climb above 90 degrees Fahrenheit, a few extra pounds of body weight make a huge difference—so much so that to maintain heat balance, a 160-pound runner would lose nearly three minutes *per mile* in a marathon against a one hundred-pound runner. In a two-hour pursuit of a deer, the Running Men would leave the Neanderthal competition more than ten miles behind.

Smothered in muscle, the Neanderthals followed the mastodons into the dying forest, and oblivion. The new world was made for runners, and running just wasn't their thing.

Privately, David Carrier knew the Running Man theory had a fatal flaw. The secret gnawed until it nearly turned him into a killer.

"Yeah, I was kind of obsessed," he admitted when I met him at his lab in the University of Utah, twenty-five years and three academic degrees since his moment of inspiration at the dissecting table in 1982. He was now David Carrier, Ph.D., professor of biology, with gray in his push-broom mustache and rimless round glasses over his intense brown eyes. "I was dying to just grab something with my own two hands and say, 'Look! Satisfied now?'"

The problem was this: Chasing an animal to death is evolution's version of the perfect crime. Persistence hunting (as it's known to anthropologists) leaves behind no forensics—no arrowheads, no spear-nicked deer spines—so how do you build a case that a killing took place when you can't produce a corpse, a weapon, or witnesses? Despite Dr. Bramble's physiological brilliance and Dr. Lieberman's fossil expertise, there was no way they could prove that our legs were once lethal weapons if they couldn't show that *someone*, somewhere, had actually run an animal to death. You can spout any theory you want about human performance ("We can suspend our own heart-beats! We can bend spoons with our brains!") but in the end, you can't make the shift from appealing notion to empirical fact if you don't come up with the goods.

"The frustrating thing is, we were finding stories all over the place," David Carrier said. Throw a dart at the map, and chances are you'll bull's-eye the site of a persistence-hunting tale. The Goshutes and Papago tribes of the American West told them; so did the Kalahari Bushmen in Botswana, the Aborigines in Australia, Masai warriors in Kenya, the Seri and Tarahumara Indians in Mexico. The trouble was, those legends were fourth- or fifth-hand at best; there was as much evidence to support them as there was that Davy Crockett kilt him a b'ar when he was only three.

"We couldn't find anyone who'd done a persistence hunt," David said. "We couldn't find someone who'd even *seen* one." No wonder the scientific community remained skeptical. If the Running Man theory was right, then at least one person on this planet of six billion should still be able to catch quarry on foot. We may have lost the tradition and necessity, but we should still have the native ability: our DNA hasn't changed in centuries and is 99.9 percent identical across the globe, meaning we've all got the same stock parts as any ancient hunter-gatherer. So how come none of us could catch a stinking deer?

"That's why I decided to do it myself," David said. "As an undergrad, I got into mountain races and had a lot of fun at those. So when it came to how humans breathe differently when we run, I think it was easier for me to see how it could affect us as a species. The idea didn't seem as strange to me as it would for someone who never left the lab."

Nor did it seem strange to him that if he couldn't find a caveman, he could become one. In the summer of 1984, David persuaded his brother, Scott, a freelance writer and reporter for National Public Radio, to go to Wyoming and help him catch a wild antelope. Scott wasn't much of a runner, but David was in great shape and fiercely motivated by the lure of scientific immortality. Between him and his brother, David figured, it should take only two hours before eight hundred pounds of proof was flopping at his feet.

"We drive off the interstate and down a dirt road for a few miles and it's a wide and open high desert of sagebrush, dry as a bone, mountains in every direction. There are antelope everywhere." That's how Scott later painted the scene for listeners on NPR's *This American Life*. "We stop the car and start running after three—a buck and two does. They run very quickly, but for short distances, and then stop and stare at us till we catch up. Then they take off again. Sometimes they run a quarter of a mile, sometimes a half mile."

Perfect! It was playing out exactly as David had predicted. The antelope weren't getting enough time to cool off before David and Scott were *yip-yip-yaahoo*ing on their tails again. A few more miles of this, David figured, and he'd be heading back to Salt Lake with a trunk full of venison and a killer video to slap down on Dr. Bramble's desk. His brother, on the other hand, sensed something very different going on.

"The three antelope look at me like they know exactly what we're proposing, and they're not the least bit worried," Scott continues. It didn't take him long to find out why they were so calm in the face of what should have been impending death. Instead of flopping over in exhaustion, the antelope pulled a shell game; when they got winded, they circled back and hid in the herd, leaving David and Scott no idea which antelopes were tired and which were fresh. "They blend and flow and change positions," Scott says. "There are no individuals, but this mass that moves across the desert like a pool of mercury on a glass table."

For two more days, the two brothers chased mercury balls across the Wyoming plains, never realizing they were in the midst of a magnificent mistake. David's failure was unwitting proof of his own theory: human running is different from any other running on earth. You can't catch other animals by copying them, and especially not by using the crude approximation of animal running we've preserved in sports. David and Scott were relying on instinct, strength, and stamina, without realizing that human distance running, at its evolutionary best, is much more than that; it's a blend of strategy and skill perfected during millions of years of do-or-die decisions. And like any other fine art, human distance running demands a brain-body connection that no other creature is capable of.

But it's a lost art, as Scott Carrier would spend the next decade discovering. Something strange happened out there on the Wyoming plains: the lure of the lost art got into Scott's blood and wouldn't let go. Despite the hopelessness of that expedition, Scott spent years researching persistence hunting on his brother's behalf. He even created a nonprofit corporation devoted to finding the Last of the Long Distance Hunters, and recruited elite ultrarunner Creighton King—the Double Grand Canyon record holder before the Skaggs bros came along—to join an expedition to the Sea of Cortez, where word had it that a tiny clan of Seri Indians had preserved the link to our distance-running past.

Scott found the clan—but he found them too late. Two elders had learned old-style running from their father, but they were a half century out of practice and too old to even demonstrate.

That was the end of the trail. By 2004, the hunt for that one person in six billion had lasted twenty years and gone nowhere. Scott Carrier gave up. David Carrier had moved on long before, and was now studying physical-combat structures in primates. The Last of the Long Distance Hunters was a cold case.

Naturally, that's when the phone rang.

"So, out of the blue, I find myself talking to this stranger," Dr. Bramble begins. He looks like an old cowpoke, with his shaggy gray hair and crisp rancher's shirt, and it's a style that perfectly matches the dried animal skulls on the walls of his lab and his enthralling, gather-round-the-campfire storytelling. By 2004, Dr. Bramble says, the Utah-Harvard team had identified twenty-six distance-running markers on the human body. With little hope of ever finding the Last Hunter, they decided to go ahead and publish their findings anyway. *Nature* magazine put them on the cover, and a copy apparently made its way to a beach town on the South African coast, because that's where this call was coming from.

"It's not hard to run an antelope to death," the stranger said. "I can show you how it's done."

"Sorry—who are you?"

"Louis Liebenberg. From Noordhoek."

Bramble knew all the top names in the running-theory field, which wasn't hard since they could fit around a diner booth. Louis Liebenberg from Noordhoek he'd never heard of.

"Are you a hunter?" Bramble asked.

"Me? No."

"Oh . . . anthropologist?"

"No."

"What's your field?"

"Math. Math and physics."

Math? "Uh . . . how did a mathematician run down an antelope?" Bramble heard a snort of laughter. "By accident, mostly."

It's eerie how the lives of Louis Liebenberg and David Carrier spiraled each other for decades without either of them knowing it. Back in the early '80s, Louis was also an undergraduate in college and, like David, he was suddenly electrified by an insight into human evolution that few others believed in.

Part of Louis's problem was his expertise: he had none. At the time, he was barely twenty and majoring in applied mathematics and physics at the University of Cape Town. It was while taking an elective course in the philosophy of science that he started wondering about the Big Bang of the human mind. How did we leap from basic survival thinking, like that of other animals, to wildly complicated concepts like logic, humor, deduction, abstract reasoning, and creative imagination? Okay, so primitive man upgraded his hardware with a bigger brain—but where did he get the software? Growing a bigger brain is an organic process, but being able to use that brain to project into the future and mentally connect, say, a kite, a key, and a lightning bolt and come up with electrical transference was like a touch of magic. So where did that spark of inspiration come from?

The answer, Louis believed, was out in the deserts of southern Africa. Even though he was a city kid who knew jack about the outdoors, he had a hunch that the best place to look for the birth of human thought was the place where human life began. "I had a vague gut feeling that the art of animal tracking could represent the origin of science itself," Louis says. Then who better to study than the

Bushmen of the Kalahari Desert, who were both masters of animal tracking and living remnants of our prehistoric past?

So, at age twenty-two, Louis decided to drop out of college and write a new chapter in natural history by testing his theory with the Bushmen. It was an insanely ambitious plan for a college dropout with zero experience in anthropology, wilderness survival, or scientific method. He spoke neither the Bushmen's native tongue, !Kabee, nor their adopted one, Afrikaans. He didn't even know anything about animal tracking, the reason he was going in the first place. But so what? Louis shrugged, and got to work. He found an Afrikaans translator, made contact with hunting guides and anthropologists, and eventually set off down the Trans-Kalahari Highway into Botswana, Namibia . . . and the unknown.

Like Scott Carrier, Louis soon discovered that he was losing a race against time. "I went village to village looking for Bushmen who hunt with bow and arrow, since they'd have the tracking skills," Louis says. But with big-game safaris and ranchers taking over their old game lands, most of the Bushmen had abandoned the nomadic life and were living on government settlements. Their decline was heartbreaking; instead of roaming the wilderness, many of the Bushmen were surviving on slave wages for farm jobs and seeing their sisters and daughters recruited by truck-stop bordellos.

Louis kept searching. Far out in the Kalahari, he finally came across a renegade band of Bushmen who, he says, "stubbornly clung to freedom and independence and wouldn't subject themselves to manual labor or prostitution." As it turned out, the search for One in Six Billion was just about mathematically correct: in all the Kalahari, only six true hunters remained.

The renegades agreed to let Louis hang around, an offer he took to the extreme; once installed, Louis acted like an unemployed in-law, basically squatting with the Bushmen for the next four years. The city kid from Cape Town learned to live on the Bushman diet of roots, berries, porcupine, and ratlike springhares. He learned to keep his campfire burning and tent zipped even on the most sweltering nights, since packs of hyenas were known to drag people from open shelters and tear out their throats. He learned that if you stumble upon an angry lioness and her cubs, you stand tall and make her back down, but in the same situation with a rhino, you run like hell.

When it comes to mentors, you can't beat survival; just trying to fill his belly every day and avoid pissing off, for instance, two black-backed jackals mating beneath a baobob was an excellent way for Louis to begin absorbing the wizardry of a master tracker. He learned to look at piles of zebra dung and distinguish which droppings came from which animal; intestines, he discovered, have ridges and grooves that leave unique patterns on feces. Learn to tell them apart, and you can single out a zebra from an exploding herd and track it for days by its distinctive droppings. Louis learned to hunch over a set of fox tracks and re-create exactly what it was doing: here, it was moving slowly as it scented around for mice and scorpions, and look, that's where it trotted off with something in its mouth. A swirl of swept dirt told him where an ostrich had taken a dust bath, and let him backtrack to find its eggs. Meerkats make their warrens in hard-pan, so why were they digging here in soft sand? Must mean there's a den of tasty scorpions. . . .

Even after you learn to read dirt, you ain't learned nothing; the next level is tracking without tracks, a higher state of reasoning known in the lit as "speculative hunting." The only way you can pull it off, Louis discovered, was by projecting yourself out of the present and into the future, transporting yourself into the mind of the animal you're tracking. Once you learn to think like another creature, you can anticipate what it will do and react before it ever acts. If that sounds a little Hollywood, then you've seen your share of movies about impossibly clairvoyant FBI profilers who can "see with the eyes of a killer." But out there on the Kalahari plains, mind-throwing was a very real and potentially deadly talent.

"When tracking an animal, one attempts to think like an animal in order to predict where it is going," Louis says. "Looking at its tracks, one visualizes the motion of the animal and feels that motion in one's own body. You go into a trancelike state, the concentration is so intense. It's actually quite dangerous, because you become numb to your own body and can keep pushing yourself until you collapse."

Visualization . . . empathy . . . abstract thinking and forward projection: aside from the keeling-over part, isn't that exactly the mental engineering we now use for science, medicine, the creative arts? "When you track, you're creating causal connections in your mind, because you didn't actually see what the animal did," Louis realized.

"That's the essence of physics." With speculative hunting, early human hunters had gone beyond connecting the dots; they were now connecting dots that existed only in their minds.

One morning, four of the renegade Bushmen—!Nate, !Nam!kabe, Kayate, and Boro/xao—woke Louis up before dawn to invite him on a special hunt. Don't eat any breakfast, they warned him, and drink all the water you can hold. Louis downed a mug of coffee, grabbed his boots, and fell in behind the hunters as they marched off across the savannah in the dark. The sun rose until it was broiling over their heads, but the hunters pushed on. Finally, after walking nearly twenty miles, they spotted a clutch of kudu, an especially agile form of antelope. That's when the Bushmen started to run.

Louis stood there, confused. He knew the standard Bushman bow-hunting drill: drop to your belly, creep into arrow range, let fly. So what the hell was this all about? He'd heard a little about persistence hunts, but he ranked them somewhere between an accident and a lie: either the animal had actually broken its neck while fleeing, or the story was out-and-out baloney. No way these guys were going to catch one of those kudus on foot. No way. But the more he said "No way," the farther away the Bushmen got, so Louis quit thinking and started running.

"This is how we do it," !Nate said when a panting Louis caught up. The four hunters ran swiftly but easily behind the bounding kudu. Whenever the animals darted into an acacia grove, one of the hunters broke from the group and drove the kudu back into the sun. The herd would scatter, re-form, scatter again, but the four Bushmen ran and swerved behind a single kudu, cutting it out of the herd whenever it tried to blend, flushing it from the trees whenever it tried to rest. If they had a doubt about which one to chase, they dropped to the ground, checked the tracks, and adjusted their pursuit.

As he gasped along behind the band, Louis was surprised to find !Nate, the strongest and most skilled hunter of the renegade Bushmen, hanging back with him. !Nate wasn't even carrying a canteen like the other hunters. Nearly ninety minutes into the pursuit, Louis discovered why: when one of the older hunters tired and dropped out, he handed his canteen to !Nate. !Nate drank it dry, then traded it for a half-full one when a second runner dropped out.

Louis staggered along behind, determined to see the hunt through to the end. He was bitterly regretting his choice of heavy bush boots; the Bushmen traditionally wore light, giraffe-skin moccasins, and now had on thin, flimsy sneakers that let their feet cool on the fly. Louis felt the way the kudu looked; he watched it weave drunkenly . . . its front knees buckled, straightened . . . it recovered and bounded away . . . then crashed to the ground.

So did Louis. By the time he got to the fallen kudu, he was so overheated he'd stopped sweating. He pitched facedown into the sand. "When you're focused on the hunt, you push to the limits. You're not aware you're exhausted," Louis later explained. In a way, he'd triumphed; Louis had managed to cross over and run as hard as if he were the one being pursued. Where he failed was not knowing to check his own footprints; because it's so easy to become numb to your own vital signs, the Bushmen learned long ago to periodically check their own tracks. If their prints looked as bad as the kudu's, they'd stop, wash their faces, hold a mouthful of water and slowly let it trickle down their throats. After the final swallow, they'd walk and check their tracks again.

Louis's head was pounding and his dry eyes were going blurry. He was barely conscious, but still alert enough to be really scared; he was lying in the desert in 107-degree heat, and he knew he had only one chance to save his life. He fumbled for his belt knife and reached toward the dead kudu. If he could slash it open, he could suck the water from its stomach.

"NO!" !Nate stopped Louis. Unlike other antelopes, kudus eat acacia leaves, which are poisonous for humans. !Nate calmed Louis, told him to hold on a little longer, and took off running: even though !Nate had already hiked twenty miles and run fifteen, he was able to run twelve more miles to bring Louis back some water. !Nate wouldn't let him drink it. First, he rinsed Louis's head, then he washed his face, and only after Louis's skin began to cool did !Nate allow him tiny sips.

Later, after !Nate had helped him back to camp, Louis marveled at the ruthless efficiency of the persistence hunt. "It's much more efficient than a bow and arrow," he observed. "It takes a lot of attempts to get a successful hunt by bow. You can hit the animal and still lose it, or scavengers can smell blood and get to it before you do, or it can take all night for the poison on the arrow tips to work. Only a small percentage of arrow shots are successful, so for the number of days hunting, the meat yield of a persistence hunt is much higher."

Louis found out only in his second, third, and fourth persistence hunts how lucky he'd gotten in the first; that debut kudu dropped after only two hours, but every one after that kept the Bushmen on the run for three to five hours (neatly corresponding, one might note, to how long it takes most people to run our latter-day version of prehistoric hunting, the marathon. *Recreation has its reasons*).

To succeed as a hunter, Louis had to reinvent himself as a runner. He'd been an excellent middle-distance athlete in high school, winning the 1,500-meter championship and finishing a close second in the 800, but to hang with the Bushmen, he had to forget everything he'd been taught by modern coaches and study the ancients. As a track athlete, he'd drop his head and hammer, but as an apprentice Bushman, he had to be eyes high and tinglingly alert every step of the way. He couldn't zone out and ignore pain; instead, his mind was constantly tap-dancing between the immediate—scratches in the dust, sweat on his own forehead—and the imaginary, as he played mental war games to think one step ahead of his prey.

The pace wasn't too fierce; the Bushmen average about ten minutes a mile, but many of those miles are in soft sand and brush, and they occasionally stop to study tracks. They'd still fire the jets and take off at a sprint, but they knew how to keep trotting afterward and recover on the run. They had to, because a persistence hunt was like showing up at the starting line without knowing if you were running a half marathon, marathon, or ultra. After a while, Louis began to look at running the way other people look at walking; he learned to settle back and let his legs spin in a quick, easy trot, a sort of baseline motion that could last all day and leave him enough reserves to accelerate when necessary.

His eating changed, too. As a hunter-gatherer, you're never off the clock; you can be walking home after an exhausting day of collecting yams, but if fresh game scuttles into view, you drop everything and go. So Louis had to learn to graze, eating lightly throughout the day rather than filling up on big meals, never letting himself get thirsty, treating every day as if he were in a race that had already started.

The Kalahari summer cooled into winter, but the hunts continued. The Utah-Harvard docs would turn out to be wrong about one
part of their Running Man theory: persistence hunting doesn't
depend on killer heat, because the ingenious Bushmen had devised
ways to run down game in every weather. In the rainy season, both the
tiny duiker antelope and the giant gemsbok, with its lancelike horns,
would overheat because the wet sand splayed their hooves, forcing
their legs to churn harder. The four-hundred-pound red hartebeest is
comfortable in waist-high grasslands, but exposed and vulnerable
when the ground parches during dry winters. Come the full moon,
antelopes are active all night and tired by daybreak; come spring,
they're weakened by diarrhea from feasting on green leaves.

By the time Louis was ready to head home from the bush and
begin writing *The Art of Tracking: The Origin of Science*, he'd gotten so
accustomed to epic runs that he almost took them for granted. He
barely mentions running in his book, focusing more on the mental
demands of the hunt than the physical. It was only after a copy of
Nature magazine fell into his hands that he fully appreciated what
he'd seen out there in the Kalahari, and grabbed the phone to dial
Utah.

Know why people run marathons? he told Dr. Bramble. Because
running is rooted in our collective imagination, and our imagination
is rooted in running. Language, art, science; space shuttles, *Starry
Night*, intravascular surgery; they all had their roots in our ability to
run. Running was the superpower that made us human—which
means it's a superpower all humans possess.

"Then why do so many people hate it?" I asked Dr. Bramble as he
came to the end of the story of Louis and the Bushmen. "If we're all
born to run, shouldn't all of us enjoy it?"

Dr. Bramble began his answer with a riddle. "This is fascinating
stuff," he said. "We monitored the results of the 2004 New York City
Marathon and compared finishing times by age. What we found is
that starting at age nineteen, runners get faster every year until they
hit their peak at twenty-seven. After twenty-seven, they start to
decline. So here's the question—how old are you when you're back to
running the same speed you did at nineteen?"

All righty. I flipped my notebook to a blank page and started jot-ting numbers. It takes eight years until you run your best time at age twenty-seven. If you get slower at the same rate you got faster, then you'd be back at your nineteen-year-old time by age thirty-six: eight years up, eight years down. But I knew there was a twist involved, and I was pretty sure it had to be whether we fade away as quickly as we improve. "We probably hang on to our speed a little longer once we get it," I decided. Khalid Khannouchi was twenty-six when he broke the marathon world record, and was still fast enough at thirty-six to finish in the top four at the 2008 U.S. Olympic trials. He'd lost only ten minutes in ten years, despite a ton of injuries. In honor of the Khannouchi Curve, I bumped my answer up to forty.

"Forty—," I started to say, until I saw the smile creasing Bramble's face. "Five," I hastily added. "I'll guess forty-five."

"Wrong."

"Fifty?"

"Nope."

"It can't be fifty-five."

"You're right," Bramble said. "It can't be. It's sixty-four."

"Are you serious? That's a—" I scribbled out the math. "That's a forty-five-year difference. You're saying teenagers can't beat guys three times their age?"

"Isn't that amazing?" Bramble agreed. "Name any other field of athletic endeavor where sixty-four-year-olds are competing with nineteen-year-olds. Swimming? Boxing? Not even close. There's something really weird about us humans; we're not only really good at endurance running, we're really good at it for a remarkably long time. We're a machine built to run—and the machine never wears out."

You don't stop running because you get old, the Dipsea Demon always said. *You get old because you stop running. . . .*

"And it's true for both genders," Dr. Bramble continued. "Women show the same results as men." That makes sense, since a curious transformation came over us when we came down from the trees: the more we became human, the more we became equal. Men and women are basically the same size, at least compared with other primates: male gorillas and orangutans weigh twice as much as their better halves; male chimps are a good one-third bigger than females; but between the average human him and the average human her, the difference in bulk is only a slim 15 percent. As we evolved, we

shucked our beef and became more sinuous, more cooperative ...
essentially, more female.

"Women have really been underrated," Dr. Bramble said.
"They've been evolutionarily shortchanged. We perpetuate this
notion that they were sitting around waiting for the men to come
back with food, but there's no reason why women couldn't be part of
the hunting party." Actually, it would be weird if women *weren't*
hunting alongside the men, since they're the ones who really need
the meat. The human body benefits most from meat protein during
infancy, pregnancy, and lactation, so why wouldn't women get as
close to the beef supply as possible? Hunter-gatherer nomads shift
their camps by the movements of the herds, so instead of hauling
food back to camp, it made more sense for the whole camp to go to
the food.

And caring for kids on the fly isn't that hard, as American ultrarunner Kami Semick demonstrates; she likes to run mountain trails
around Bend, Oregon, with her four-year-old daughter, Baronie, riding along in a backpack. Newborns? No problem: at the 2007
Hardrock 100, Emily Baer beat ninety other men and women to finish eighth overall while stopping at every aid station to breast-feed
her infant son. The Bushmen are no longer nomadic, but the equal-
partners-in-hunting tradition still exists among the Mbuti Pygmies
of the Congo, where husbands and wives with nets pursue the giant
forest hog side by side. "Since they are perfectly capable of giving
birth to a child while on the hunt, then rejoining the hunt the same
morning," notes anthropologist Colin Turnbull, who's spent years
among the Mbuti, "mothers see no reason why they should not con-
tinue to participate fully."

Dr. Bramble's picture of the past was taking on clarity and color. I
could see a band of hunters—young and old, male and female—running tirelessly across the grasslands. The women are up front, leading the way toward fresh tracks they spotted while foraging, and hard
behind are the old men, their eyes on the ground and their minds
inside a kudu skull a half mile ahead. Crowding their heels are teens
eager to soak up tips. The real muscle hangs back; the guys in their
twenties, the strongest runners and hunters, watching the lead track-
ers and saving their strength for the kill. And bringing up the rear?
The Kami Semicks of the savannah, toting their kids and grandkids.

After all, what else did we have going for us? Nothing, except we ran like crazy and stuck together. Humans are among the most communal and cooperative of all primates; our sole defense in a fang-filled world was our solidarity, and there's no reason to think we suddenly disbanded during our most crucial challenge, the hunt for food. I remembered what the Seri Indians told Scott Carrier after the sun had set on their persistence-hunting days. "It was better before," a Seri elder lamented. "We did everything as a family. The whole community was a family. We shared everything and cooperated, but now there is a lot of arguing and bickering, every man for himself."

Running didn't just make the Seris a people. As Coach Joe Vigil would later sense about his own athletes, it also made them *better* people.

"But there's a problem," Dr. Bramble said. He tapped his forehead. "And it's right up here." Our greatest talent, he explained, also created the monster that could destroy us. "Unlike any other organism in history, humans have a mind-body conflict: we have a body built for performance, but a brain that's always looking for efficiency." We live or die by our endurance, but remember: endurance is all about conserving energy, and that's the brain's department. "The reason some people use their genetic gift for running and others don't is because the brain is a bargain shopper."

For millions of years, we lived in a world without cops, cabs, or Domino's Pizza; we relied on our legs for safety, food, and transportation, and it wasn't as if you could count on one job ending before the next one began. Look at !Nate's wild hunt with Louis; !Nate sure wasn't planning on a fast 10k immediately after a half-day hike and a high-speed hunt, but he still found the reserve energy to save Louis's life. Nor could his ancestors ever be sure that they wouldn't become food right after catching some; the antelope they'd chased since dawn could attract fiercer animals, forcing the hunters to drop lunch and run for their lives. The only way to survive was to leave something in the tank—and that's where the brain comes in.

"The brain is always scheming to reduce costs, get more for less, store energy and have it ready for an emergency," Bramble explained. "You've got this fancy machine, and it's controlled by a pilot who's thinking, 'Okay, how can I run this baby without using any fuel?' You and I know how good running feels because we've made a habit of it." But lose the habit, and the loudest voice in your ear is your ancient survival instinct urging you to relax. And there's the bitter irony: our fantastic endurance gave our brain the food it needed to grow, and now our brain is undermining our endurance.

"We live in a culture that sees extreme exercise as crazy," Dr. Bramble says, "because that's what our brain tells us: why fire up the machine if you don't have to?"

To be fair, our brain knew what it was talking about for 99 percent of our history; sitting around was a luxury, so when you had the chance to rest and recover, you grabbed it. Only recently have we come up with the technology to turn lazing around into a way of life; we've taken our sinewy, durable, hunter-gatherer bodies and plunked them into an artificial world of leisure. And what happens when you drop a life-form into an alien environment? NASA scientists wondered the same thing before the first space flights. The human body had been built to thrive under the pressure of gravity, so maybe taking away that pressure would act as an escape-trajectory Fountain of Youth, leaving the astronauts feeling stronger, smarter, and healthier. After all, every calorie they ate would now go toward feeding their brains and bodies, instead of pushing up against that relentless downward pull—right?

Not by a long shot; by the time the astronauts returned to earth, they'd aged decades in a matter of days. Their bones were weaker and their muscles had atrophied; they had insomnia, depression, acute fatigue, and listlessness. Even their taste buds had decayed. If you've ever spent a long weekend watching TV on the sofa, you know the feeling, because down here on earth, we've created our own zero-gravity bubble; we've taken away the jobs our bodies were meant to do, and we're paying for it. Nearly every top killer in the Western world—heart disease, stroke, diabetes, depression, hypertension, and a dozen forms of cancer—was unknown to our ancestors. They didn't have medicine, but they did have a magic bullet—or maybe two, judging by the number of digits Dr. Bramble was holding up.

"You could literally halt epidemics in their tracks with this one remedy," he said. He flashed two fingers up in a peace sign, then slowly rotated them downward till they were scissoring through space. The Running Man.

"So simple," he said. "Just move your legs. Because if you don't think you were born to run, you're not only denying history. You're denying who you are."

CHAPTER 29

The past is never dead. It's not even past.

—WILLIAM FAULKNER, *Requiem for a Nun*

I WAS ALREADY awake and staring into the dark when Caballo came scratching at my door.

"Oso?" he whispered.

"C'mon in," I whispered back. I blinked on my watch: 4:30.

In half an hour, we were supposed to start out for our rendezvous with the Tarahumara. Months earlier, Caballo had told them to meet us in a little glen of shade trees on the trail up Batopilas mountain. The plan was to push up and over the peak, then down the back side and across the river to the village of Urique. I didn't know what Caballo would do if the Tarahumara didn't show up—or what I'd do if they did.

Travelers on horseback give themselves three days for the thirty-five-mile journey from Batopilas to Urique; Caballo planned to do it in one. If I fell behind, would I be the one wandering lost in the canyons this time? And what if the Tarahumara didn't show—would Caballo lead us into no-man's-land to search for them? Did he even know where he was going?

Those were the thoughts that kept me from sleeping. But Caballo, it turned out, had worries of his own. He came in and sat on the edge of my bed.

"Do you think the kids are up for it?" he asked.

Remarkably, they seemed fine after their near-death day in the canyons. They'd put away a good meal of tortillas and frijoles that evening, and I hadn't heard any sounds of distress from the bathroom during the night.

"How long till giardia hits?" I asked. Giardia parasites, I knew, had to incubate for a while in the intestines before erupting into diarrhea, fever, and stomach cramps.

"A week or two."

"So if they don't come down with something else by this morning, they might be okay till after the race."

"Hmm," Caballo muttered. "Yeah." He paused, obviously chewing over something else. "Look," he went on. "I'm going to have to pop Barefoot Ted between the eyes." The problem this time wasn't Ted's feet; it was his mouth. "If he gets in the face of the Rarámuri, they're going to get real uncomfortable," Caballo said. "They're going to think he's another Fisher and split."

"What are you going to do?"

"I'm going to tell him he's got to keep it shut tight. I don't like telling people what to do, but he's got to get the message."

I got up and helped him roust the others. The night before, a friend of Caballo's had loaded our bags on a burro and set off for Urique, so all we had to carry was enough food and water to get us there. Bob Francis, the old backcountry guide, had volunteered to drive Luis's father the long way around the mountain in his 4×4 pickup, sparing him the hike. Everyone else turned out quickly, and by 5 a.m., we were picking our way over the boulders toward the river. The canyon moon glittered on the water and bats were still darting overhead as Caballo led us to a faint footpath skirting the water line. We fitted into single file and shuffled into an easy jog.

"The Party Kids are amazing," Eric said, watching them glide along behind Caballo.

"They're more like the Comeback Kids," I agreed. "But Caballo's big worry is—" I pointed ahead to Barefoot Ted, whose outfit for the hike consisted of red shorts, his green FiveFinger toe shoes, and an anatomically correct skeleton amulet around his neck. Instead of a shirt, he wore a red raincoat with the hood knotted under his chin and the rest flapping loose over his shoulders like a cape. Jingling from his ankle was a string of bells, which he'd gotten because he'd read somewhere that Tarahumara elders wore them.

"Good mojo," Eric grinned. "We've got our own witch doctor."

By sunup, we'd left the river and turned up into the mountains. Caballo was pushing hard, even harder than he had the day before. We ate on the move, chomping down quick bites of tortilla and energy bars, sipping conservatively on our water in case it had to last all day. When it got light enough to see, I turned and looked back to get my bearings. The village had vanished like Brigadoon, swallowed whole by the forest. Even the trail behind us seemed to dissolve into the thick green foliage as soon as we passed. It felt like we were sinking into a bottomless green sea.

"Not too much farther," I could hear Caballo saying. He was pointing to something I couldn't make out yet. "See that cluster of trees? That's where they'll be."

"*The* Arnulfo," Luis said, wonder in his voice. "I'd rather meet him than Michael Jordan."

I got closer and saw the trees. I didn't see any people.

"The flu's been going around," Caballo said, slowing down and tilting back his head to squint at the hills above us for signs of life. "There's a chance some of the runners will come later. If they're sick. Or if they have to take care of their families."

Eric and I glanced at each other. Caballo had never mentioned anything about the flu before. I eased my hydration pack off my shoulders and got ready to sit down and rest. *Better take a break now till we see what's next*, I thought, dropping the pack at my feet. When I looked back up, we were surrounded by half a dozen men in white skirts and pirate blouses. Between blinks, they'd materialized from the forest.

We all stood, silent and stunned, waiting for a cue from Caballo.

"Is he here?" Luis whispered.

I scanned the ring of Tarahumara until I spotted that familiar whimsical smile on that handsome mahogany face. Wow; he really came. Just as unbelievably, his cousin Silvino was right beside him.

"That's him," I whispered back. Arnulfo heard and glanced over. His lips twitched in a slight smile when he recognized me.

Caballo was overcome with emotion. I thought it was just relief, until he reached out with both hands toward a Tarahumara runner with a mournful, Geronimo-like face. "Manuel," Caballo said.

Manuel Luna didn't return the smile, but he sandwiched both Caballo's hands with his own. I walked over. "I knew your son," I said. "He was very good to me, a real *caballero*."

"He told me about you," Manuel said. "He wanted to be here."

That emotional reunion between Caballo and Manuel broke the ice for everyone else. The rest of Caballo's crew circulated among the Tarahumara, trading the special Tarahumara handshake Caballo had taught them, that light rasping of finger pads that is simultaneously less grasping and more intimate than a big ol' powerpump.

Caballo began introducing us. Not by name—in fact, I don't think I ever heard him use our names again. He'd been studying us over the past three days, and just as he'd seen an *oso* in me and Barefoot Ted had spotted a monkey in himself, Caballo felt he'd identified spirit animals for everyone else.

"El Coyote," he said, laying a hand on Luis's back. Billy became El Lobo Joven—the young wolf. Eric, quiet and ever watchful, was El Gavilán, the hawk. When he got to Jenn, I saw a flicker of amused interest briefly light up Manuel Luna's eyes. "La Brujita Bonita," Caballo called her. To the Tarahumara, steeped in tales of their two magnificent years at Leadville and the epic battle between Juan Herrera and Ann "the Bruja" Trason, calling a young runner "The Pretty Little Witch" had exactly the punch of nicknaming an NBA rookie "Heir Jordan."

"*¿Hija?*" Manuel asked. Was Jenn really Ann Trason's daughter?

"*Por sangre, no. Por corazón, sí,*" Caballo replied. Not the same blood, but the same heart.

Finally, Caballo turned to Scott Jurek. "El Venado," he said, which even got a reaction out of too-cool Arnulfo. Now, what was the crazy gringo playing at? Why would Caballo call the tall, lean, and supremely confident-looking guy "the Deer"? Was he giving the Tarahumara a foot tap under the table, a little hint how to play their cards on race day? Manuel remembered very well the way Caballo had urged the Tarahumara in Leadville to sit patiently on Ann Trason's heels and "run her down like a deer." But would Caballo favor the Tarahumara over his own compatriot? Or maybe it was a setup— maybe Caballo was trying to trick the Tarahumara into holding back while this American built an unbeatable lead. . . .

It was all mysterious and complicated and thoroughly entertaining to the Tarahumara, whose love of race strategy rivaled their taste for corn beer. Quietly, they began to banter among themselves, until Barefoot Ted barged in. Whether accidentally or prophylactically, Caballo had bypassed Ted in the introductions, so Ted presented himself.

"*Yo soy* El Mono!" he announced. "The Monkey!" Hang on, Barefoot Ted thought; do they even *have* monkeys in Mexico? Maybe the Tarahumara don't know what a *mono* is. Just in case, he began hooting and scratching like a chimp, his ankle bells jingling and the sleeves of his red raincoat flapping in his face, somehow thinking that impersonating a thing they'd never heard of would let them know what that thing was.

The Tarahumara stared. None of them, incidentally, wore bells.

"Okay," Caballo said, eager to drop the curtain on this show. "*¿Vámonos?*"

We reshouldered our packs. We'd been on the climb for nearly five straight hours, but we had to keep racing the sun if we were going to have a chance of fording the river before dark. Caballo took point, while the rest of us shuffled into single file among the Tarahumara. I tried to put myself last so I wouldn't slow down the parade, but Silvino wouldn't hear of it. He wouldn't move till I moved first.

"*¿Por qué?*" I asked. Why?

Habit, Silvino said; as one of the top ball-racers in the canyons, he was used to keeping tabs on his teammates from the rear and letting them pull the pace until it was time for him to slingshot off for the final miles. I was tickled to think of myself as part of an All-Star Mixed Tarahumara-American Ultrarunning Team, until I translated what Silvino had said for Eric.

"Maybe," Eric said. "Or maybe the race already started." He nodded farther ahead. Arnulfo was walking right behind Scott, watching him intently.

CHAPTER 30

Poetry, music, forests, oceans, solitude—they were what developed enormous spiritual strength. I came to realize that spirit, as much or more than physical conditioning, had to be stored up before a race.

—HERB ELLIOTT, Olympic champion and
world-record holder in the mile who trained in bare feet,
wrote poetry, and retired undefeated

"*OYE, OSO,*" a shopkeeper called, waving me inside.

Two days after we'd arrived in Urique, we were known everywhere by the spirit-animal nicknames Caballo had given us. "Everywhere," of course, meant about five hundred yards in every direction; Urique is a tiny, Lost World village sitting alone at the bottom of the canyon like a pebble at the bottom of a well. By the time we'd finished breakfast on our first morning, we'd already been folded into the local social life. An army squad encamped on the outskirts would salute Jenn as they passed through on patrol, calling, "*¡Hola, Brujita!*" Kids greeted Barefoot Ted with shouts of "*Buenos días*, Señor Mono." Good morning, Mr. Monkey.

"Hey, Bear," the shopkeeper continued. "Do you know that Arnulfo has never been beaten? Do you know he's won the one-hundred-kilometer race three times in a row?"

No Kentucky Derby, presidential election, or celebrity murder trial has ever been handicapped as passionately and personally as Caballo's race was by the people of Urique. As a mining village whose best days were over more than a century ago, Urique had two things left to be proud of: its brutally tough landscape and its Tarahumara neighbors. Now, for the first time, a pack of exotic foreign runners had traveled all this way to test themselves against both, and it had exploded into much more than a race: for the people of Urique, it was the one chance in their lifetime to show the outside world just what they were made of.

And even Caballo was surprised to find that his race had surpassed his hopes and was growing into the Ultimate Fighting Competition of underground ultras. Over the past two days, Tarahumara runners had continued trickling in by ones and twos from all directions. When we awoke the morning after our hike from Batopilas, we saw a band of local Tarahumara traipsing down from the hills above the village. Caballo hadn't even been sure the Urique Tarahumara still ran anymore; he'd been afraid that, as in the tragic case of the Tarahumara of Yerbabuena, government upgrades to the dirt road had converted the Urique Tarahumara from runners into hitchhikers. They certainly looked like a people in transition; the Urique Tarahumara still carried wooden *palia* sticks (their version of the ball race was more like high-speed field hockey), but instead of traditional white skirts and sandals, they wore running shorts and sneakers from the Catholic mission.

That same afternoon, Caballo was overjoyed to see a fifty-one-year-old named Herbolisto come jogging in from Chinivo, accompanied by Nacho, a forty-one-year-old champion from one of Herbolisto's neighboring settlements. As Caballo had feared, Herbolisto had been laid up with the flu. But he was one of Caballo's oldest Tarahumara friends and hated the idea of missing the race, so as soon as he felt a little better, he grabbed a *pinole* bag and set off on the sixty-mile trip on his own, stopping off on the way to invite Nacho along for the fun.

By the eve of Race Day, our numbers had tripled from eight to twenty-five. Up and down Urique's main street, debate over who was now the true top seed was running hot: Was it Caballo Blanco, the wily old veteran who'd poached the secrets of both American and Tarahumara runners? Or the Urique Tarahumara, experts on the local trails who had hometown pride and support on their side? Some money was riding on Billy Bonehead, the Young Wolf, whose surf-god physique drew admiring stares whenever he went for a swim in the Urique River. But the heaviest street action was divided between the two stars: Arnulfo, king of the Copper Canyons, and El Venado, his mysterious foreign challenger.

"*Sí, señor,*" I replied to the shopkeeper. "Arnulfo won a one-hundred-kilometer race in the canyons three times. But the Deer has won a one-hundred-*mile* race in the mountains *seven* times."

"But it's very hot down here," the shopkeeper retorted. "The Tarahumara, they eat heat."

"True. But the Deer won a one-hundred-thirty-five-mile race across a desert called Death Valley in the middle of summer. No one has ever run it faster."

"No one beats the Tarahumara," the shopkeeper insisted.

"So I've heard. So who are you betting on?"

He shrugged. "The Deer."

The Urique villagers had grown up in awe of the Tarahumara, but this tall gringo with the flashy orange shoes was unlike anyone they'd ever seen. It was eerie watching Scott run side by side with Arnulfo; even though Scott had never seen the Tarahumara before and Arnulfo had never seen the outside world, somehow these two men separated by two thousand years of culture had developed the same running style. They'd approached their art from opposite ends of history, and met precisely in the middle.

I first saw it up on Batopilas mountain, after we'd finally gotten to the top and the trail flattened as it circled the peak. Arnulfo took advantage of the plateau to open it up. Scott locked in beside him. As the trail curled into the setting sun, the two of them vanished into the glare. For a few moments, I couldn't tell them apart—they were two fiery silhouettes moving with identical rhythm and grace.

"Got it!" Luis said, dropping back to show me the image in his digital camera. He'd sprinted ahead and wheeled around just in time to capture everything I'd come to understand about running over the past two years. It wasn't Arnulfo's and Scott's matching form so much as their matching smiles; they were both grinning with sheer muscular pleasure, like dolphins rocketing through the waves. "This one is going to make me cry when I get back home," Luis said. "It's like getting Babe Ruth and Mickey Mantle in the same shot." If Arnulfo had an advantage, it wouldn't be style or spirit.

But I had another reason to put my money on Scott. During the last, hardest miles of the hike to Urique, he kept hanging back with me and I'd wondered why. He'd come all this way to see the best runners in the world, so why was he wasting his time with one of the worst? Didn't he resent me for holding everyone up? Seven hours of descending that mountain eventually gave me my answer:

What Coach Joe Vigil sensed about character, what Dr. Bramble conjectured with his anthropological models, Scott had been his entire life. The reason we race isn't so much to beat each other, he understood, but to be *with* each other. Scott learned that before he had a choice, back when he was trailing Dusty and the boys through the Minnesota woods. He was no good and had no reason to believe he ever would be, but the joy he got from running was the joy of adding his power to the pack. Other runners try to disassociate from fatigue by blasting iPods or imagining the roar of the crowd in Olympic Stadium, but Scott had a simpler method: it's easy to get outside yourself when you're thinking about someone else.*

That's why the Tarahumara bet like crazy before a ball race; it makes them equal partners in the effort, letting the runners know they're all in it together. Likewise, the Hopis consider running a form of prayer; they offer every step as a sacrifice to a loved one, and in return ask the Great Spirit to match their strength with some of his own. Knowing that, it's no mystery why Arnulfo had no interest in racing outside the canyons, and why Silvino never would again: if they weren't racing for their people, then what was the point? Scott, whose sick mother never left his thoughts, was still a teenager when he absorbed this connection between compassion and competition.

The Tarahumara drew strength from this tradition, I realized, but Scott drew strength from *every* running tradition. He was an archivist and an innovator, an omnivorous student who gave as much serious thought to the running lore of the Navajo, the Kalahari Bushmen,

---

*Any doubts I had about this theory were laid to rest the following year, when I went to crew for Luis Escobar at Badwater. At three o'clock in the morning, I drove ahead to check on Scott and found him bearing down in the midst of a four-mile-high hill. He'd already run eighty miles in 125-degree heat and was on pace for a new course record, but when he saw me, the first words out of his mouth were, "How's Coyote?"

and the Marathon Monks of Mount Hiei as he did to aerobic levels, lactate thresholds, and the optimal recruitment of all three types of muscle-twitch fiber (not two, as most runners believe).

Arnulfo wasn't going up against a fast American. He was about to race the world's only twenty-first-century Tarahumara.

While the shopkeeper and I were busy setting the over-under, I saw Arnulfo strolling past. I grabbed a couple of Popsicles to pay him back for the sweet limes he'd given me at his house, and together we went looking for a shady spot to relax. I saw Manuel Luna sitting under a tree, but he looked so alone and lost in thought, I didn't think we should disturb him. Barefoot Monkey, however, saw it differently.

"MANUEL!" Barefoot Ted shouted from across the street.

Manuel's head jerked up.

"Amigo, am I glad to see you," Barefoot Ted said. He'd been looking around for some tire rubber so he could make his own pair of Tarahumara sandals, but figured he needed some expert advice. He grabbed mystified Manuel by the arm and led him into a tiny shop. As it turned out, Ted was right; all tire rubber is not the same. What Ted wanted, Manuel demonstrated with his hands, was a strip with a groove right down the middle, so the knot for the toe strap can be countersunk and not get torn off by the ground.

Minutes later, Barefoot Ted and Manuel Luna were outside with their heads together, tracing Ted's feet and slicing away at the tire tread with my big-bladed Victorinox knife. They worked through the afternoon, trimming and measuring, until, just before dinner, Ted was able to do a test run down the street in his new pair of Air Lunas. From then on, he and Manuel Luna were inseparable. They arrived for dinner together and hunted around the packed restaurant for a place to sit.

Urique has only one restaurant, but when it's run by Mamá Tita, one is plenty. From daybreak till midnight for four straight days, this cheerful sixty-something woman kept the four burners on her old propane stove blazing full blast, bustling away in a kitchen hot as a boiler room as she turned out mountains of food for all Caballo's runners: stewed chicken and goat, batter-fried river fish, grilled beef, refried beans and guacamole, and minty, tangy salsas, all garnished with sweet limes and chili oil and fresh cilantro. For breakfast, she served eggs scrambled with goat cheese and sweet peppers, and on the side, heaping bowls of *pinole* and flapjacks that tasted so much like pound cake, I volunteered to apprentice in her kitchen one morning to learn the secret recipe.*

As the American and Tarahumara runners squeezed around the two long tables in Tita's back garden, Caballo banged on a beer bottle and stood up. I thought he was going to deliver our final race instructions, but he had something else on his mind.

"There's something wrong with you people," he began. "Rarámuri don't like Mexicans. Mexicans don't like Americans. Americans don't like *anybody*. But you're all here. And you keep doing things you're not supposed to. I've seen Rarámuri helping *chabochis* cross the river. I've watched Mexicans treat Rarámuri like great champions. Look at these gringos, treating people with respect. Normal Mexicans and Americans and Rarámuri don't act this way."

Over in the corner, Ted thought he could help Manuel by translating Caballo's clumsy Spanish into clumsier Spanglish. As Ted yammered, a faint smile kept flitting across Manuel's face. Finally, it just stayed there.

"What are you doing here?" Caballo went on. "You have corn to plant. You have families to take care of. You gringos, you know it can be dangerous down here. No one has to tell the Rarámuri about the danger. One of my friends lost someone he loved, someone who could have been the next great Rarámuri champion. He's suffering, but he's a true friend. So he's here."

Everyone got quiet. Barefoot Ted laid a hand on Manuel's back. Of all the Tarahumara he could have asked for help with his huaraches, I realized, he hadn't picked Manuel Luna by accident.

"I thought this race would be a disaster, because I thought you'd be too sensible to come." Caballo scanned the garden, found Ted in the corner, and locked eyes with him. "You Americans are supposed to be greedy and selfish, but then I see you acting with a good heart. Acting out of love, doing good things for no reason. You know who does things for no good reason?"

---

*Tita's secret (it's okay, she won't mind): she whips boiled rice, overripe bananas, a little cornmeal, and fresh goat milk into her batter. Perfection.

"CABALLO!" the shout went up.

"Yah, right. Crazy people. *Más Locos.* But one thing about crazy people—they see things other people don't. The government is putting in roads, destroying a lot of our trails. Sometimes Mother Nature wins and wipes them out with floods and rock slides. But you never know. You never know if we'll get a chance like this again. Tomorrow will be one of the greatest races of all time, and you know who's going to see it? Only crazy people. Only you Más Locos."

"Más Locos!" Beers were shoved in the air, bottles were clinking. Caballo Blanco, lone wanderer of the High Sierras, had finally come out of the wild to find himself surrounded by friends. After years of disappointments, he was twelve hours from seeing his dream come true.

"Tomorrow, you'll see what crazy people see. The gun fires at daybreak, because we've got a lot of running to do."

"CABALLO! VIVA CABALLO!"

CHAPTER 31

Often I visualize a quicker, like almost a ghost runner,
ahead of me with a quicker stride.

—GABE JENNINGS, 2000 U.S. Olympic Trial 1,500-meter winner

BY 5 A.M., Mamá Tita had pancakes and papayas and hot *pinole* on
the table. For their prerace meal, Arnulfo and Silvino had requested
pozole—a rich beef broth with tomatoes and fat corn kernels—and
Tita, chirpy as a bird despite only getting three hours of sleep,
whipped it right up. Silvino had changed into a special race outfit, a
gorgeous turquoise blouse and a white *zapete* skirt embroidered with
flowers along the hem.

"*Guapo*," Caballo said admiringly; looking good. Silvino ducked
his head bashfully. Caballo paced the garden, sipping coffee and fret-
ting. He'd heard that some farmers were planning a cattle drive on
one of the trails, so he'd tossed awake all night, planning last-minute
detours. When he got up and trudged down for breakfast, he discovered that Luis Escobar's dad had already ridden to the rescue with
old Bob, Caballo's fellow wandering gringo from Batopilas. They'd
come across the *vaqueros* the evening before while shooting photos in
the backcountry and warned them off the course. Now without a
stampede to sweat over, Caballo was searching for something else.
He didn't have to look far.

"Where are the Kids?" he asked.

Shrugs.

"I better go get them," he said. "I don't want them killing themselves without breakfast again."

When Caballo and I stepped outside, I was stunned to find the entire town there to greet us. While we'd been inside having breakfast, garlands of fresh flowers and paper streamers had been strung across the street, and a mariachi band in dress sombreros and torero suits had begun strumming a few warm-up tunes. Women and children were already dancing in the street, while the mayor was aiming a shotgun at the sky, practicing how he could fire it without shredding the streamers.

I checked my watch, and suddenly found it hard to breathe: thirty minutes till the start. The thirty-five-mile hike to Urique had, as Caballo predicted, "chewed me up and crapped me out," and in half an hour, I had to do it all over again and go fifteen miles farther. Caballo had laid out a diabolical course; we'd be climbing and descending sixty-five hundred feet in fifty miles, exactly the altitude gain of the first half of the Leadville Trail 100. Caballo was no fan of the Leadville race directors, but when it came to choosing terrain, he was just as pitiless.

Caballo and I climbed the hill to the little hotel. Jenn and Billy were still in their room, arguing over whether Billy needed to carry the extra water bottle which, it turned out, he couldn't find anyway. I had a spare I was using to store espresso, so I hustled to my room, dumped the coffee, and tossed it to Billy.

"Now eat something! And hustle up!" Caballo scolded. "The mayor is gonna blast that thing at seven sharp."

Caballo and I grabbed our gear—a hydration backpack loaded with gels and PowerBars for me, a water bottle and tiny bag of *pinole* for Caballo—and we headed back down the hill. Fifteen minutes to go. We rounded the corner toward Tita's restaurant, and found the street party had grown into a mini–Mardi Gras. Luis and Ted were twirling old women and fending off Luis's dad, who kept cutting in. Scott and Bob Francis were clapping and singing along as best they could with the mariachis. The Urique Tarahumara had set up their own percussion brigade, beating time on the sidewalk with their *palia* sticks.

Caballo was delighted. He pushed into the throng and began a

Muhammad Ali shuffle, bobbing and weaving and punching his fists in the air. The crowd roared. Mamá Tita blew him kisses.

"¡*Ándale!* We're going to dance all day!" Caballo shouted through his cupped hands. "But only if nobody dies. Take care out there!" He turned to the mariachis and dragged a finger across his throat. Kill the music. Showtime.

Caballo and the mayor began corraling dancers off the street and waving runners to the starting line. We crowded together, forming into a crazy human quilt of mismatched faces, bodies, and costumes. The Urique Tarahumara were in their shorts and running shoes, still carrying their *palias*. Scott stripped off his shirt. Arnulfo and Silvino, dressed in the bright blouses they'd brought especially for the race, squeezed in beside Scott; the Deer hunters weren't letting the Deer out of their sight for a second. By unspoken agreement, we all picked an invisible line in the cracked asphalt and toed it.

My chest felt tight. Eric worked his way over beside me. "Look, I got some bad news," he said. "You're not going to win. No matter what you do, you're going to be out there all day. So you might as well just relax, take your time, and enjoy it. Keep this in mind—if it feels like work, you're working too hard."

"Then I'll catch 'em napping," I croaked, "and make my move."

"No moves!" Eric warned, not even wanting the thought to creep into my skull as a joke. "It could hit one hundred degrees out there. Your job is to make it home on your own two feet."

Mamá Tita walked from runner to runner, her eyes puddling as she pressed our hands. "*Ten cuidado, cariño*," she urged. Be careful, dearie.

"¡*Diez!* . . . ¡*Nueve!* . . ."

The mayor was leading the crowd in the countdown.

"¡*Ocho!* . . . ¡*Siete!* . . ."

"Where are the Kids?" Caballo yelled.

I looked around. Jenn and Billy were nowhere in sight.

"Get him to hold off!" I shouted back.

Caballo shook his head. He turned away and got into race-ready position. He'd waited years and risked his life for this moment. He wasn't postponing it for anyone.

"¡*BRUJITA!*" The soldiers were pointing behind us.

Jenn and Billy came sprinting down the hill as the crowd hit "*Cuatro.*" Billy wore surf baggies and no shirt, while Jenn had on black compression shorts and a black jog bra, her hair knotted in two tight Pippi braids. Distracted by her military fan club, Jenn whipped the drop bag with her food and spare socks to the wrong side of the street, startling spectators, who hopped over it as it flew between their legs and disappeared. I raced over, snagged it, and got it to the aid table just as the mayor jerked the trigger.

BOOM!

Scott leaped and screamed, Jenn howled, Caballo hooted. The Tarahumara just ran. The Urique team shot off in a pack, disappearing down the dirt road into the predawn shadows. Caballo had warned us that the Tarahumara would go out hard, but whoa! This was just ferocious. Scott fell in behind them, with Arnulfo and Silvino tucked in on his heels. I jogged slowly, letting the pack flow past until I was in last place. It would be great to have some companionship, but at this point, I felt safer alone. The worst mistake I could make would be getting lulled into someone else's race.

The first two miles were a flat ramble out of town and along the dirt road to the river. The Urique Tarahumara hit the water first, but instead of charging straight into the shallow fifty-yard crossing, they suddenly stopped and began rooting around the shore, flipping over rocks.

What the hell . . . ? wondered Bob Francis, who'd gone ahead with Luis's dad to take photos from the far side of the river. He watched as the Urique Tarahumara pulled out plastic shopping bags they'd stashed under rocks the night before. Tucking their *palias* under their arms, they slipped their feet into the bags, pulled them tight by the handles, and began sloshing across the river, demonstrating what happens when new technology replaces something that has worked fine for ten thousand years: afraid of getting their precious Salvation Army running shoes wet, the Urique Tarahumara were hobbling along in homemade waders.

"Jesus," Bob murmured. "I've never seen anything like it."

The Urique Tarahumara were still stumbling over slippery rocks when Scott hit the riverbank. He splashed straight into the water, Arnulfo and Silvino hard behind. The Urique Tarahumara reached shore, kicked the bags off their feet, and stuffed them into their shorts to use again later. They began scrambling up the steep sand dune with Scott closing fast, sand spraying from his churning feet. By the time the Urique Tarahumara hit the dirt trail leading up the mountain, Scott and the two Quimares had made contact.

Jenn, meanwhile, was already having a problem. She, Billy, and Luis had crossed the river side by side with a pack of Tarahumara, but as Jenn tore up the sand dune, her right hand was bugging her. Ultra-runners rely on "handhelds," water bottles with straps that wrap around your hand for easy carrying. Jenn had given Billy one of her two handhelds, then rigged a second for herself with athletic tape and a springwater bottle. As she fought her way up the dune, her homemade handheld felt sticky and awkward. It was a tiny hassle, but it was a hassle she'd have to deal with every minute of the next eight hours. So should she keep it? Or should she once again risk running into the canyons with only a dozen swallows in her hand?

Jenn began gnawing through the tape. Her only hope of compet-ing with the Tarahumara, she knew, was to go for broke. If she gam-bled and crashed, fine. But if she lost the race of a lifetime because she'd played it safe, she'd always regret it. Jenn tossed the bottle and immediately felt better. Bolder, even—and that led to her next risky decision. They were at the bottom of the first meat grinder, a steep three-mile hill with little shade. Once the sun came up, she had little hope of sticking with the heat-eating Tarahumara.

"Ah, fuck it," Jenn thought. "I'm just gonna go now while it's cool." Within five strides, she was pulling away from the pack. "Later, dudes," she called over her shoulder.

The Tarahumara immediately gave chase. The two canny old vets, Sebastiano and Herbolisto, boxed Jenn in from the front while the three other Tarahumara surrounded her on the sides. Jenn looked for a gap, then burst loose and pulled away. Instantly, the Tarahumara swarmed and bottled her back up. The Tarahumara may be peace-loving people at home, but when it came to racing, it was bare knuckles all the way.

"I hate to say it, but Jenn is going to blow up," Luis told Billy as they watched Jenn dart ahead for the third time. They were only three miles into a 50-mile race, and she was already going toe-to-toe with a five-man Tarahumara chase pack. "You don't run like that if you want to finish."

"Somehow she always pulls it off," Billy said.

"Not on this course," Luis said. "Not against these guys."

Thanks to the genius of Caballo's planning, we'd all get to witness the battle in real time. Caballo had laid out his course in a Y pattern, with the starting line dead in the middle. That way, the villagers would see the race several times as it doubled back and forth, and the racers would always know how far they were trailing the leaders. That Y-formation also provided another unexpected benefit: at that very moment, it was giving Caballo plenty of reason to be very suspicious of the Urique Tarahumara.

Caballo was about a quarter mile back, so he had a perfect view of Scott and the Deer hunters as they closed the gap with the Urique Tarahumara on the hill across the river. When he saw them heading back toward him after the first turnaround, Caballo was astounded: in the space of just four miles, the Urique crew had opened up a *four-minute lead*. They'd not only dropped the two best Tarahumara racers of their generation, but also the greatest climber in the history of Western ultrarunning.

"No. Way. In. HELL!" growled Caballo, who was running in a pack of his own with Barefoot Ted, Eric, and Manuel Luna. When they got to the five-mile turnaround in the tiny Tarahumara settlement of Guadalupe Coronado, Caballo and Manuel started asking the Tarahumara spectators some questions. It didn't take them long to find out what was going on: the Urique Tarahumara were taking side trails and shaving the course. Rather than fury, Caballo felt a pang of pity. The Urique Tarahumara had lost their old way of running, he realized, and their confidence along with it. They weren't Running People anymore; they were just guys trying desperately to keep up with the living shadows of their former selves.

Caballo forgave them as a friend, but not as a race director. He put out the word: the Urique Tarahumara were disqualified.

I got a shock of my own when I hit the river. I'd been concentrating so much on watching my footing in the dark and reviewing my mental checklist (*bend those knees . . . bird steps . . . leave no trace*) that when I started to wade through the knee-deep water, it suddenly hit me: I'd just run two miles and it felt like nothing. Better than nothing—I felt light and loose, even more springy and energized than I had before the start.

"Way to go, Oso!" Bob Francis was calling from the opposite bank. "Little bitty hill ahead. Nothing to worry about."

I scrambled out of the water and up the sand dune, growing more hopeful with every step. Sure, I still had forty-eight more miles, but the way it was going, I might be able to steal the first dozen or so before I had to make any real effort. I started climbing the dirt trail just as the sun was slanting over the top of the canyon. Instantly, everything lit up: the glittering river, the shimmering green forest, the coral snake coiled at my feet. . . .

I yelped and leaped off the trail, sliding down the steep slope and grabbing at scrub brush to stop my fall. I could see the snake above me, silent and curled, ready to strike. If I climbed back up, I risked a fatal bite; if I climbed down toward the river, I could plunge off the side of the cliff. The only way out was to maneuver sideways, working my way from one scrub-brush handhold to the next.

The first clump held, then the next. When I'd made it ten feet away, I cautiously hauled myself back onto the trail. The snake was still blocking the trail, and for good reason—it was dead. Someone had already snapped its back with a stick. I wiped the dirt out of my eyes and checked the damage: rock rash down both shins, thorns in my hands, heart pounding through my chest. I pulled the thorns with my teeth, then cleaned my gashes, more or less, with a squirt from my water bottle. Time to get going. I didn't want anyone to come across me bleeding and panicky over a rotting snake.

The sun got stronger the higher I climbed, but after the early-morning chill, it was more exhilarating than exhausting. I kept thinking about Eric's advice—"If it feels like work, you're working too hard"—so I decided to get outside my head and stop obsessing about my stride. I began drinking in the view of canyon around me, watching the sun turn the top of the foothill across the river to gold. Pretty soon, I realized, I'd be nearly as high as that peak.

Moments later, Scott burst around a bend in the trail. He flashed me a grin and a thumbs-up, then vanished. Arnulfo and Silvino were right behind him, their blouses rippling like sails as they flew past. I must be close to the five-mile turnaround, I realized. I climbed around the next curve, and there it was: Guadalupe Coronado. It was little more than a whitewashed schoolhouse, a few small homes, and a tiny shop selling warm sodas and dusty packs of cookies, but even from a mile away, I could already hear cheers and drumbeats.

A pack of runners was just pulling out of Guadalupe and setting off in pursuit of Scott and the Quimares. Leading them, all by herself, was the Brujita.

The second Jenn saw her chance, she pounced. On the hike over from Batopilas, she'd noticed that the Tarahumara run downhill the same way they run up, with a controlled, steady flow. Jenn, on the other hand, loves to pound the descents. "It's the only strength I've got," she says, "so I milk it for all I'm worth." So instead of exhausting herself by dueling with Herbolisto, she decided to let him set the pace for the climb. As soon as they reached the turnaround and started the long downhill, she broke out of the chase pack and began speeding off.

This time, the Tarahumara let her go. She pulled so far ahead that by the time she hit the next uphill—a rocky single track climbing to the second branch of the Y at mile 15—Herbolisto and the pack couldn't get close enough to swarm her. Jenn was feeling so confident that when she reached the turnaround, she stopped to take a breather and refill her bottle. Her luck with water so far had been fabulous; Caballo had asked Urique villagers to fan out through the canyons with jugs of purified water, and it seemed that every time Jenn took her last swallow, she came across another volunteer.

She was still gurgling her full bottle when Herbolisto, Sebastiano, and the rest of the chase pack finally caught her. They spun around without stopping, and Jenn let them go. Once she was rewatered, she began pounding down the hill. Within two miles, she'd once again reeled them in and left them behind. She began mentally scanning the course ahead to calculate how long she could keep pulling away. Let's see . . . upcoming was two miles of descent, then four flat miles back into the village, then—

Wham! Jenn landed facedown on the rocks, bouncing and sliding on her chest before coming to a stunned stop. She lay there, blinded with pain. Her kneecap felt broken and an arm was smeared with blood. Before she could gather herself to try getting to her feet, Herbolisto and the chase pack came storming down the trail. One by one, they hurdled Jenn and disappeared, never looking back.

They're thinking, That's what you get for not knowing how to run on the rocks, Jenn thought. *Well, they've got a point.* Gingerly, she pulled herself to her feet to assess the damage. Her shins looked like pizza, but her kneecap was only bruised and the blood she thought was pouring from her hand turned out to be chocolaty goo from an exploded PowerGel packet she'd stashed in her handheld. Jenn walked a few cautious steps, then jogged, and felt better than she expected. She felt so good, in fact, that by the time she reached the bottom of the hill, she'd caught and passed every one of the Tarahumara who'd jumped over her.

"¡*BRUJITA!*" The crowd in Urique went crazy when Jenn came racing back through the village, bloody but smiling as she hit the twenty-mile mark. She paused at the aid station to dig a fresh goo out of her drop bag, while a deliriously happy Mamá Tita dabbed at Jenn's gory shins with her apron and kept shouting "¡*Cuarto! ¡Estás en cuarto lugar!*"

"I'm a what? A room?" Jenn was halfway out of town again before her rickety Spanish let her figure out what Mama Tita was talking about: she was in fourth place. Only Scott, Arnulfo, and Silvino were still ahead of her, and she was nibbling steadily at their lead. Caballo had picked her spirit name perfectly: twelve years after Leadville, the Bruja was back with a vengeance.

But only if she could handle the heat. The temperature was nearing 100 degrees just as Jenn was entering the furnace—the jagged up-and-down climb to the Los Alisos settlement. The trail hugged a sheer rock wall that plunged and soared and plunged again, gaining and losing some three thousand feet. Any of the hills in the Los Alisos stretch would rank among the hardest Jenn had ever seen, and there were at least half a dozen of them, strung one behind the other. The heat shimmering off the rocks felt as if it was blistering her skin, but she had to stick tight to the canyon wall to avoid slipping off the edge and into the gorge below.

Jenn had just reached the top of one of the hills when she suddenly had to leap against the wall: Arnulfo and Silvino were *blazing* toward her, running shoulder to shoulder. The Deer hunters had taken everyone by surprise; we'd expected the Tarahumara to haunt

Scott's heels all day and then try to blast past him at the finish, but instead, the Deer hunters had pulled a fast one and jumped out first.

Jenn pressed her back against the hot rock to let them pass. Before she had time to wonder where Scott was, she was leaping back against the wall again. "Scott is running up this goddamn thing with the most intensity I've ever seen in a human being," Jenn said later. "He's *booking*, going, '*Huh-Huh-Huh-Huh.*' I'm wondering if he's even going to acknowledge me, he's so in the zone. Then he looks up and starts screaming, 'Yaaaah, Brujita, *whooooo*!' "

Scott stopped to brief Jenn on the trail ahead and let her know where to expect water drops. Then he quizzed her about Arnulfo and Silvino: How far ahead were they? How did they look? Jenn figured they were maybe three minutes out and pushing hard.

"Good," Scott nodded. He swatted her on the back and shot off.

Jenn watched him go, and noticed he was running on the very edge of the trail and sticking tight to the turns. That was an old Marshall Ulrich trick: it made it harder for the guy in the lead to glance back and see you sneak up from behind. Scott hadn't been surprised by Arnulfo's big move after all. The Deer was hunting the hunters.

"Just beat the course," I told myself. "No one else. Just the course."

Before I tackled the climb to Los Alisos, I stopped to get myself under control. I ducked my head in the river and held it there, hoping the water would cool me off and the oxygen debt would snap me back to reality. I'd just hit the halfway point, and it had only taken me about four hours. Four hours, for a hard trail marathon in desert heat! I was so far ahead of schedule, I'd started getting competitive: *How hard can it be to pick off Barefoot Ted? He's got to be hurting on those stones. And Porfilio looked like he was struggling. . . .*

Luckily, the head-dunking worked. The reason I was feeling so much stronger today than I had on the long haul over from Batopilas, I realized, was because I was running like the Kalahari Bushmen. I wasn't trying to overtake the antelope; I was just keeping it in sight. What had killed me during the Batopilas hike was keeping pace with Caballo & Co. So far today, I'd only competed against the racecourse, not the racers.

Before I got too ambitious, it was time to try another Bushman tactic and give myself a systems check. When I did, I noticed I was in rougher shape than I'd thought. I was thirsty, hungry, and down to just half a bottle of water. I hadn't taken a leak in over an hour, which wasn't a good sign considering all the water I'd been drinking. If I didn't rehydrate soon and get some calories down my neck, I'd be in serious trouble in the roller coaster of hills ahead. As I started sloshing the fifty yards across the river, I filled the bladder of my empty hydration pack with river water and dropped in a few iodine pills. I'd give that a half hour to purify, while I washed down a ProBar—a chewy raw-food blend of rolled oats, raisins, dates, and brown rice syrup—with the last of my clean water.

Good thing I did. "Brace yourself," Eric called as we passed each other on the far side of the river. "It's a lot rougher up there than you remember." The hills were so tough, Eric admitted, that he'd been on the verge of dropping out himself. A bad-news burst like that could come across as a punch in the gut, but Eric believes the worst thing you can give a runner midrace is false hope. What causes you to tense up is the unexpected; but as long as you know what you're in for, you can relax and chip away at the job.

Eric hadn't exaggerated. For over an hour, I climbed up and down the foothills, convinced I was lost and on the way to disappearing into the wilderness. There was only one trail and I was on it—but where the hell was the little grapefruit orchard at Los Alisos? It was only supposed to be four miles from the river, but I'd felt as if I'd covered ten and I still couldn't see it. Finally, when my thighs were burning and twitching so badly I thought I was going to collapse, I spotted a cluster of grapefruit trees on a hill ahead. I made it to the top, and dropped down next to a group of the Urique Tarahumara. They'd heard they were disqualified and decided to cool off in the shade before walking back to the village.

"*No hay problema*," one of them said. It's not a problem. "I was too tired to keep going anyway." He handed me an old tin cup. I scooped into the communal *pinole* pot, giardia be damned. It was cool and deliciously grainy, like a popcorn Slushee. I gulped down a cupful, then another, as I looked back at the trail I'd just covered. Far below, the river was faint as fading sidewalk chalk. I couldn't believe I'd run here from there. Or that I was about to do it again.

———

"It's *unbelievable*!" Caballo gasped.

He was slick with sweat and bug-eyed with excitement. As he struggled to catch his breath, he sluiced sweat off his dripping chest and flung it past me, the shower of droplets sparkling in the blazing Mexican sun. "We've got a world-class event going on!" Caballo panted. "Out here in the middle of nowhere!"

By the forty-two-mile mark, Silvino and Arnulfo were still ahead of Scott, while Jenn was creeping up behind all three. On her second pass through Urique, Jenn had dropped into a chair to drink a Coke, but Mamá Tita grabbed her under the arms and hauled her to her feet.

"¡*Puedes, cariño, puedes!*" Tita cried. You can do it, sweetie!

"I'm not dropping out," Jenn tried to protest. "I just need a drink."

But Tita's hands were in Jenn's back, pushing her back into the street. Just in time, too; Herbolisto and Sebastiano had taken advantage of the flat road into town to move back within a quarter mile of Jenn, while Billy Bonehead had broken free of Luis to move within a quarter mile of *them*.

"This is anybody's day!" Caballo said. He was trailing the leaders by about a half hour, and it was driving him batty. Not because he was losing; because he was in danger of missing the finish. The suspense was so unbearable, Caballo finally decided to drop out of his own race and cut back to Urique to see if he could get there in time for the final showdown.

I watched him run off, desperate to follow. I was so tired, I couldn't find my way to the skinny cable bridge over the river and somehow ended up under it, forcing me to splash through the river for the fourth time. My soaked feet felt too heavy to lift as I shuffled through the sand on the far side. I'd been out here all day, and now I was at the bottom of that same endless Alpine climb I'd almost fallen off this morning when I'd gotten spooked by the dead snake. There was no way I'd get down before sunset, so this time, I'd be stumbling back in the dark.

I dropped my head and started trudging. When I looked up again, Tarahumara kids were all around me. I closed my eyes, then opened them again. The kids were still there. I was so glad they weren't a hallucination, I was almost weepy. Where they'd come from and why they'd chosen to tag along with me, I had no idea. Together, we made our way higher and higher up the hill.

After we'd gone about half a mile, they darted up a nearly invisible side trail and waved for me to follow.

"I can't," I told them regretfully.

They shrugged, and ran off into the brush. "*¡Gracias!*" I rasped, missing them already. I kept pushing up the hill, shambling along at a trot that couldn't have been faster than a walk. When I hit a short plateau, the kids were sitting there, waiting. So *that's* how the Urique Tarahumara were able to break open such big leads. The kids hopped up and ran alongside me until, once again, they vanished into the brush. A half mile later, they popped out again. This was turning into a nightmare: I kept running and running, but nothing changed. The hill stretched on forever, and everywhere I looked, Children of the Corn appeared.

What would Caballo do? I wondered. He was always getting himself into hopeless predicaments out here in the canyons, and he always found a way to run his way out. *He'd start with easy*, I told myself. *Because if that's all you get, that's not so bad. Then he'd work on light. He'd make it effortless, like he didn't care how high the hill is or how far he had got to go*—

"OSO!" Heading toward me was Barefoot Ted, and he looked frantic.

"Some boys gave me some water and it felt so cold, I figured I'd use it to cool down," Barefoot Ted said. "So I'm squirting myself all over, spraying it around . . ."

I had trouble following Barefoot Ted's story, because his voice was fading in and out like a badly tuned radio. My blood sugars were so low, I realized, I was on the verge of bonking.

". . . and then I'm going, 'Crap, oh crap, I'm out of water—' "

From what I could make out from Barefoot Ted's yammering, it was maybe a mile to the turnaround. I listened impatiently, desperate to push on to the aid station so I could chow down an energy bar and take a break before tackling the final five miles.

". . . So I tell myself if I've got to pee, I'd better pee into one of these bottles in case I'm down to the last, you know, the last of the last. So I pee into this bottle and it's like, *orange*. It's not looking good. And it's *hot*. I think people were watching me pee in my bottle and thinking, 'Wow, these gringos are really tough.' "

"Wait," I said, starting to understand. "You're not drinking piss?"

"It was the *worst!* The worst-tasting urine I've ever tasted in my entire life. You could bottle this stuff and sell it to bring people back from the dead. I know you can drink urine, but not if it's been heated and shaken in your kidneys for forty miles. It was a failed experiment. I wouldn't drink that urine if it was the last liquid on planet Earth."

"Here," I said, offering the last of my water. I had no idea why he hadn't just gone back to the aid station and refilled if he was so worried, but I was too exhausted to ask any more questions. Barefoot Ted dumped his whiz, refilled his bottle, and padded off. Odd as he was, there was no denying his resourcefulness and determination; he was less than five miles from finishing a 50-mile race in his rubber toe slippers, and he'd been willing to drink bodily waste to get there.

Only after I arrived at the Guadalupe turnaround did it finally penetrate my woozy mind why Barefoot was dry in the first place: all the water was gone. All the people, too. Everyone in the village had trooped into Urique for the postrace party, closing up the little shop and leaving no one behind to point out the wells. I slumped down on a rock. My head was reeling, and my mouth was too cottony to let me chew food. Even if I managed to choke down a few bites, I was way too dehydrated to make the hour-long run to the finish. The only way to get back to Urique was on foot, but I was too wasted to walk.

"So much for compassion," I muttered to myself. "I give something away, and what do I get? Screwed."

As I sat, defeated, my heavy breathing from the hard climb slowed enough for me to become aware of another sound—a weird, warbling whistle that seemed to be getting closer. I pulled myself up for a look, and there, heading up this lost hill, was old Bob Francis.

"Hey, amigo," Bob called, fishing two cans of mango juice out of his shoulder bag and shaking them over his head. "Thought you could use a drink."

I was stunned. Old Bob had hiked five miles of hard trails in 95-degree heat to bring me juice? But then I remembered: a few days before, Bob had admired the knife I'd lent Barefoot Ted to make his sandals. It was a memento from expeditions in Africa, but Bob had been so kind to all of us that I had to give it to him. Maybe Bob's miracle delivery was just a lucky coincidence, but as I gulped the juice and got ready to run to the finish, I couldn't help feeling that the last piece of the Tarahumara puzzle had just snapped into place.

Caballo and Tita were jammed into the crowd at the finish line, craning their necks for the first glimpse of the leaders. Caballo pulled an old, broken-strapped Timex out of his pocket and checked the time. Six hours. That was probably way too fast, but there was a chance that—

"¡*Vienen!*" someone shouted. They're coming!

Caballo's head jerked up. He squinted down the straight road, peering through the bobbing heads of dancers. False alarm. Just a cloud of dust and—no, there it was. Bouncing dark hair and a crimson blouse. Arnulfo still had the lead.

Silvino was in second, but Scott was closing fast. With a mile to go, Scott ran Silvino down. But instead of blowing past, Scott slapped him on the back. "C'mon!" Scott shouted, waving for Silvino to come with him. Startled, Silvino reached deep and managed to match Scott stride for stride. Together, they bore down on Arnulfo.

Screams and cheers drowned out the mariachi band as the three runners made their last push toward the finish. Silvino faltered, surged again, but couldn't hold Scott's pace. Scott drove on. He'd been in this spot before, and he'd always found something left. Arnulfo glanced back and saw the man who'd beaten the best in the world coming after him with everything he had. Arnulfo blazed through the heart of Urique, the screams building as he got closer and closer to the tape. When he snapped it, Tita was in tears.

The crowd had already swallowed Arnulfo by the time Scott crossed the line in second. Caballo rushed over to congratulate him, but Scott pushed past him without a word. Scott wasn't used to losing, especially not to some no-name guy in a pickup race in the middle of nowhere. This had never happened to him before—but he knew what to do about it.

Scott walked up to Arnulfo and bowed.

The crowd went crazy. Tita rushed over to hug Caballo and found him wiping his eyes. In the midst of this pandemonium, Silvino struggled across the finish line, followed by Herbolisto and Sebastiano.

And Jenn? Her decision to win or die trying had finally caught up with her.

By the time she arrived at Guadalupe, Jenn was ready to faint. She slumped down against a tree and dropped her dizzy head between her knees. A group of Tarahumara clustered around, trying to encourage Jenn back to her feet. She lifted head and mimed drinking.

"¿*Agua?*" she asked. "¿*Agua purificada?*"

Someone shoved a warm Coke into her hand.

"Even better," she said, and smiled wearily.

She was still sipping the soda when a shout went up. Sebastiano and Herbolisto were running into the village. Jenn lost sight of them when the crowd thronged around to offer congratulations and *pinole*. Then Herbolisto was standing over her, stretching out his hand. With the other, he pointed toward the trail. Was she coming? Jenn shook her head. "Not yet," she said. Herbolisto started to run, then stopped and walked back. He put out his hand again. Jenn smiled and waved him off. "Get going, already!" Herbolisto waved good-bye.

Soon after he disappeared down the trail, the shouting began again. Someone relayed Jenn the information: the Wolf was coming.

Bonehead! Jenn saved him a long sip of her Coke, and pulled herself to her feet while he downed it. For all the times they'd paced each other and all the sunset runs they'd done on Virginia Beach, they'd never actually finished a race side by side.

"Ready?" Billy said.

"You're toast, dude."

Together, they flew down the long hill and thundered across the swaying bridge. They came into Urique whooping and hollering, redeeming themselves magnificently; despite Jenn's bloody legs and Billy's narcoleptic approach to prerace prep, they'd beaten all but four of the Tarahumara as well as Luis and Eric, two highly experienced ultrarunners.

Manuel Luna had dropped out halfway. Though he'd done his best to come through for Caballo, the ache of his son's death left him too leaden to compete. But while he couldn't get his heart into the racing, he was fully committed to one of the racers. Manuel prowled up and down the road, watching for Barefoot Ted. Soon, he was joined by Arnulfo . . . and Scott . . . and Jenn and Billy. Something odd began to happen: as the runners got slower, the cheers got wilder. Every time a racer struggled across the finish—Luis and Porfilio, Eric and Barefoot Ted—they immediately turned around and began calling home the runners still out there.

From high on the hill, I could see the twinkle of the red and green lights strung above the road to Urique. The sun had set, leaving me running through that silvery-gray dusk of the deep canyons, a moonlike glow that lingers, unchanging, until you feel everything is frozen in time except you. And then, from out of those milky shadows, emerged the lone wanderer of the High Sierras.

"Want some company?" Caballo said.

"Love it."

Together, we clattered across the swaying bridge, the cool air off the river making me feel oddly weightless. When we hit the last stretch into town, trumpets began blasting. Side by side, stride for stride, Caballo and I ran into Urique.

I don't know if I actually crossed a finish line. All I saw was a pigtailed blur as Jenn came flying out of the crowd, knocking me staggering. Eric caught me before I hit the ground and pushed a cold bottle of water against the back of my neck. Arnulfo and Scott, their eyes already bloodshot, pushed a beer into each of my hands.

"You were amazing," Scott said.

"Yeah," I said. "Amazingly slow." It had taken me over twelve hours, meaning that Scott and Arnulfo could have run the course all over again and still beaten me.

"That's what I'm saying," Scott insisted. "I've been there, man. I've been there *a lot*. It takes more guts than going fast."

I limped over toward Caballo, who was sprawled under a tree as the party raged around him. Soon, he'd get to his feet and give a wonderful speech in his wacky Spanish. He'd bring forward Bob Francis, who'd walk back into town just in time to present Scott with a ceremonial Tarahumara belt and Arnulfo with a pocketknife of his own. Caballo would hand out prize money, and get choked up when the Party Kids, who could barely pay for the bus back to El Paso, immediately gave their cash to the Tarahumara runners who'd finished behind them. Caballo would roar with laughter as Herbolisto and Luis danced the Robot.

But that would all come later. For now, Caballo was content to just sit alone under a tree, smiling and sipping a beer, watching his dream play out before his eyes.

CHAPTER 32

That head of his has been occupied with contemporary
society's insoluble problems for so long, and he is
still battling on with his good-heartedness and boundless
energy. His efforts have not been in vain, but he will
probably not live to see them come to fruition.

—THEO VAN GOGH, 1889

"YOU'VE GOT TO HEAR THIS," Barefoot Ted said, grabbing my arm.

Damn. He caught me just as I was trying to slink away from the madness of the street party and limp off to the hotel to collapse. I'd already heard Barefoot Ted's entire postrace commentary, including his observation that human urine is both nutrient-rich and an effective tooth whitener, and I couldn't imagine anything he could possibly say that would be more compelling than a deep sleep in a soft bed. But it wasn't Ted telling stories this time. It was Caballo.

Barefoot Ted pulled me back into Mamá Tita's garden, where Caballo was holding Scott and Billy and a few of the others spellbound. "You ever wake up in an emergency room," Caballo was saying, "and wondered whether you wanted to wake up at all?" With that, he launched into the story I'd been waiting nearly two years to hear. It didn't take me long to grasp why he'd chosen that moment. At dawn, we'd all be scattering and heading home. Caballo didn't want us to forget what we shared, so for the first time, he was revealing who he was.

———————

He was born Michael Randall Hickman, son of a Marine Corps gunnery sergeant whose postings moved the family up and down the West Coast. As a skinny loner who constantly had to defend himself in new schools, young Mike's first priority every time they moved was to find the nearest Police Athletic League and sign up for boxing lessons.

Brawny kids would smirk and pound their gloves together as they watched the geek with the silky hippie hair gangle his way into the ring, but their grins died as soon as that long left arm began snapping jabs into their eyes. Mike Hickman was a sensitive kid who hated hurting people, but that didn't stop him from getting really good at it. "The guys I liked best were the big, muscular ones, 'cause they'd keep coming after me," he recalled. "But the first time I ever knocked out a guy, I cried. For a long time after that, I didn't knock out anybody."

After high school, Mike went off to Humboldt State to study Eastern religions and Native American history. To pay tuition, he began fighting in backroom smokers, billing himself as the Gypsy Cowboy. Because he was fearless about walking into gyms that rarely saw a white face, much less a vegetarian white face spouting off about universal harmony and wheatgrass juice, the Cowboy soon had all the action he could handle. Small-time Mexican promoters loved to pull him aside and whisper deals in his ear.

"*Oye, compay*," they'd say. "Listen up, my friend. We're going to start a *chisme*, a little whisper, that you're a top amateur from back east. The gringos are gonna love it, man. Every *gabacho* in the house is going to bet their kids on you."

The Gypsy Cowboy shrugged. "Fine by me."

"Just dance around so you don't get slaughtered till the fourth," they'd warn him—or the third, or the seventh, whichever round the fix had been set for. The Cowboy could hold his own against gigantic black heavyweights by dodging and clinching up until it was time for him to hit the canvas, but against the speedy Latino middleweights, he had to fight for his life. "Man, sometimes they had to haul my bleeding butt out of there," he'd say. But even after leaving school, he stuck with it. "I just wandered the country fighting. Taking dives, winning some, losing but really winning others, mostly putting on good shows and learning how to fight and not get hurt."

After a few years of scrapping along in the fight game's under-world, the Cowboy took his winnings and flew to Maui. There, he turned his back on the resorts and headed east, toward the damp, dark side of the island and the hidden shrines of Hana. He was look-ing for a purpose for his life. Instead, he found Smitty, a hermit who lived in a hidden cave. Smitty led Mike to a cave of his own, then began guiding him to Maui's hidden sacred sites.

"Smitty is the guy who first got me into running," Caballo told us. Sometimes, they'd set out in the middle of the night to run the twenty miles up the Kaupo Trail to the House of the Sun at the top of 10,000-foot Mount Haleakala. They'd sit quietly as the first rays of morning sparkled on the Pacific, then run back down again, fueled only by wild papayas they'd knocked from the trees. Gradu-ally, the backroom brawler named Mike Hickman disappeared. In his place arose Micah True, a name inspired by "the courageous and fearless spirit" of the Old Testament prophet Micah and the loy-alty of an old mutt called True Dog. "I don't always live up to True Dog's example," Caballo would say. "But it's something to shoot for."

During one of his vision-seeking runs through the rain forest, the newly reborn Micah True met a beautiful young woman from Seattle who was visiting on vacation. They couldn't have been more differ-ent—Melinda was a psychology grad student and the daughter of a wealthy investment banker, while Micah was, quite literally, a cave-man—but they fell in love. After a year in the wilderness, Micah decided it was time to return to the world.

Wham! The Gypsy Cowboy knocked out his third opponent . . .

. . . and his fourth . . .

. . . and his fifth . . .

With Melinda in his corner and those rain-forest runs powering his legs, Micah was virtually untouchable; he could dance and shuffle until the other fighter's arms felt like cement. Once his fists drooped, Micah would dart in and hammer him to the canvas. "I was inspired by love, man," Micah said. He and Melinda settled in Boulder, Colorado, where he could run the mountain trails and get bouts in Denver arenas.

"He sure didn't look like a fighter," Don Tobin, then the Rocky Mountain lightweight kickboxing champion, later told me. "He had real long hair and was carrying this crusty old pair of gloves, like they were handed down from Rocky Graziano." Don Tobin became the Cowboy's friend and occasional sparring partner, and to this day, he marvels at the Cowboy's work ethic. "He was doing unbelievable training on his own. For his thirtieth birthday, he went out and ran thirty miles. *Thirty miles!*" Few American marathoners were putting up those numbers.

By the time his unbeaten streak reached 12–0, the Cowboy's reputation was formidable enough to land him on the cover of Denver's weekly newspaper, *Westword.* Under the headline FIST CITY was a full-page photo of Micah, bare-chested and sweaty, fists cocked and hair swinging, his eyes in the same glower I saw twenty years later when I surprised him in Creel. "I'll fight anybody for the right amount of money," the Cowboy was quoted as saying.

Anybody, eh? That article fell into the hands of an ESPN kickboxing promoter, who quickly tracked down the Cowboy and made an offer. Even though Micah was a boxer, not a kickboxer, she was willing to put him in the ring for a nationally televised bout against Larry Shepherd, America's fourth-ranked light heavyweight. Micah loved the publicity and the big payday, but smelled a rat. Just a few months before, he had been a homeless hippie meditating on a mountaintop; now, they were pitting him against a martial artist who could break cinder blocks with his head. "It was all a big joke to them, man," Micah says. "I was this long-haired hippie they wanted to shove into the ring for laughs."

What happened next summarizes Caballo's entire life story: the easiest choices he ever had to make were the ones between prudence and pride. When the bell clanged on ESPN's *Superfight Night,* the Gypsy Cowboy abandoned his usual canny strategy of dodging and dancing. Instead, he sprinted self-righteously across the ring and battered Shepherd with a furious barrage of lefts and rights. "He didn't know what I was doing, so he covered up in the corner to figure it out," Micah would recall. Micah cocked his right arm for a haymaker, but got a better idea. "I kicked him in the face so hard, I broke my toe," Micah says. "And his nose."

Dingdingding.

Micah's arm was jerked into the air, while a doctor began probing Shepherd's eyes to make sure his retinas were still attached. Another KO for the Gypsy Cowboy. He couldn't wait to get back home to celebrate with Melinda. But Melinda, he discovered, had a knockout of her own to deliver. And long before that conversation was over— long before she'd finished telling him about the affair and her plans to leave him for another man and move back to Seattle—Micah's brain was buzzing with questions. Not for her; for him.

He'd just smashed a man's face on national TV, and why? To be great in someone else's eyes? To be a performer whose achievements were only measured by someone else's affection? He wasn't stupid; he could connect the dots between the nervous boy with the Great Santini dad and the lonely, love-hungry drifter he'd become. Was he a great fighter, in other words, or just a needy one?

Soon after, *Karate* magazine called. The year-end rankings were about to come out, the reporter said, and the Gypsy Cowboy's upset had made him the fifth-ranked light-heavyweight kickboxer in America. The Cowboy's career was about to skyrocket; once *Karate* hit the stands and the offers started pouring in, he'd have plenty of big-money opportunities to find out whether he truly loved fighting, or was fighting to be loved.

"Excuse me," Micah told the reporter. "But I just decided to retire."

Making the Gypsy Cowboy disappear was even simpler than dispensing with Mike Hickman. Everything Micah couldn't carry on his back was discarded. The phone was disconnected, the apartment abandoned. Home became a '69 Chevy pickup. By night, he slept in a sleeping bag in the back. By day, he hired himself out to mow lawns and move furniture. Every hour in between, he ran. If he couldn't have Melinda, he'd settle for exhaustion. "I'd get up at four-thirty in the morning, run twenty miles, and it would be a beautiful thing," Micah said. "Then I'd work all day and want to feel that way again. So I'd go home, drink a beer, eat some beans, and run some more."

He had no idea if he was fast or slow, talented or terrible, until one summer weekend in 1986 when he drove up to Laramie, Wyoming, to take a stab at the Rocky Mountain Double Marathon. He surprised even himself by winning in six hours and twelve minutes, knocking off back-to-back trail marathons in a scratch over three hours each. Racing ultras, he discovered, was even tougher than prizefighting. In the ring, the other fighter determines how hard you're hit, but on the trail, your punishment is in your own hands. For a guy looking to beat himself into numbness, extreme running could be an awfully attractive sport.

Maybe I could even go pro, if I could just get over these nagging injuries. . . . That thought was running through Micah's mind as he coasted on his bike down a steep Boulder street. Next thing he knew, he was blinking into bright lights in the emergency room of Boulder Community Hospital, his eyes caked with blood and his forehead full of stitches. Best he could recall, he'd hit a gravel slick and sailed over the handlebars.

"You're lucky you're alive," the doctor told him, which was one way of looking at it. Another was that death was still a problem hanging over his head. Micah had just turned forty-one, and despite his ultrarunning prowess, the view from that ER gurney was none too pretty. He had no health insurance, no home, no close family, and no steady work. He didn't have enough money to stay overnight for observation, and he didn't have a bed to recover on if he checked out.

Poor and free was the way he'd chosen to live, but was it the way he wanted to die? A friend let Micah mend on her sofa, and there, for the next few days, he pondered his future. Only lucky rebels go out in a blaze of glory, as Micah knew very well. Ever since second grade, he'd idolized Geronimo, the Apache brave who used to escape the U.S. cavalry by running through the Arizona badlands on foot. But how did Geronimo end up? As a prisoner, dying drunk in a ditch on a dusty reservation.

Once Micah recovered, he headed to Leadville. And there, during a magical night running through the woods with Martimano Cervantes, he found his answers. Geronimo couldn't run free forever, but maybe a "gringo Indio" could. A gringo Indio who owed nothing, needed no one, and wasn't afraid to disappear from the planet without a trace.

"So what do you live on?" I asked.

"Sweat," Caballo said. Every summer, he leaves his hut and rides buses back to Boulder, where his ancient pickup truck awaits him behind the house of a friendly farmer. For two or three months, he resumes the identity of Micah True and scrounges up freelance furniture-moving jobs. As soon as he has enough cash to last another year, he's gone, vanishing down to the bottom of the canyons and stepping back into the sandals of El Caballo Blanco.

"When I get too old to work, I'll do what Geronimo would've if they'd left him alone," Caballo said. "I'll walk off into the deep canyons and find a quiet place to lie down." There was no melo-drama or self-pity in the way Caballo said this, just the understanding that someday, the life he'd chosen would require one last disappear-ing act.

"So maybe I'll see you all again," Caballo concluded, as Tita was killing the lights and shooing us off to bed. "Or maybe I won't."

By sunup the next morning, the soldiers of Urique were waiting by the old minibus that was idling outside Tita's restaurant. When Jenn arrived, they snapped to attention.

"*Hasta luego*, Brujita," they called.

Jenn blew them screen-siren kisses with a big sweep of her arm, then climbed aboard. Barefoot Ted got on next, climbing up gin-gerly. His feet were so thickly swathed in cloth bandages, they barely fit inside his Japanese bathhouse flip-flops. "They're not bad, really," he insisted. "Just a little tender." He squeezed in next to Scott, who willingly slid over to make room.

The rest of us filed in and made our sore bodies as comfortable as possible for the jouncing trip ahead. The village tortilla-maker (who's also the village barber, shoemaker, and bus driver) slid behind the wheel and revved the rattling engine. Outside, Caballo and Bob Francis walked the length of the bus, pressing their hands against each of our windows.

Manuel Luna, Arnulfo, and Silvino stood next to them as the bus pulled out. The rest of the Tarahumara had set off already on the long hike home, but even though these three had the greatest distance to travel, they'd waited around to see us off. For a long time afterward, I could see them standing in the road, waving, until the entire town of Urique disappeared behind us in a cloud of dust.

ACKNOWLEDGMENTS

BACK IN 2005, Larry Weissman read a pile of my magazine clips and synthesized them into one smart question. "Endurance is at the heart of all your stories," he said, or something to that effect. "Got one you haven't told yet?"

"Well, yeah. I heard about this race in Mexico. . . ."

Since then, Larry and his brilliant wife, Sascha, have served as my agents and higher brain functions, teaching me how to turn a clutter of ideas into a legible proposal and yanking hard on the choke chain whenever I miss deadlines. Without them, this book would still be just a tale I told over beers.

Runner's World magazine, and especially then-editor Jay Heinrichs, first sent me into the Copper Canyons and even briefly (*very* briefly) entertained my notion of publishing an all-Tarahumara issue. I'm indebted to James Rexroad, ace photographer, for his companionship and gorgeous photos on that trip. For a man with such a huge brain and lung capacity, *Runner's World* editor emeritus Amby Burfoot is extraordinarily generous with his time, expertise, and library. I still owe him twenty-five of his books, which I promise to return if he'll join me for another run.

But I'm especially grateful to *Men's Health* magazine. If you don't read it, you're missing one of the best and most consistently credible magazines in the country, bar none. It's staffed by editors like Matt Marion and Peter Moore, who encourage absurd ideas such as sending oft-injured writers into the wilderness for footraces with invisible Indians. *Men's Health* allowed me to train for the race on their dime, then helped me shape the resulting story. Like everything I've written for Matt, it came into his hands like an unmade bed and came out with crisp hospital corners.

For a clan so consistently misrepresented by the media, the ultra community was extraordinarily supportive of my research and personal experimentation. Ken, Pat, and Cole Chlouber always made me feel at home in Leadville and taught me more than I ever wanted to learn about burro racing. Likewise, Leadville race director Merilee O'Neal filled every request I could think of and gave me a race-finisher's hug even though I hadn't earned it. David "Wild Man" Horton, Matt "Skyrunner" Carpenter, Lisa Smith-Batchen and her husband Jay, Marshall and Heather Ulrich, Tony Krupicka—they all shared their remarkable stories and secrets of the trail. Sunny Blende, the ace ultra nutritionist, staved off disaster in the desert when Jenn, Billy, Barefoot Ted, and I fumblingly crewed for Luis Escobar at the 2006 Badwater, and provided the best definition of the sport I've ever heard: "Ultras are just eating and drinking contests, with a little exercise and scenery thrown in."

If you didn't feel overwhelmed by weird digressions while reading this book, you and I both owe thanks to Edward Kastenmeier, my editor at Knopf, and his assistant, Tim O'Connell. Also to Lexy Bloom, a senior editor at Vintage Books, who offered her valuable insight and comments down the stretch. Somehow, they figured out how to cut the fat out of my writing without sacrificing any flavor. Likewise, my friend Jason Fagone, author of the excellent *Horsemen of the Esophagus*, helped me understand the difference between storytelling and self-indulgence. Max Potter first let me write about Leadville for *5280* magazine and is the rare writer noble enough to cheerlead another writer on. Patrick Doyle, *5280*'s amazing researcher, confirmed many facts about Caballo's mysterious life, and even unearthed that lost newspaper photo from "The Gypsy Cowboy's" prizefighting days. Years ago, Susan Linnee gave me a job at the Associated Press that I didn't deserve, then taught me how to do it. If more people knew Susan, fewer would bash journalism.

To be a great athlete, you need to pick your parents wisely. To survive as a writer, you should do likewise with your family. My brothers, sisters, nieces, and nephews have all been tremendously supportive and forgiving of missed birthdays and obligations. Most of all, I'm indebted to my wife, Mika, and my glorious daughters, Sophie and Maya, for the joy that I hope is evident in these pages.

I now know why the Tarahumara and the Más Locos got along so beautifully. They are rare and wonderful people, and spending time with them is one of the greatest privileges of my life. I wish I had time for one more mango juice with that great gringo Indio, Bob Francis. Shortly after the race, he died. How, I don't know. Like most deaths in the Copper Canyons, his death remains a mystery.

While still absorbing the loss of his loyal old friend, Caballo got the offer of a lifetime. The North Face, the popular outdoor sports company, offered to become his race sponsor. Caballo's future, and his race's, would finally be secure.

Caballo thought it over. For about a minute.

"No, thanks," he decided. "I don't want anyone to do anything except come run, party, dance, eat, and hang with us. Running isn't about making people buy stuff. Running should be free, man."